nobody's boy

Other books by Roland Hegstad:
   *Who Causes Suffering?*
   *Rattling the Gates*
   *Pretenders to the Throne*

Visit us at www.reviewandherald.com for information on other Review and Herald® products.

# Grover Wilcox
## with Roland R. Hegstad

# nobody's boy

**A TRUE STORY**

REVIEW AND HERALD® PUBLISHING ASSOCIATION
HAGERSTOWN, MD 21740

The author assumes full responsibility for the accuracy of all facts and quotations as cited in this book.

Texts credited to NIV are from the *Holy Bible, New International Version*. Copyright © 1973, 1978, 1984, InternationaL Bible Society. Used by permission of Zondervan Bible Publishers.

This book was
Edited by Jeannette R. Johnson
Designed by Leumas Design/Willie Duke
Cover photos by Corbis Images/Helen King, discouraged child; Corbis Images/Norbert
　　　　Schaefer, boy walking on beach
Typeset: 11/14 Bembo

PRINTED IN U.S.A.

08 07 06 05 04　　　　5 4 3 2 1

**R&H Cataloging Service**
Wilcox, Grover, 1946-
　　Nobody's boy: An incredible
story of darkness and light. With
Roland R. Hegstad.

　　1. Wilcox, Grover. I. Hegstad, Roland R.

　　　　　[B]

ISBN 0-8280-1817-0

# DEDICATION

## *To Jack*

**I began to write** *Nobody's Boy* six years ago. Because of a life-threatening illness, progress was slow. But my Father, who told me to write, also sent help and encouragement.

Foremost was Jack.

His modesty is such that he has asked me not to reveal his true surname. In the book I refer to him as Jack Milford. (There are probably enough "Jacks" in the world to assure his anonymity.) I can find no words sufficient to express my love for a friend who has indeed been closer than a brother. At every crisis of my illness he has been there for me, assuring me of his and his Father's love. When I stood on the bank of the Jordan, ready at last to give up my struggle for life, it was Jack who assured me that my Father had a job for me to do down here. Because I could not actually go into my Father's throne room, He gave me Jack as the next-best thing available on earth.

Jack once told me that there were two reasons I was still alive: My Father had a work for me to do, and I was too stubborn to lay down on the job. I have added another: "You, Jack, with your love for God and for me, are the third reason."

So I often refer to him as R-3—my brother, my friend, and God's child.

# ACKNOWLEDGMENTS

**Five years ago I met** a husky doctor with a glowing face and sparkling eyes. Kindness jumped out from a heart that belongs to the King. Dr. Steven C. Stewart is that rare doctor who shoulders his patients' burdens. He has read every draft of this book as I wrote and rewrote. Every time I go to his office my courage and joy shoot up like a thermometer immersed in boiling water. Every other day for two months I was on a jug of amphotericin B infusions. After each one, somehow I would throw off the pile of blankets, stagger to my feet, and amble down the long hospital hall to the elevator. Down I would go for nine floors to the A level. On rubbery legs I would shuffle to the very end of the hall, where a tasteful plastic sign on the wall reads: "Steven C. Stewart, M.D." There I would place a shaking hand on the sign and thank my Father for him. He has been with me every page of this journey, and I love him.

One day I met a dynamo in the RV park where I lived. It took all of 30 seconds to become brothers, because our Daddy had planned the event. I asked him to look over my book notes—and he did. But he said he had too many projects to work with me on the book. However, the good Lord brought him back a few months later for a three-month stay. His wife, Stella, looked at him and said, "Roland, I believe the Lord wants you to work with Grover on his book." And Roland replied, "I realize that the Lord brought me back here for that very purpose." So it was that Roland R. Hegstad, a creative editor and writer with a number of books on his résumé, and Grover Wilcox, with none, became partners. Best of all was the love that grew between us as we worked together. *Nobody's Boy* is truly our book.

*A special thanks also to:*
   Mike Hagelgantz—God's smile on you
   Bob and Judi Wilcox—His caring ones
   Anne Spradlin—for her daily support and love
   Chris Brooks—God's joy
   Rick Masterson—God's boy

Drs. Keith Colburn, Gregory Cheek, Lennard Spetcht,
 and Eric Baumann—His boys
Saul Silva—One of the four "zeroes"
Dr. Phil Kitchen—My brother in Christ

*And more thanks to:*
 Karen Bekoweis, Chris McLaughlin, Bud Bradbury, Wynne
 Robertson, Mark Self

*A thank you for the love and friendship of my nieces:*
 Ambre Otten, Dion Chuzel, and Sherri Crook

*Also:*
 Chuck McKinstry, Don Schneider, Ivan and Elizabeth Reeve, Roger
 and Bonnie Morrisey, and Isobel and J. V. Sudds

*For the love of my daughters:*
 Julia and Bonnie

*And for my mom and dad:*
 Whose future rests in the hands of a merciful and loving God,
 so loving that He has put it in my heart to love them.

# CONTENTS

# FOREWORD

## The Story of an Exceptional Person

This book tells the story of an exceptional person. The victim from a childhood of neglect and abuse in its worst forms, Grover Wilcox has never quit looking for—and expecting—the good in people. Now facing the relentless onslaught of a life-threatening disease, he has grasped the hand of God so firmly that he communicates peace and love to other sufferers. An inspiring, true story.

*—Steven C. Stewart, M.D.*
*Chief of Urology, Veterans Hospital;*
*Professor, Loma Linda University School of Medicine*

## A Close-up View of His Battle

I have observed with a great deal of interest and admiration the struggles experienced by Grover Wilcox. As one of the doctors taking care of him for a very serious and often fatal disease, I have had a close-up view of his battle to survive major catastrophic events in a life that has known more than its share of hard times. His determination not to give up, coupled with his mission to share compassion and empathy with a multitude of critically or terminally ill patients is an inspiration to those of us privileged to know him.

Most patients with his illness would focus on their own desperate need; Grover spends his time and energy and modest means on hundreds of patients and their concerned loved ones. His faith in the "Daddy" he never had on earth is profound. I feel honored to be his doctor and share in the battle against the disease that seeks to end his mission on earth.

*—Keith Colburn, M.D.*
*Chief of Rheumatology and Professor of Medicine*
*Loma Linda University School of Medicine*

## The Most Important Day of My Life

As a newspaperman of long experience I know a good story when I see one. I also know when the story is well written. *Nobody's Boy* is both. But it's even more. It's the story of the most exceptional character I have ever met. Even our meeting was under exceptional circumstances. Join me at Denver International Airport and experience it for yourself.

It's late in the afternoon, and my flight has been canceled. I'm looking for a flight home after another long business trip. Off I go to exercise my survivor-learned handling of airline employees.

"I must get on a Chicago flight with another major airline. *Please!*" (that magic word). Success! Headed for the alternate airline, I get a sinking feeling. I've never heard of it. And it's a discount outfit. Does that mean they discount safety and security? I've given up my leather seat, great food, and free booze to cram into a cattle car instead of a Boeing 777, and it's storming to boot.

As I board the discount I see that my beloved aisle seat and the two next to it are empty. In fact, most of the plane is empty. Then two young men who look like football players board. They have that look we experienced travelers know so well: they'll crush your suit jacket in the overhead and talk of plane crashes while consuming $3 Bud Lights for the entire flight. And—how did I know it would be?—they hold tickets 6A and 6B, right next to my 6C.

My traveling instincts tell me to move toward peace and quiet as soon as the doors are shut. But to where? The plane is virtually empty. I have my choice of several seats. Halfway down the aisle I plop into an aisle seat, hand the flight attendant $3 for a glass of red wine, and ready myself for my "flight of enchantment."

It isn't until the plane is being pushed back that I realize someone is hunched down in the window seat, coughing and moaning. I turn to see a man, probably in his late 40s or early 50s, obviously in distress. Assuming he might be afraid of flying, I tell him not to worry; I have flown many times, and even the storm will not prevent us from arriving safely. He assures me he is not afraid. Further, he is happy I have chosen this seat. I have, he says, "friendly eyes."

*A weirdo,* I think. Then I got a better look at him. He's smiling through tears and pain. Is he fearful—or even near death? He explains that he has a disease called Wegener's granulomatosis, "so rare and devastating that even today doctors know little about it, other than it kills very quickly, usually within a few weeks." His name is Grover Wilcox. He is sick from the chemo he has taken. With my journalist-trained questions I soon learn that his illness has cost him everything—his position as a teacher, friendships, home, security.

I find that Grover doesn't touch people; he connects with them. As he tells me of people he has met in the hospital, of accompanying some to the brink of death, in some strange way I walk with him into their rooms, hear his words of comfort; I even feel good about being part of his quest to make them feel loved. When Grover speaks of God healing them, it is I who feel tortured memories slip away. When he speaks of God's love touching them, it is I who feel the warmth of His love and acceptance. When he speaks of his heavenly "Daddy," it is I who feel His hug.

What I experienced that night changed my life—at 30,000 feet in a thunderstorm.

> *"At the heart of the cyclone tearing the sky*
> *And flinging the clouds and the towers by,*
> *Is a place of eternal calm."*

The words are from Edwin Markham. Grover quotes them in *Nobody's Boy*. Pull up a copy and prepare for connections. Grover will tell you with whom.

*Rich Masterson*
*Owner-Publisher, Chicago* Bugle
*Former National Director, Circulation Division*
*Chicago* Tribune *Media Services*

# INTRODUCTION

*I liked the feel of sand between my toes. Especially early in the morning before the sun heated the beach. But what child wouldn't? And it was mine. All mine. Of course, I didn't know that it was Long Beach, and that on a summer day a thousand other children would claim it.*

*I loved the silence. Even the waves seemed strangely gentled, and the sun's rays caressed me as they peeked over the horizon. The morning gulls swept overhead, sliding on unseen currents. To my untutored eyes they seemed held aloft by unseen hands—perhaps those of someone or something called "God."*

*At the margin of the gentle waters, I could see the homes of unseen little creatures, tiny bubbles marking their presence. Occasionally a crab would scuttle across in front of me, and I would curl my toes protectively. It wouldn't do to cry out and shatter the silence. Strangely, even then I observed that silence has a sound. It hovers at the verge of consciousness, a muted something that vanishes if you concentrate on it. Maybe, I thought, like the sound of an army of ants marching to war against another little army. I wondered whether they wore uniforms and what they used for weapons.*

*In the years since, as I've retraced my childhood steps, I've heard the waves roaring as they attack the beach. And the gulls lecture their fellows and human alike with raucous abandon. Freeway traffic plays its basso profundo background, and children chitter and chatter the lyrics of summertime. Strange it is that the once silent beach has become a babel; strange, too, that a silent child now dares to disturb the sound of silence.*

*Those who have heard my story find it incredible. "Your parents must have spoken to you kindly sometime."*

*No. They never spoke a kind word to me. In fact, other than curses, I heard few words at all. The usual sound I heard was the sound of silence. It became my refuge. . . . The refuge for* **Nobody's Boy.**

★ ★ ★

I was a child of nowhere and everywhere, for we—my family—were street people during my childhood. We lived in tents on a California beach, along railroad tracks near Riverside, in cow pastures and deserted shacks, campgrounds along the roads to Arrowhead and Big Bear lakes, a log cabin, and scores of houses where we never paid rent and usually disappeared by night. By the time I was a teenager we had moved more than 100 times. My father never worked a steady job, nor did my mother. We children— seven of us, of which I was the next-to-youngest—learned to survive on booty from farmers' orchards and vegetable fields, supplemented by begging from relatives and strangers alike. We often went days without a meal. There was an even darker side. Our homes, if they can be called that, were dark places of abuse—physical, emotional, and sexual. Tension and fear hung like black clouds over our days, as we children watched fearfully for telltale signs of violent eruptions. During my childhood years my parents choked and beat me, resulting in my attempt to escape deep within myself. I became the invisible child, never speaking to an adult. I never heard the words "I love you," never knew the security of a hug.

My parents professed to be Seventh-day Adventists.

Digest that for a moment. *Church members!* Professing to know the Lord. Talking heaven but living hell. When I was 7 years old, my mother went to prison and my father abandoned us. We children lived for a few weeks by stealing from a neighbor's farm—even eating chicken feed we found on the barn floor. One midnight police broke into the shack where we lived and took all seven of us to the Riverside juvenile hall. During the year we were confined, we would look through the barred windows and over the barbed-wire fence and see well-dressed children playing in their yards. A year later our parents claimed us, and it was back to the nomadic existence that had been our lot from birth.

Recite the scenario above to a psychiatrist, and you'll be told that I surely grew up hating my parents—and my heavenly Parent as well. That I've likely been in jail, and at the least am a rebel who cannot stand authority figures—including God. One psychologist, Dr. Alane Samarza of Redlands, California, has spoken of the lasting damage to be expected from such an abusive childhood: "The early experiences of maltreatment, abuse, and neglect," she says, "may result in depression, fears, anxieties, and problems in relationships—including distrust and intimacy dysfunctions—as well as poor self-esteem." She couldn't have described us children better if she had written our case histories.

Dr. Samarza would understand why I feel almost impelled to jump ahead in my story, to evade the dark years, to deny the reality of what happened, as several of my siblings have done. It is only the publishing of this book that has enabled them to move from years of denial to facing honestly the trauma our parents inflicted on us. And it is only writing it that has brought me a measure of deliverance. It has also brought us siblings together. For the first time an older brother has brushed aside the façade of respectability he had constructed—his way of retaining sanity. For the first time in 28 years a sister has called me—and called and called (five times in one afternoon)! And now others of my brothers and sisters are shattering the years of silence and shame. As this book goes to the publisher, we've had a family reunion! I find myself almost unable to believe the joy of seeing brothers and sisters who had disappeared for decades. You'll learn how incredible this development is as the painfully honest saga of the Wilcox family unfolds.

Many products come with a warning label. Ironically, many such labels are affixed to medications advertised to cure everything from hair loss to weight gain. Especially emphatic are those that warn you not to take sure cure B if you are taking sure cure A. Or, if your problem is theology—for example, "Why in the world didn't God act to stop the abuse of the Wilcox kids?—you may be told (1) "You're looking for the answer in the wrong church"; (2) Just "trust and obey, for there's no other way," as a well-worn song in some hymnals advises; or as another song offers: (3) "Someday He'll make it plain to me" (which not only puts off the answer but prolongs the pain).

When you're young and abused, as I was, neither theology nor theory (of whatever discipline) helps you sleep better at night. Not that I didn't wonder the big "Why?" I'd slip out into the night and ponder the universe, with its distant and unfeeling stars. Was there really a God, as I had heard on our family's occasional excursions to church? Somehow I believed there was. But He wasn't my Father, and He didn't care about me. Still, I sometimes threw a silent prayer heavenward and clutched at a tenuous thread of faith, only to awaken to the harsh reality of betrayal, beatings, sexual abuse, abandonment, hunger, shame.

I remember seeing a rainbow one afternoon while playing with a childhood chum. I had endured my mother slapping me around that morning and was not in the best of moods. But this rainbow was not the run-of-the-mill sort. As we watched, it turned into a brilliant double arch.

I had never seen such vivid colors. They seemed to pulse, as if communicating a message in some celestial code. "You know the story about rainbows, don't you?" my companion asked.

I nodded. "God destroyed the wicked world by flood and He sent Noah and"—I couldn't remember the names of the others—"and He sent a rainbow as a promise that He wouldn't do that again."

"Do you really believe that?" my friend asked.

There were times that I did, and there were times that I didn't. My chum had to be content with my shrugged shoulders. I've seen many more skies filled with threatening clouds than with rainbows. Still, just the other day I saw another magnificent rainbow and across the years remembered the question and my indecision. But this time it seemed to communicate a promise: Someday the world will sing again! Maybe I will too.

> *O mystic sense of sudden quickening!*
> *Hope's lark-song rings, or life's deep undertone*
> *Wails through my heart—and then I needs must sing.*
> —*William James Dawson*

# 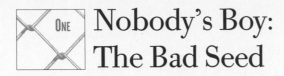 Nobody's Boy: The Bad Seed

*And so beside the silent sea*
*I wait the muffled oar;*
*no harm from Him can come to me*
*on ocean or on shore.*

— John Greenleaf Whittier, "The Eternal Goodness"

**On a windy March 5, 1946,** if medical convention prevailed, a doctor at Riverside Hospital swatted my rear, and I told him to lay off or I'd tell my mother. Aunt Jen, a delightful woman who lived a few miles from the hospital, says I was a handsome, broad-shouldered baby with a large head topped by a generous swath of black, curly hair. A few days later I spent my first day on the beach, in the arms of my sister Pam, who was to become my de facto mother. For the next 18 years I was just another face in the crowd to my parents. It was as though I didn't exist. Why? How I wish I knew! Maybe in mother's case it was because I resembled my womanizing father. He may have had an instinctive aversion to me because she named me Grover, after a brother-in-law whom my father hated. As a missionary he represented everything our family was not in his love of God and his commitment to Christian service. So little Grover had two strikes against him before he even heard of baseball.

At 6 months I was a solitary, independent, and curious child. Our Long Beach home was a ragged tan tent with a canvas floor and a flap for the door. Two adults and six children called it home. Fred, of the fire-engine hair and green-hued freckles, and his blond twin, Ned, were 6 years old. They and their toothpick-legged 4-year-old brother, Edward, were inseparable. Even at 9, Pam knew she was gorgeous. People who noticed her velvet eyes and wavy black hair flowing down her back would call her Elizabeth Taylor. Three-year-old Clara's waist-length blond hair bounced becomingly as she ran about the beach. She not only resembled her mother, she was the light of her mother's life to the exclusion of her siblings—a status that didn't endear her to them or her father.

Back to the threesome—Fred, Ned, and Edward. Children don't grow without eating. And often our parents would disappear without making any provision for meals. So my brothers would wander the beach, searching for anything that would quiet their protesting stomachs. Eagle-eyed Edward would nervously keep watch outside an unoccupied tent while his brothers slipped inside to look for an icebox or a footlocker. If they found one, Fred, the best domesticated, would quickly fix sandwiches, then carefully replace everything, and they would slip away. Already they were learning the tools of survival.

I was not. At 6 months I was investigating the tools of extinction. Fred tells me that it's a miracle I'm still around. A miracle (an event or action that apparently contradicts known scientific laws) it was not; a providence (the care or benevolent guidance of God or nature) it might have been. My brothers say it happened this way: While my parents were absent and the boys were seeking breakfast, I crawled out of the tent and down to the ocean. When they returned to find the tent empty, the three rushed up and down the beach, calling my name. Babies hunting a baby. Overhead, gulls mocked their futility and dove at the distraught boys. Whatever the culpability of our parents, my brothers knew the punishment that would be theirs if I were drowned on their watch. So it was, I've been told, that Edward fell to the sand, crying, "He's dead! I just know he's dead! What are we going to do?"

From down the beach came a cry through Ned's cupped hands: "Fred! Edward! Look over there!"

"Where? We don't see anything!"

"There!"

The three musketeers have retold the story many times, but for the first several tellings, never in the presence of our parents. According to their account, a diaper bobbed to the surface. Running into the surf, they saw a pair of legs sticking up. They grabbed them and pulled. Who was at the other end but me! I was wearing a sand "cap" of awesome dimensions; they had to wash it off before I could raise my head. But you know how stories grow. It is believable, however, that they dragged me from the surf and back to the tent. And their memory of delivering an unsolicited lecture to me seems to have merit: "Don't *ever* go out of the tent again! Do you hear me?" (That allegedly from Fred.) "How do we keep him here?" (That, I'm told, from Edward.) Both knew they would be severely punished if the incident became known. It would be their fault, not that of their parents. You blame the kids if an unsupervised baby drowns on a public beach. Thus began Edward's and Fred's training in parenthood, a role that would stretch into years. Of course, my parents heard what had happened. Fred was punished because he didn't do his job of covering for them. Someone else was always to blame. Irresponsible Fred!

Just a few weeks later baby Grover disappeared again. This time when my brothers ran through the waves that assaulted the beach, their thin cries were unrewarded. In defeat the three white-faced boys headed back to the empty tent. When they were almost there, Fred heard a train whistle echoing from the tracks that paralleled the beach just 50 yards behind our tent. Jerking his head around, he saw me sitting smack in the middle of the track, facing the oncoming train, just as calm as you please. Sprinting like an Olympic champion, he grabbed me up a heartbeat or two before the

train sped by. Again I got a lecture. Again my parents heard of it. No thanks to Fred. The brothers were punished. Again our parents assumed no blame. Again. And again.

At last the police decided our tent had been around too long to be a legitimate residence for weekend tourists. So we became tourists in fact, finally ending up in, as my father put it, a suburb of Palm Springs, then a winter haven for Hollywood's well-heeled. Actually, we set-

**The "Bad Seed"—able to get in trouble, even while sitting down.**

tled 20 miles northwest of Palm Springs amid a small collection of shacks nestled among boulders on a dry creek bed that dove out of the mountains. My father spent much of his time in Los Angeles, where he worked as a chauffeur for various Hollywood celebrities of the day. It was to be the last time in 25 years he held a steady job. Unfortunately, from my mother's perspective, he was gifted with rugged good looks—a look-a-like, many said, for Clark Gable, the male heart-stopper of the day. With his manicured mustache, Father was a magnet for the women, with whom he enjoyed many a dalliance while his wife and children sought to survive in the isolated, coyote-ridden canyon called Whitewater.

Through the years, with the aid of Aunt Jen and my brothers, I've been able to fill in a few of the blank spaces in father's profile. Wendon Wilcox was 12 when his father died, and, subsequently, his mother did everything a mother could do to spoil him. She saw to it that he was one of the few high school students to have his own car, a large 1920s sedan with chromed headlights and a shiny black paint job. To this gift she added a long fur coat. His muscular frame enhanced many a hockey game in the Adirondack mountains of upstate New York. As a youth he developed into a world-class speed skater. Even before acquiring the car he was known, it is said, as a "dandy." Not that his popularity was without challenge; he is said to have had a "dark side." More prominent in memory, however, was his golden-tongued role as an actor, which survived into his Hollywood years and beyond.

I think it likely that his mother's indulgence contributed to his utter lack of responsibility, as exhibited so often during his marriage. Certainly, fatherhood was alien to his personality and practice. All this despite his coming from a heritage of hard-working English immigrants. With them, however, also came what is known as the family temper. According to family lore, passed from one generation to another, children were known to suffer abuse at the hands of parents. In one account they went off to school with black eyes and strap marks on their backs. Women in the family, it was said, often had to deal with wandering husbands. My father seemed determined to contribute his own chapters of shame, though his stated aim seemed more laudable. He determined to become rich. It sounded good, but all his children knew something was wrong—terribly wrong!

My mother, Sarah Thompson, came from a long line of successful people dating back to Edward Winslow, one of the men who stepped off the Mayflower onto Plymouth Rock. Also in her family line was Queen Elizabeth. Her mother immigrated to the United States in the mid-1800s. My mother's father was a gambler who often abandoned his family. During the Great Depression of the 1930s, he got into financial difficulty because of his gambling. His solution? The family packed their few possessions into a small cart and started walking south. When their feet gave out, they acquired a decrepit old Model T (by what means no-

body knows) and nursed it into Mobile, Alabama. The family knew neither serenity nor stability. Relatives remember Grandmother to be a
pretty and talented woman who sacrificed her life in a hopeless marriage.

Mother had classical features—
long blond hair, and the slim figure
of the "after" in a diet ad. In her
youth, her large doe eyes captured
the attention of numerous young
men. One, from Lake Placid, met
her as he visited New York City.
She was 17 when they married.
Though beautiful outside, much
was lacking inside, most notably

18-year-old Wendon Wilcox, with his black
sedan, and his sister, Jen

self-esteem and stability. Her husband did nothing to meet these needs;
rather, he stripped her of any values that could have contributed to motherhood. Her response to his infidelities was to become pregnant. The more
children, she reasoned, the more reason for him to stay home. She catered
to his every whim, trying desperately to be what she could never be. At
times she was even the family wage earner. She gave the role of wife a
pretty good try, but lost among all the trying was the role of mother. By
the time I came along, poverty and father's sexual peccadilloes had trans-
formed her into a depressed caricature of the once promising young
woman he had promised to love and cherish until death should them part.
Instead of baking bread, she hurled dishes; instead of raising children, she
raised cane.

When the money ran out we fled Whitewater for Cabazon, Cabazon
for Palm Springs, Palm Springs for La Sierra, La Sierra for Los Angeles, and
so it went. One day, right out of the blue, my father announced that we
were going to New York City. We had gone there by train three years before as my father dodged the draft in the waning days of World War II. This
time, however, we were to travel by car, and not just any car. Father ushered us outside and voilá! There, obscuring a major portion of the horizon
(or so it seemed to my brothers), sat a huge 1932 Cadillac convertible. As I
envision it across the years, I've wondered whether he picked it or it picked
him! For sure, it furthered his fantasy of riches. He likely hoped that, at
worst, people seeing us in it would assume we were an elite family of aris-

tocrats, momentarily down on their luck. No question, that behemoth and he belonged together. It was as black as sin and had a mammoth 16-cylinder engine that could have driven an army tank to a new speed record. My brothers have never forgotten its purr as we rolled through the desert, its snarl as we headed up a mountain road. For the first time in their short lives, Fred and Ned thought maybe we were rich; maybe we would always have enough to eat. They watched other people's children turn and look enviously as we passed. Maybe they wished they were rich like us! My brothers never voiced their thoughts. Somehow they knew.

**The Behemoth: The 16-cylinder 1932 Cadillac convertible that conveyed nine of us to Long Island, New York.**

As it turned out, the aged Cadillac was not without problems. That mighty engine had to be fed both gas and oil—the latter of which it seemed to need about as often as it needed gas. For whatever reason, maybe just to keep company with other failing components, it clattered to a stop several times on the trip. We children, all seven of us, would curl up and try to sleep while father sought a solution. A laconic reporter might have described the trip as "on again, off again, gone again." But finally, several weeks after leaving California, we arrived at what New Yorkers called the Big Apple. I was too young to question this designation; but when my brothers heard it, it's likely they felt a yearning in their undernourished tummies. We headed out to Long Island, where we were to stay again with Aunt Anne, my mother's sister, and Uncle Marty. Aunt Anne was a secretary at the *Faith for Today* telecast. A kind and generous person, she welcomed us as if we were royalty. My brothers thought Aunt Anne looked like Queen Elizabeth. The best we could do for Uncle Marty's family tree was a tobacco farm in Kentucky. He wore an odd-shaped shoe on his left foot with a lift to compensate for a short leg, the result of a kick from a cranky old mule "down on the farm" when he was 12 years old. The tuberculosis that developed had eaten away six inches of bone. Uncle Marty's leg was bum, but his heart was gold, and we kids loved him.

Anne and Marty shared church fellowship with my parents. But as I was to learn, there are church members and there are church members. My aunt and uncle really believed that God had walked among His fallen children on two very human legs. They really believed that He loved His sinful creation so much that He paid the penalty for their sins by dying on a cross. They really believed that He rose from the grave and went back to His Father with the good news. They really believed that He was going to come again, confer immortality on His children, punish the children of the devil, and take His children home. I knew that my parents believed in the devil, and since they, too, were church members, one would assume they believed in God. Trouble was, the devil seemed much more in control of them than God was, as Anne and Marty were about to discover. I've told you about our New York relatives' commitment to the Adventist church because father had come up with a plan (maybe "scheme" is a better word), and its success depended on our hosts' sincere belief that the gospel—the Bible's way of saying "good news"—must be shared with all the world.

The way father put it to Anne and Marty, in his best golden-voiced counterfeit of sincerity, was simple: The gospel must, indeed, go to all the world and the best way to see that sinners got the genuine gospel was to put a Bible in their hands. Of course, he said, there were Bibles and there were Bibles. He, providentially, had come into possession of a new, illustrated H.M.S. Richards' Bible that would have double—no, triple—the impact of all other Bibles put together! And he had one to show them, fresh off the press. Not only that, this Bible had a concordance that would direct people to the *true* gospel. Across the years I can almost hear what followed.

Looking furtively about, he said, "You know these liberal translators are doing things like taking the 'virgin' out of that text in Isaiah, and making Mary just an ordinary Jewish girl who got in trouble and had to get married. And you couldn't guess what they're doing with some of those texts in the book of Revelation."

Whatever his sales talk, I came to know him well enough to believe that he knew what buttons to push and that he pushed them all.

Now, the new Bible he was about to introduce to the world—this illustrated Bible with none of those liberal problems—was guaranteed not only to win the relatives everyone was praying for, but also to fill the empty pews in all the Adventist churches of New York City! And he, my father of the golden voice, was willing to visit those churches and help them do just what God ordered His chosen people to do. All he needed were introductions to their pastors. He got them. He also got an introduction to the church members, many of whom he visited in their homes, where he prayed that the Lord would anoint their sacrificial commitment. One pastor introduced him to another, and so it went, his golden voice dramatically calling the Adventists who really believed Christ was soon to return, to stand up and be counted! In the evenings we watched him sit and count their money.

Our hosts little knew what they were getting into when they invited us to stay. But enlightenment was not long delayed. The behavior that had traumatized us children could not be turned on and off at will. When Mother became angry, as she did a few days into our stay, she threw things. Dishes smashed against the kitchen wallpaper. Father's rage was incandescent; he was more likely to throw a fist or a child than dishes. And that, too, was to happen. I was to be the victim.

It happened on a happy Friday. Thirteen people crowded my aunt's house. (I don't know why I still don't think of it as Uncle Marty's house. Maybe it was because of the new outfit Aunt Anne bought me that I was wearing that day.) Sometime in midafternoon I wandered into the bathroom—their one bathroom. And there, just for me, was a fascinating toy! A roll of toilet paper that virtually demanded I play with it. Soon it was on the floor, leaving me with the empty wooden spool, which I shoved down into the toilet. I then pulled the interesting little handle nearby. I was happily contemplating my wet shoes when my mother walked in. She took one look at me and the water running out into the hallway and promptly "lost it." Grabbing me by the arm, she dragged me to the bedroom, where my father joined us. Without even closing the door (as an onlooker said), they "beat the hell out of me," choked me, and threw me on the bed. The shocked silence of the onlookers was broken only by my agonized gasping for breath. Later, there was an effort to exert damage control. *This did not happen, did it? We just lost it for a moment, didn't we? It won't happen again, will it?* Of course it did. And of course there was no doubt that it all was my fault. I was, after all, as my mother often said, the "bad seed."

Unbelievably, my parents repeated their performance only a few days later after I stained my aunt's dressing table by pouring perfume on it.

Again I was beaten and almost strangled. I do not know at what point I decided to become a shadow because shadows can't be beaten. My brothers recall that my father began referring to me as "Mysterious Al." From birth, my older siblings recall, I was the silent child, the cardboard cutout wandering aimlessly. From the age of 3—the limit of my memory—I can recall little verbal communication with either parent. No hello, no goodbye. No "I love you." Nothing other than accusations and curses. I was never touched tenderly. Rather, I was a punching bag. Of course, I always made them do it. However, I never shouldered the blame, as many victims of abuse do. But, as many do, I buried a truckload of hate and fury deep inside. Maybe things would have been even worse had I known what a functional home was.

About that money my parents collected from the New York City Adventist churches for Bibles to bless the heathen—my folks used it for bars, dancing, and drinking. Some went for an affair Father had. Not one Bible was delivered. Finally, our long-suffering relatives had enough. Uncle Marty threw us out. In a rage, blaming our gracious benefactors, my parents loaded up the Cadillac, and we took off for Maine to camp in the woods. Left behind were two wonderful people to face a host of angry church members. I regret exposing this sordid chapter in the history of the Wilcox family, but you could never understand what follows without having met my parents. They are, after all, the ones who created Nobody's Boy, who never said the words "mama" or "daddy" until he wrote this book.

Our stay in Maine lasted only a few weeks. Maine folks are known for their common sense. My father's golden tongue may have waxed eloquent, but amid a frugal people who measure men by their deeds rather than their words, there were no free handouts. We hit the road back to La Sierra, California, where Aunt Jen and Uncle Ross always responded graciously to a sob story. Simple but hardworking folk, they toiled at blue-collar jobs and, despite their hospitality, were scorned by my parents and avoided—until their money ran out.

Aunt Jen, a large woman, was hard of hearing and wont to yell her questions and responses. Further, she backed down from nobody. Uncle Ross was even louder and rowdier, but he had a talent that endeared him to all us children. He could down a dozen doughnuts in a flash—a talent likely related to his jolly belly that jiggled when he walked. In addition to sweets, he had two addictions—black Oldsmobiles and Coca-Cola.

We lived off these gracious people again and again until the day Mother lost it again. Angered by a firmly and loudly expressed opinion from Aunt Jen, my mother threw a hot iron across the room at her.

Enraged, her teenage daughter, Tonya, unloaded on our parents, concluding, I've been told, by calling Father a "lazy bum who needs to get out and get a job!" We didn't have much to pack.

This time Father called on a Hollywood friend for whom he had been chauffeur. Summoning up his considerable charm, he sought advice

One of the 15 or 16 times the six of us were dumped off on Aunt Jen in La Sierra, California. She bought our clothes. (L-R) Pam, Fred, Ned, Edward, Clara, and Grover.

on a home suitable for his illustrious family. Maybe it was the coming season of Christmas. Maybe it was a whiff of the upper side of fantasyland. Whatever, what failed in Maine succeeded in Hollywood. We moved into a Frank Lloyd Wright house on the beach in Newport Beach. Using the address as a credit reference, Father bought a fire-engine-red MG sports car, which he parked in the large garage beneath the house. But again, it was here today, gone tomorrow. Six weeks later the MG was repossessed. We fled our mansion late one night, having paid no rent. Father traded our venerable Cadillac for an old bus, which he and his brother turned into an early RV. A nearby park became our home. With no utilities, we had to use the shower and public bathroom located by the laundry room. With two adults and seven children, our RV was not just crowded, it was *crowded* crowded, so crowded that I slept in the luggage rack. So crowded that I found it difficult to retain the invisibility I coveted and cultivated. Though I was only 3 years old, I can remember life there as if it were yesterday. It's a funny thing about memory: sweet times and bad times alike seem to stay best in memory. Only the beatings and chokings in New York City and a bear in Maine remain of my earlier memories.

It seemed miles to that public bathroom in the dark night, so I began to wet my bed. One morning as I climbed quietly from my wet quarters, I heard my father's guttural voice: "You little bastard!" He lunged for me and began swinging a belt against my naked backside. I hung there for a moment before dropping to the floor. There was no place to go, no escape hatch in a small busload of nine occupants. I lay on the floor as Father kicked me and beat me until his rage subsided.

As an adult, I've rationalized the incident as the rage of an unemployed man with eight hungry mouths to fill, who lived in a poverty that belied his fantasies of riches and respect. In his mind we were the burdens who ruined his life. He hated us, and we hated him. So he stormed at us children and the wife who held him back from the status his breeding warranted. Ours was a world of cold, brutal harshness mixed with a rigid religious ideology. God really had no place in our loveless environment, but we had a strange, sick connection to religion, hanging on to it while criticizing everything about it. Our liturgy consisted of information on all the ways to go to hell and all the rules to get to heaven. Of course, at 3 I entertained no theology. All I knew was that there was supposed to be a bad devil and a good God who answered the prayers of little children. The devil I could believe in; in my early years I saw his footprints wherever my parents stepped. God? In my worst moments of unbelief, Aunt Anne and Uncle Marty would come to mind. Surely it wasn't the devil who made them good. It had to be someone . . .

An incident that occurred when I was 3 ½ years old left me convinced that God and I had a speaking relationship. I was sitting in a public sandbox, not far from our old bus, when Eddie, the 5-year-old neighborhood bully, threw sand on me. I had come to know him and fear him. Conditioned to nonresponse by the many brutal beatings I had endured from my parents, I sat silent and still. He had stolen my only toy, a small plastic rake. Now he added injury to insult by using it to hit me on my head, and in that moment, I erupted. Screaming like a banshee, I jumped on his back, grabbed his neck, and rode him, facedown, into the sand.

"I hate you! I hate you!" I shouted, digging my fingers deep into his flesh.

Unable to breathe, Eddie struggled desperately, but the more desperate he became, the more violently I squeezed and shoved. Deep guttural noises escaped my throat as I rode him like a wild animal in a death struggle with its prey. Suddenly I heard a voice within my head command, *"Let him up; you're killing him—he's going to die."* Stunned, I jumped from his back.

He lay there, struggling for air. In what seemed eons later, he crawled shakily across the sandbox, got to his feet, and ran home. I just sat, frightened by the feeling of rage out of control. I didn't learn until later that my mother had witnessed the whole affair from our RV window. I've wondered whether my parents felt the same adrenalin rush, the same out-of-control rage of my sandbox war while they were beating me. More important to me, however, even as I stumbled from the sandbox, was the source of the voice that had urged me to release my death grip on the bully who had assaulted me. And now, as well as then, my conclusion is the same: It was God. *Maybe,* I thought, *He spoke through an angel. Or maybe it was what the Bible calls the Holy Spirit who spoke.*

It's too bad I never told my mother about that voice in the sandbox. She might have understood. But then I don't recall that she ever stopped beating me, and surely something—or someone—must have told her to stop. Maybe even my father got the word. And, maybe again, the voice was what we call conscience. Did my parents have one? The preachers say that when we repeatedly override our conscience, it grows fainter and fainter. Psychologists say it differently, but they seem to arrive at the same conclusion. My conclusion remains: It was the voice of God that spoke to me in that sandbox, however conveyed.

My brothers and I did get into fights after that. We were all fighters, rough and ready to leap at a perceived offense, except at home. There, we never uttered a challenging word. We had learned by experience that even a spontaneous show of happiness could be rewarded with violence.

Another experience when I was 3½ confronted me with quite another challenge: not that there is no God, but if there is, why doesn't He speak up when you really need Him? It started on a breezy August day with another trip to the trailer park bathroom, which was right next to the laundry. Several times during my daytime visits I'd encountered a loudmouthed camper named Gertrude. She had a long, bony nose that dominated her thin face, and looked 100 years old. She always carried a yellow broom that all the boys in the camp were sure she could ride. If we strayed from the pebble walkway, she would yowl at us and often follow up with a swing of her broom, as she did at me that morning.

"Get off the grass, you brat," she yelled, swinging her broom threateningly.

I "got" back around the building and into the men's room from the far side. In and out of the stall I went, congratulating myself for taking care of my business without help. As I turned toward the door, a hot, smelly hand clamped over my face, while another hand dragged me by the arm into the shower area. A guttural voice growled in my ear, "Shut up, _____ it, or I'll kill you!"

I was paralyzed with fear. Even as I write this my hand is shaking. My assailant, a large man, pulled my pants down, spun me around, and forced himself into me. Though the pain was excruciating, I made no sound; my conditioning held. In what seemed forever—but was only a minute or two—he was gone, and I stood there, shaking, humiliated, not knowing the name for what had happened but having no doubt it was bad, very bad. I suppose most other boys would have run home, sobbing, and their fathers would have held them, comforted them, and then, maybe, gone for a gun. Nobody's Boy had nobody to run to, nobody who cared.

Until recently I had never told anyone what happened. The words, "sexual abuse," somehow seem too clinical, too academic to describe "it." On that painful August day when I was little more than a baby, I pulled my pants up and walked back to our homemade RV. The pain was not only physical it burned deep down in my psyche. I knew I had gotten what I deserved. A big person had hurt me because I was a bad boy.

In the days and weeks that followed, I retreated still further into my private hell. Nobody noticed. Not father. Not mother. Not brothers or sisters. Always in my mind were the words with which mother had defined me—"bad seed." I knew that she must be right. If I were not, they would not beat me and choke me and hurt me. I would be hugged, and maybe even kissed. But I was bad, and bad people do bad things to bad boys. Now I had something else to hate. That park. Our bus. My parents— No, I had already hated them.

Modest as the park charge was, there came a day, as usual, when it could not be paid. And there came a night, as usual, when we hit the road. Where would it take us this time—to a place of rainbows? No, that was too much to hope for.

# Big Troubles

*I remember, I remember*
*The house where I was born,*
*The little window where the sun*
*Came peeping in at morn;*
*He never came a wink too soon,*
*Nor brought too long a day,*
*But now, I often wish the night*
*Had borne my breath away.*

—Thomas Hood

**San Bernardino is a city** of about 183,000 souls, located at the base of the San Bernardino Mountains. It has its attractions, but affluence is not one of them. Even state welfare has been unable to upgrade the income of San Bernardino's poor materially. A friend has said that it is the only city he knows whose downtown is distinguished by a discount grocery and a pawn shop. He's exaggerating, of course, but it is true that nearly half of San Bernardino's inhabitants are on welfare. (The very thought stirs a sense of kinship.)

Come in to Los Angeles by plane, rent a car, and you can make it to San Bernardino in an hour and a half—at midday, that is, and then only occasionally. At high-traffic times (twice a day, and sometimes all day) your trip may take five hours. To your left, as you drive east, are the San Gabriel Mountains; to the right and ahead you may see Mount San Jacinto, which looms up behind Palm Springs. To get there you drive three miles east from San Bernardino, through Loma Linda and Redlands, and then up you'll go a thousand feet onto the desert. Often, returning to Loma Linda from a visit with my brother Edward in Palm Springs, I've come to the dropoff looking down toward San Bernardino and been unable to see anything—the valley would be covered by a blanket of smog. Two decades ago it was so thick that a healthy adult couldn't walk two blocks without gasping for breath. Stringent regulations imposed by California have greatly improved the air quality in the valley.

Was it after four or five moves that Father nursed our old car 6,000 feet up the switchbacks of the San Bernardino Mountains to a tiny town called Skyforest? Calling it a town stretches reality. I can recall only a few shacks scattered through the pine trees. Today's would-be house owners would die for our location, which was on the mountain rim overlooking, at that time, the smog-free and lightly populated valley. Our site was ideal, so far as my parents were concerned, for a second reason. It was a haven for abject poverty and abuse because nobody bothered anybody for any reason. It also seemed a step up from our previous homes, if only because we were on welfare and had more to eat. As we children wandered through the forest we could hear warblers welcoming us. However, squirrels jerked their tails nervously as we neared them, and jays warned us to mind our own business. An old oak near our house had been struck by lightning and was partially hollowed out. We called it the "Bear Tree," and hid there from imaginary bruins.

We lost Fred from our games when, at 12 years of age, he became the only one in the family to get a job. Not skilled labor, to be sure, but honorable—babysitting and raking pine needles. His income bought us food. He also brought us some excitement. One night, after working late, he hurried home along the mountain highway. Coming to a shortcut through the woods that he had taken a few times in the daylight, he decided to chance it in the dark. Using his best imitation of an Indian scouting for game, he slipped along the trail until he heard twigs snapping, and he wasn't anywhere near the bear tree. That's when he abandoned his Indian fantasy, shifted his gait into high gear, and flew through the woods. Just as he reached the pavement, a car coming around a corner framed him in its headlights. He looked back and, to his dismay, saw the big black bear that had been his unseen companion in the woods. If his previous sprint would have qualified him for a high school medal, his inspired second run (as he described it) was of Olympic quality, rivaling his pace of a few years before when he had snatched me from the train tracks on Long Beach. I'll never forget his face as he rushed right past the bear tree and into the house, pale as a ghost and shaking as if he had palsy. His account of a bear the size of a hippo and fast as a bill collector on the trail of an overdue account was couched in words we could understand. The next night he worked late again, but he didn't take the shortcut through the woods.

Up to this point our stay in Sky Forest had offered a welcome respite. Food, shelter, and a bit of stability might have seemed less than a blessing to many families. To us children it seemed heaven on earth. But if the theology I've heard has any validity, heaven isn't on earth—yet. And until it is, earth will continue to offer up its sad realities, as we children well knew. It didn't take Father long to confirm our fears.

Blue Jay, a small town nearby, had a skating rink. Father's athleticism included several years of skating during his youth in upstate New York. The rink owners thought he would make a great instructor. He did, but he didn't confine his instruction to skating. He seduced his female clients. (Yes, we knew. And so did Mother.)

One breezy afternoon we were ordered to go outside and play. We smelled trouble. A couple hours later an ambulance drove into our yard, lights flashing on its roof. Two men jumped out and wheeled a cot into the house. We didn't have long to wait. When it came out, Mother was on it with a white sheet over her. The men put her into the back of the ambulance and shut the door. Then, with siren wailing, they sped away.

In a normal family, Father would call the kids in, sit them down, and seek to lessen their anxiety. But our family was anything but normal.

"Are those men stealing Mama?" a wide-eyed Annie questioned as they drove away.

"I don't know, Annie," I whispered.

"I'm scared," Annie said. "Let's go up to the bear tree. She grabbed my hand to lead the way. Later, she said she was hungry.

"Let's go over to the big house," I responded.

No one seemed to be at home, so we crept around the side and found an unlocked door. In the kitchen we found crackers and a jar of sweet pickles, which we consumed while we wondered what was wrong with Mother and what would happen to us now. Weeks later we learned that Mother, depressed by her husband's repeated infidelity, had tried to kill herself. What about us? Would we be given away? Would we ever see each other again?

In the weeks of her absence our circumstances worsened, but there was nothing new: secrecy, tension, violent eruptions, depression, disappearances, screaming, punching, grabbing, choking, silence, poverty, starvation, shame, embarrassment, isolation. Things didn't change when Mother came home. We moved. And moved. And moved. From

September 1952 to September 1953 we moved 19 times. Our residences included cow pastures, campgrounds, and shacks.

The last move, however, seemed to offer a new start. It took us to Malibu, where my father joined Ron Chapita, a Hollywood star of the day, in producing parts for military aircraft. Our house was a rich man's residence, a beachfront, with a four-car garage. Though we had money for once, there were ever new crises to further crush my spirit. Above all was my parents' continued refusal to see my need to be validated, affirmed, and loved. To be ignored by one's own parents exacts a heavy penalty. It left my soul wandering in a wasteland of bewilderment and depression. Much of my life I've searched for real parents without even realizing it. As a teenager I sought and received solace from my brother Ned, but no relationship can substitute for a missing mother and father. As Nobody's Boy, I was starved for affection, a searcher for love, but not even knowing how to define these needs. If there was a God, He walked with me in the flesh of my little sister Annie, whose love kept me from total mental isolation and, I believe on reflection, mental collapse.

And, of course, there was no new start. Wherever we moved, our baggage traveled with us. None of us children were surprised when, one morning, we heard the crashing of thrown dishes. We didn't have to be told; our father was having another affair. When my mother blew up, she lost all reason. The needs of her children meant nothing.

It was at such a time that my needs peaked. I would hide in a closet with Annie, and we would silently plead for the chaos to stop. It didn't. What did it feel like to be held and cared about and maybe even hugged? I was not the only child asking these questions. And I was not the only one hiding somewhere. But I was the only one my folks seldom spoke to, and then usually to curse me. All of us crept quietly about like small animals, waiting for a giant to step on us and crush us. My stomach was a tight mass as I internalized every rejection.

This time when Mother blew up because of her husband's affair with a secretary, he left. He had borrowed money from his Hollywood partner and never paid it back. Mr. Chapita sent the law to collect the debt. Of course, Father couldn't pay it; in fact, we were about to be evicted from our beach paradise. His reaction was nothing new. He put six of us into our current vehicle—a 1951 Chevy panel delivery truck—and headed for the sanctuary of the San Bernardino mountain wilderness. Left behind were our mother and our brother Edward, who had an eye infection. We took nothing but a few blankets and pillows. Leading us was a violent madman who hated children, especially those who burdened his life.

The first night we pulled into a remote cow pasture, deep in the mountains, unhitched the barbed-wire gate, jolted down a dusty cow path, and, by the light of the Chevy's headlights, spread our blankets in the truck and on the ground, hoping they would keep us warm at the 7,000-foot elevation. Where were we? Where were we going? What would happen to Mother and Edward? What would happen to us? It's called anxiety. It burdens one's mind during the day and banishes sleep during the night. There we hid from the law and waited, while Mother dealt with the police.

A few weeks later we were reunited in a run-down two-story, three-bedroom house on the corner of a large farm near Riverside, which is about 20 miles south of San Bernardino. For the record, our address was 12710 Magnolia Avenue. Tall skinny palms alternated with short fat ones lining the highway in front of our house. We didn't mind the broken panes of glass or the flaking paint of our new residence. It had a roof, and we wouldn't be there long anyway.

Our neighbors across the street kept a goat that was less friendly than its owners. Our back door faced a barn with its array of cats and cows. We boys explored every inch of the place as we meandered across the onion fields and green pastures. We often played in the small pond where the cattle drank. One of those cattle was a large, white Brahma bull, with loose hanging skin and two huge horns. When he was elsewhere in the pasture, I would push a stick with a cloth on it into a piece of wood, call it a boat, and, as its captain, sail it across the ocean. Lest our home site seem attractively bucolic, I should mention that our house was next to the four-lane highway that led from Riverside to the coast cities. I remember sitting on the front porch with my brothers and sisters as mother read a book about the end of the world. I can't say that it was frightening; rather, given life as we knew it, even hell didn't seem too fearsome.

I spent as much time as I could outside, away from the yelling and abuse that hung like fog within the house. Sometimes I wondered whether God didn't go inside houses. While playing on the farm, I could almost feel His presence. Inside the house, I couldn't. Then I remembered the happy atmosphere in Aunt Jen's house, also in Riverside, and made an adjustment in my theology. God did go into some houses, but not into houses like ours.

In late August, just a few weeks after we had moved to Riverside, Mother disappeared, just as she had once before. This time I didn't see any strange cars come into our yard. One day she was there, and the next she had vanished. A week went by, and still she was gone. I didn't ask, and neither did my siblings. We all knew that a question could trigger an explosion. We learned later that the sheriff had arrested her for writing checks on a nonexistent account to cover my father's unpaid loans in Los Angeles. In due course she was tried, convicted, and sentenced to one year in prison in Vista, California.

Neglected by a father who would disappear for days at a time, we scavenged for food like animals, on some days not eating at all. The phrase "justice is blind" is meant to emphasize that all who come before the law—whether poor or rich, male or female, young or old, Black or White—are treated equally. If sentencing a mother to prison for a year without investigating the competency of her husband or the status of her children represents justice, I don't even now know the meaning of the word.

Then, only a few days later, Father disappeared; again, with no warning. No explanation. No provision made for our survival. We learned later that he had gone to stay with friends in Hollywood. Once in a while, during succeeding weeks, he would materialize, not to provide money or food, but rather to send Fred to borrow money from one relative or another. On another occasion, not wanting to face his wife alone, he took Fred to the prison with him. Fred never told us about the visit.

The calm before the storm: A missing mother and father; a terror-filled midnight soon to come. (L-R, back) Edward, Pam, Ned, Fred; (front) Grover, Annie, Clara.

I am unable even from an adult perspective to explain why we missed the false stability we had grown up with. It was as if we were addicted to the constant chaos, tension, and insecurity. Any change in status was terrifying. I did not miss my mother's temper or my father's violence. I hated them for their indifference to me as a needy child. When they disappeared, one cold unknown was simply replaced by another. I joined my brothers and sisters in this new struggle for survival. We gathered the fallen nuts from several gnarled walnut trees that grew beside the dusty road. We husked them carefully, making sure not to lose even the smallest particle. We stole a number of white onions from the farm next door and put them in a burlap sack kept in the hallway. Our daily "feast" consisted of an onion and a handful of nuts.

Ned got a job at a small chicken ranch up in the hills behind our house. I helped him. We got no money but were permitted to keep any eggs that were cracked or spotted with blood. We could not have carried a pot of gold back to our hungry siblings with more pride than we carried those eggs. When hunger would overwhelm us, we would sneak into the nearby barn. At the back, near the hay, was a barrel filled with chicken feed made up of cereal, ground animal parts, and other things that no sane adult would eat. But were it not for that chicken feed, we would have starved.

I knew something was happening to me but didn't know what. The sun no longer shone down in yellow warmth; rather it had a greenish cast. The music of the birds had turned into scolding. Even the warm August breeze conveyed a strange chill.

One day a gray pickup truck pulled up next to the barn in a cloud of dust. Three men jumped out and went inside. I hurried over to see what was going on and watched, wide-eyed, as they put a rope around the neck of one of the cows and led it into the yard. One of the men—a burly six-footer with brown chewing tobacco dribbling down his chin—leveled what looked like a .30 caliber Winchester at the cow and pulled the trigger. My ears were still ringing when the cow fell to its knees. With a quick flash of a knife, one of the men slit its throat. Blood spurted into their faces and spattered against the side of the barn and onto my feet. The other cattle smelled the blood, and panic set in. One of the men shoved a rifle into my shaking hands and, laughing, told me to shoot another cow that was being dragged from the barn. Its eyes were rolled back in terror, and foam flew from its mouth. I dropped the gun and, trying to escape the nightmare of my 7-year-old life, ran blindly toward the pond.

There I sat and silently wept. The big bull I had avoided stood look-ing at me with his large, penetrating eyes. It was as if he were asking, "Who is this strange boy who never makes a sound?"

With the first week of September came school days. We watched the school buses go by our house. Our parents had never registered us for school. Our schooling had been interrupted so many times that we had no idea where our records were. We were afraid that the teachers would find that we had no parents, no food, no school clothes, no nothing. So we stayed out of sight during the day, fearful that the authorities might know that our mother was in prison and be watching for us. During the early evenings we ate what food we had on hand and played games. We moved our jars of walnuts out of the way and played hopscotch. When it was dark, we watched for the headlights of a truck. Our goal was to race around the house before the truck sped by. If you failed, a monster was supposed to get you. The monster did get us—the hunger, the dirty bod-ies, the daily fear, the isolation, the fatigue, and other monsters unknown. Then we would drift off to bed.

One hot day Fred rode his rusty bike on an errand to La Sierra, a col-lege town only two miles away. Father had returned, and at his command Fred went to beg for money from a nearby stranger who owned an orange grove. We had relatives in La Sierra, but they were drained from previous solicitations. One was my father's sister, Aunt Jen. She was standing in her front yard watering the grass when Fred pedaled by. She called out to him, but he ignored her. Alarmed, she watched him until he disappeared. Something was wrong, she decided. Little did we know the far-reaching consequences of her concern.

September 11, 1953, was an especially hot day. My stomach growled as I wandered around, scavenging for food. A sniff or two at my torn shirt reminded me that it probably had not been washed since we had left Malibu two months before. My ripped jeans had holes in the knees, but, as I saw it, a knee was not a knee until it had viewed the world through a man-sized hole. I rummaged the onion bag in the hall and appropriated a specimen that would not have passed muster in a grocery store. The wal-nuts had disappeared, along with Father, the week before. We wandered through an orange grove only to find that all had been picked. We had previously tried the tar on the telephone poles, which proved to be chewable but did little to assuage stomach pains.

That evening I slipped over to the barn and appropriated a couple handfuls of chicken feed. With my stomach pains eased, I curled up in a warm corner of the barn near the stacked hay and drifted off to sleep. I was jerked back to reality a half hour later by my 5-year-old sister, Annie. She was calling my name as she wandered toward the hay.

"Grover, where are you? Grover, I'm so hungry." She said it as though I could do something about it.

I scraped up a handful of chicken feed for her, and she sat munching it contentedly.

"Good night, Palsie," I said affectionately as she headed back to the house to sleep with her two sisters. I worried about her; she was so frail and pale. We were pals, and I loved her so. She was the one I talked to when the fog that clouded my mind threatened to send me tumbling into an abyss from which there might be no return. At last, reluctantly, I stumbled back to the house and dragged myself up the creaky stairs in the dark, for we had no electricity. We four boys shared a room with two beds. Our room faced the highway, and our window was always open to get some fresh air. We had no screens on the windows, and the insects crowded in for their nightcap. It's a wonder we didn't all need blood transfusions, but at least we got some cool night air.

I flip-flopped onto the old metal-framed bed with its thin mattress, but I couldn't seem to sleep. I was still trying to when the midnight train whistled its intention as it prepared to cross the highway just up the road. I listened to the metal wheels clanking against the tracks. They seemed to be repeating the refrain my stomach was voicing: *I'm so hungry in the dark; I'm so hungry in the dark; I'm so hungry—*

I shifted my body on the bed. My feet were dirty from the cow-piled yard, and my hair was matted and unwashed. I slept in my shorts and ragged shirt. It was hard to find a comfortable position in which to curl up, for the bed sagged terribly in the middle. With the frogs and crickets and heavy breathing from my three brothers for an accompaniment, I finally slipped into a troubled sleep.

I came half awake soon after to what sounded like keys rattling at the top of the stairs. Out of the blackness a gruff voice called out a command: "GET UP AND GET DRESSED!"

Fred stirred and sat up as a beam of light swept across his startled face. Ned and Edward were rubbing their eyes and sitting up, terrified, not knowing what was happening. They grabbed for their clothes and struggled into them. In my room, on hands and knees, I sought for my pants and pulled them over sleep-heavy legs.

What was happening? Were we being kidnapped? Surely no one would have come to our house to rob us! Fear speeded our steps as we stumbled down the stairs and out the front door. All seven of us stood in the darkness, searching one another's face. I could hear Annie sobbing quietly as a flashlight splashed across our faces. Across the years all seven of us are agreed that the invaders—the police, as we were to learn—never spoke another word.

Our eyes blinded by the light, we could see only two shadows in the driveway. But we got! Fast, without protest. We all had years of training. We knew how to be quiet, orderly, and herded. There were no questions from any of us as we climbed into two cars. I looked toward the front seat, desperately searching for a glimpse of my brothers, but a wire screen between the front and back seats blocked my view. The night creatures were momentarily quiet. Who were these men? What did they want? Where were they taking us?

I hadn't left much behind. There was a tiny boat floating on the pond for some other child to find on a sunny afternoon. A few onions waited in a burlap sack for 14 dirty hands to treasure. The other nonmaterial items— the pain, the shame, the hurt, the fear—traveled with us.

The men drove in silence. As we passed under a streetlight I saw that the driver wore a black cap, and the windshield reflected a silver badge on his chest. The police had us. Why, then, was there not one word of kindness? Didn't these men have children at home that they may have tucked into bed? Had they kissed a child's forehead before going to work? And where was God? I wondered. Did He see the cars pull into the yard? Was He on the stairs watching as we stumbled past? If He was there, if angels folded their wings as we filed by, I never knew it. All I knew was that the smallest members of the Wilcox family were in trouble. Big trouble.

**THREE**

# Juvie Hall

*A child, I,*
*so little understood*
*and understanding,*
*Abandoned,*
*Denied,*
*Why?*

—*The Chronicles of Grover,* I, IV

**No other cars were on the road** that night a half century ago. It seemed that we drove forever on a road that went nowhere. Later I would find that we covered only a few miles. At 1:00 in the morning our captors stopped in front of a large building with a chain-link fence around it. The headlights lit up a sign. I sounded out the words to myself: "juvenile hall." I had no idea what that meant. I could see a large glass door with shiny metal around it. Then the car doors opened, and we were gruffly told to get out. The glass door opened with a buzzing sound, and we entered a semi-dark room and huddled together.

"Follow me," a voice commanded my sisters.

I looked up to see a huge woman with greasy black hair and eyes that bugged out like those in a fish I once saw. I watched my three sisters walk down the hall, clinging to each other as if they could not face the unknown alone. We four boys stood silent, our empty stomachs churning. The police had gone. They had appeared out of the night, grabbed us from our beds, stolen us away, spoken their five words, and disappeared. There was no explanation, no gentle pat on the head. Like all the other big people, they lived only to hurt us. They were the enemy.

The big woman returned with a tall skinny woman. "Take them to the bathroom, wash them, and delouse them," she ordered. "They're always the same—dirty."

As I turned to follow my brothers, she grabbed me by the arm and spun me around. "You're staying here!" She lifted me and tossed me into a crib.

I was stunned. Small for my age, yes; a baby, no! But alone. Oh, *so* alone! Alone in this strange, dark building. Alone in Bug Eye's room. Alone in my mind and soul. Alone in a crib. *Dear God, if You exist, do something for me!* I could hear my brothers somewhere down the hall. Someone was crying. One was demanding to go home. A woman shouted, "QUIET!" Gradually I became aware of the ticking of the large round clock that hung on the wall across from the crib. *Tick. Tick. Tick. Where am I?* As I sat up, I heard the wild yells of a small child. I was later to learn that her name was Sybil, and that she was mentally challenged. At the moment her incoherent cries seemed to answer my question—I was in a madhouse. *Where are my brothers and sisters? What is happening to us?*

At last I slept. Panic gripped me when I awakened. Events of the night had been bad enough, but now I found I had wet the bed. What would that woman—the big woman who had thrown me into the crib—do to me? *O God, where are You?*

As I've reflected on the terrors of that September night I've thought how much better I would have slept had one of the policemen patted me on the head and said, "Son, everything's going to be all right." How much less apprehensive I would have been had the bug-eyed woman hugged me and gently laid me in the crib. Real compassion, real caring, real love: these seem so alien to much of the human race. And, I've come to believe, their absence removes much of what the term *human* was meant to encompass. We are left afraid to reach out, and when fear controls us, we hide behind defense mechanisms. Just one hug for a terrified child that terrible September night could have turned my life around.

With morning came the bug-eyed woman storming into the room. "You kids are all alike—dirty, and you always wet the ——— bed! I can smell it in the hall!" She grabbed me out of the crib, dragged me into a bathtub, scrubbed me red with a stiff brush, and then cut off my hair. Finally she walked over to a large closet and opened the doors. "Get some clothes on," she said tersely.

I stood with my mouth open. The shelves were filled with neat stacks of striped T-shirts, socks, and underwear. They may have been donated by the Salvation Army or some other charitable organization, but I'd never seen anything like it! The clothing would have outfitted my brothers and me until we were in high school. And there were shoes without flapping soles. I didn't know there was a closet like that in the whole wide world!

"I'm going to throw away these disgusting rags," the woman said, grabbing up my old clothes. She picked out a brightly striped shirt and pulled it over my head. "Wet the bed again, and no more new clothes for you."

I may have heard her, but it didn't register. I was too busy putting on a pair of new black shoes. I thought that closet must have had an opening somewhere that connected with heaven! I wasn't left standing and staring long. Bug Eyes marched me into a large room with tables. Kids were sitting around them eating. It seemed to me that they all stopped and stared at me, as I sat down. I couldn't see my brothers and sisters anywhere. I guessed that kids were seated by age. I could see a little colored box by each person and hear the clicking of spoons against the white dishes. Later someone told me that we were eating dry cereal. It tasted good, but it would have tasted even better if I could have sat by my brothers. I wondered if we would be fed only once a day.

Just as I finished my cereal, some adult shouted a command and everyone got up, pushed their chair against the table, and filed out into what they called the "dorm." It was a long, rectangular room with a concrete floor and lights high up in the ceiling. Cots lined each wall. Each had a thin mattress, white sheets, one blanket, and a pillow. Everyone seemed to move like everyone else, and there was no talking or laughing. Something familiar made me feel at home. I realized later, much later, that it was the loneliness, the hopelessness, the hollowness.

Moving again in concert with others, I walked down a corridor and into a large room with a gray cement floor. A sofa faced a strange-looking piece of furniture that had a white glass window in the middle. Someone whispered that it was a "TV," whatever that was. Within a few hours we were ushered into what they called a "dining room," where there seemed to be food everywhere. Despite having overworked my salivary glands while examining my new clothing and shoes, I had enough juice left to down a huge meal. There seemed to be food everywhere. I decided they would probably not feed us more than once a week. And this time I caught sight of my brothers at a table across the room. Again, all I could hear was the clanging of spoons or forks against the bowls. Everything in this strange place seemed worthy of superlatives. But again, nobody was talking or laughing. It all seemed so strange to Nobody's Boy, who had so often been hungry, so often been beaten. Things got even better when my sister Pam was put to work in the kitchen, from which she would slip us extra treats. Incarceration in juvenile hall in 1953 seemed filled with endless blessings for the Wilcox family.

Clothing. (I hadn't noticed that our shirts had numbers printed on them.)

Shelter. No rain through the roof. (I was yet to learn what juvenile hall was.) And that new piece of furniture, called a television, to entertain.

What more could one want? I was soon to find out.

During the first week at juvenile hall, I saw there was more than one building. All were made of the same red brick. One building had windows painted blue just below the roof line. A tall chain-link fence, taller than my oldest brother, Fred, surrounded the property. It was even taller than the bug-eyed woman. All around the top of the fence were strands of what was called "barbed wire." Nobody could go in or out the front door without a key. My brothers told me we were in jail. What had we done? We'd stolen a few apples and chicken feed and oranges. Surely they couldn't know of the sandwiches Ned had made when he slipped into tents on Long Beach. He had never taken more than we needed just to survive.

Juvenile hall in 1953 was a detention facility for children from birth to 18 years of age. There you could find the criminals, the incorrigibles, and the runaways, as well as the abused and the abandoned. We all breathed the same air and shared the same space. Youth who gave special trouble were kept in a separate area. We were the "throwaway kids." If anyone had wanted us, we would not have landed in this place.

As the months passed, we spent many hours trying to figure out why our relatives never came to see us. Aunt Jen lived only three miles from juvenile hall, but she, as we saw it, was the culprit who had turned us in to the authorities. When she came to visit, we refused to see her. We did not, of course, expect either of our parents to show up. As usual, we were on our own. But we had enough to eat, and I had my very own bed. There were problems, however, as I soon learned.

"Hey, you better watch out here."

"Oh, what do you mean?"

"Watch out for the big kids; they'll hurt you. I hate them all. They always beat me up and do other stuff to you. I hate my parents, too."

"So do I," I whispered. "Why are you here?"

"I kept choking my sister. They hate me and don't want me," my informant said, with a quiver in his voice.

I eyed this angry boy. His name was Tom. He was 10 years old. When the lights went out, I lay there, afraid to go to sleep. A guy who chokes his sister was in a bed only three feet away. The older boys slept at the other end of the room. Nighttime brought out all the strange noises, especially poor Sybil's anguished cries. I didn't sleep much the first few nights. The rules were strict and the repercussions severe. The counselors did what they wanted since nobody was there to check on them. I was too young to understand why they beat the boys regularly. Inside juvenile hall and out, child abuse was looked on as a family matter. Punishment was physical and often violent. The bug-eyed woman loved to pull you along by the arm. The tall skinny one liked to pull your hair. The female counselors were nicer to the girls for reasons I was too young to understand.

I soon learned that we were designated wards of the State of California. We had lacked supervision and were unwanted, it was said. What did that make us? What did that make me? Was I so worthless, so bad, that I wasn't worth feeding or being loved? Me, Grover Winslow Wilcox, an unwanted child. An inmate of a juvenile jail, ward of a piece of land called California, My number was 10114. It was right on my shirt. I'll never forget it. Yes, for once I had enough food, but it wasn't food for my soul. I let the tears roll as I pressed my face into the flat pillow. The authorities had confirmed it: I was Nobody's Boy.

Aunt Jen had a different view. According to her, I had a Father—a heavenly Daddy who loved me so much that He had sent His Son to die for me. He had a real home all ready for me, and had even written my name on His hand. I was not Nobody's Boy. I was His boy! It would be some time before I realized it, but He was willing to wait. Sadly, I knew only the God my parents had modeled for my siblings and me. And I hated Him!

Nobody ever said what we were supposed to do until they yelled because we were not doing it. On my second morning in juvenile hall I got up, pulled my clothes on, and went to breakfast. Because I was only 7 years old, I couldn't eat with my brothers. As I ate, I heard the other kids talking about school. I knew what a school was because I had finished the first grade in Malibu. But there was, so far as I knew, no school in juvenile hall.

After breakfast, Fish Eyes told us to follow her, and we marched out the front gate and onto the sidewalk. The door was locked behind us as we turned down a street lined with pepper trees laden with small, red, BB-like berries. I noticed brightly dressed kids from the neighborhood walking in the direction we were. The boys were carrying Roy Rogers lunch pails; the girls had pails with Dale Evan's picture on them. *Wham!* "Keep your eyes straight ahead!" Fish Eye snarled. The other kids kept as far from us as they could. However, a narrow gate behind the school drew us together as we arrived on the school grounds. A group of boys taunted us: "Hey, here they come, the juvie kids in the prison clothes!" Laughter became general as they read aloud the numbers on our shirts. One of the larger juvies swung at a tormenter, and war broke out. As I rolled in the dust with a tormentor, I swung my fists wildly but well. We no-goods were used to protecting ourselves.

"Get up out of the dirt, you no-good riffraff," shouted an under-nourished-looking male teacher. "You don't deserve to be here! All you are is trouble!"

I knew the script well: We were automatically at fault. We didn't even have to vie for that status. Separated from the good guys at last, we shuffled on toward the school, rubbing the dirt from our clothes as best we could. My classroom was the first building we came to, right next to the bike rack, I noticed. I slipped through the door and into the second-grade classroom and sought a desk in the back row, where my number wouldn't be so conspicuous.

The teacher, a short, squatty blond, didn't seek an explanation. It wasn't needed. "Why do you J.H. kids always cause trouble every time you come to school?" It wasn't a question; it was an indictment. She stared straight at me. "Are you Grover Wilcox? I understand they brought you in just two days ago. Seven years old and already in trouble. Well? Speak up!"

I felt like crawling under the desk. I said nothing. Maybe I was bad and worthless. Every big person said so. In that moment I bonded with my juvie partners. I hated all these kids with clean clothes, lunch pails, and books. And I was sure they hated me. Despite my best efforts to suppress them, two tears trickled down my cheeks and onto the desk. With a quick swipe of my arm, I brushed them away. I hated every student. I hated the teacher. They would never see me cry again. If I had to cry, it would be on the inside.

The school's name, Liberty Elementary, was a cruel daily reminder that we came from behind bars. It was for grades one through six. One day a student asked my brother Edward why he was in juvenile hall. He looked about, as if to make sure no one else was listening, then whispered, "I killed somebody." Nobody bothered him after that.

Soon after we arrived at juvenile hall, Pam and Fred got all seven of us together out under the walnut trees. "Don't let anybody try to be nice to you," Pam warned. "They're all bad. We must stick together against the enemy." Here, on reflection, is the dysfunctional motto of isolation and loneliness. I adopted it. I talked to no one. But one day as I sat under the walnut trees two big boys came up behind me. "Hey, you ———; you're going to get it now!" They jumped me and began punching me in the stomach. They chose that target because bruises there didn't show up as they would on the face; the counselors would see blood that ran down a shirt. They finished up by kicking me in the back and telling me that I would get it worse if I told. No matter what I did or didn't do, I got beat up regularly. Some weeks it was once a day. So the shadows continued to be my best friend.

The highlight of each day was gathering in the TV room where we would watch a movie. Our favorites were shootouts between cowboys and Indians. Favorites for the boys, that is. The girls liked more peaceful themes, such as Shirley Temple playing with dolls. One day one of the bigger girls switched the channel during a movie Fred and Ned particularly liked. That led to an argument that escalated into a fistfight. As a result, my brothers were put into a restricted area for 14- to 18-year-old criminals. Edward soon followed his brothers. We had no communication for 10 months. By peering through the chain-link fence I could see them marching in formation. Though without communication with my parents through the years, I'd had my brothers and sisters. Now I had no one. "Mysterious Al" sank further into the shadows.

One day I discovered what would become a lifelong passion—basketball. If I stood in a long line of would-be athletes, I would get one shot at the basket when I reached the front. I felt a glow all over on the rare occasions that the ball went in. On a Friday afternoon, after an unusually long wait, I was about to shoot the ball when a girl we called "the witch" knocked it loose and grabbed it. "Get out of here, skinny punk! Your brothers aren't here to protect you anymore."

"Give me that ball; it's my turn!" I shouted, surprising even myself.

When she slapped me in the face, I hit her back with a full, round-house swing. It landed just as Bug Eye came by. She asked no questions, just grabbed my arm and screamed, "Get out of here and go to bed! All you brats have been a problem. No-goods!"

I fought the urge to tell her what had really happened. I hated the un-fairness. But I went. I had to stay in bed for the whole weekend. I was given only one meal a day until Monday breakfast.

On a cool October day I sat in the sand by the walnut trees, playing my pretend game. I made believe stones were cars, and sticks were trucks. I made a highway by dragging my fingers through the sand. Somehow I sensed I was being watched. There, under a walnut tree, stood a boy who was about my age. His eyes followed my truck as I steered it around a corner. Something about his silence touched me, a connoisseur of silence. Did I dare? I beckoned him over. Close up, he didn't look threatening. Brown hair stuck out from his head but did little to cover his most notable feature—ears that stuck out so far I could visualize his flying over the fence in a strong wind. "Do you want to play with me?" I asked.

He nodded.

"Here, you be the gas truck—that's the long piece of wood. What's your name?" I whispered.

No reply.

"Can you talk?"

"Yes, but those big boys punched me and told me to shut my mouth for the rest of the day."

"You just stay with me for the rest of the day. What's your name?"

"Ben. I'm 6."

"Grover. I'm 7."

We played until dinner; then we sat together.

"Why are you here, Ben?" I whispered.

"I don't know. I think my mother ran away. Why are you here?"

"I don't know either. My parents just left, and we were kidnapped here."

I had noticed that Ben's eyes looked kind of vacant, as if part of him wasn't in there anymore. I understood. I knew Ben needed a friend.

That evening I checked my eyes in the mirror.

★ ★ ★

Every once in a while Annie (I called her my Palsie) and I would get together under the walnut tree. I made sure she had the shadiest spot. She was my baby sister, you know. Annie seemed to me to be wasting away. When she grinned at me, her tiny, thin face seemed almost to disappear. When we had been together at home, I would always share some of the food I got. Her eyes would light up, and somewhere, deep down in me, something would seem to come to life.

"Oh, Annie, I'm so glad to see you!"

"Me too, Grover. I miss you and our hiding place!"

"Yeah. I wonder if that brown cat still comes and hides in the hayloft. Do you think we'll ever go back there?"

"I don't know. Anyway, we have food now."

"I know. Pam gave me part of a doughnut last night."

We sat silent, peering across the yard where the older boys were confined. "I was hoping to see our brothers," Palsie said.

"What do you do all day when we're in school?" I asked.

"Oh, mostly I play with Sybil and color. Did you know that I have my own coloring book now?"

"No! Your very own? What's in it?"

"It has horsies and cows and kittens. There's a farm, but not like where we lived. I don't have my own colors; they have a big box for all of us. We kind of share."

"What are the girls like, Palsie? Do they hurt you?"

"Sometimes; but Pam always sticks up for me. I love her, you know."

"I miss Pam too," I told her. "I hardly ever get a chance to see her. The big boys beat us up all the time. There's nobody here with me now, so I hide a lot. They— *Look, there they are!*"

We pressed our faces against the fence and watched our brothers walk by.

"Grover, why don't you run away when you go to school?"

"We can't. Crow Face watches us all the way, and she said she would hurt us if we tried. Besides, where would we go?"

"You could run home."

"Home? Nobody's there. I don't know where our parents are. They hate me anyway."

Annie began to cry. "I want to go home. I miss home!" Tears cascaded down her face.

"Everybody loves you, Pet-horse. Do you think of me?"

"Yes, all the time!" She grinned at me through the tears.

We heard the dinner bell. We jumped up and ran for the food building. I could run faster than she could, but I let her win.

My concern about Annie's health proved all too well founded. Three months into our juvie confinement, she became deathly ill. When Aunt Jen offered to take her in, the court was all too happy to release not only her but Pam as well. Aunt Jen worked, so Pam's help was necessary. Annie recovered, but remained at Jen's. The rest of us were left to wonder why the judge could not—in fact, should not—have released us as well.

After Annie left, the days dragged. Occasionally I would go to our spot by the walnut trees, stand against the fence, and press my face so tight against the links that my nose would push through. I tried to convince myself that part of me was free. I would wonder if Annie was somewhere out there in the distant fields, and whether there was anyone in the whole wide world who loved Grover Wilcox. Several times I reached up and touched a barb on the wire that imprisoned me. Could anyone make it over that? Once in a while someone would try and be brought back, hands covered with blood.

One night the whole compound was electric with the news that one of the older boys had gotten away. We had no idea how, and we didn't care. We just knew that if he did it, we could, too. However, within a few days the escapee was captured, returned, and put into a tiny cell in solitary confinement. He was our hero and, in a sense, our priest, for escaping had become not only our obsession but our religion.

No one ever perused the Bible more diligently than I perused books that had something about escape in them—escaping from Indians, escaping from animals, from storms, even from marriage, an unanticipated institution from which to flee. *Even if I escaped,* I thought, *where would I go?* I mentally compared the morning breakfast with the chicken feed I'd left behind. My stomach sent a quick message to my brain: "Don't even think about it!"

My obsession with freedom gave way every night to vigilance. *Keep your eyes open. Be alert for danger. Look over your shoulder. Read the room for vi-*

*brations*. These were security tools with which I had a nearly lifetime familiarity. From my earliest memory at home, I had practiced it. Fail, and you got a beating—or worse. What went on in the juvenile hall dormitory was worse.

*As I turned toward the door, a hot, smelly hand clamped over my face while another dragged me by the arm into the shower area. A guttural voice growled in my ear, "Shut up or I'll kill you!"*

The memory remained. And on some nights, like this one, it returned.

The lights had been turned out. As my eyes had adjusted to the darkness I heard a commotion about six beds down on my left. The dorm was aligned with beds only three feet apart. I lifted my head and turned to see several of the big boys, who had sneaked in, pull a blanket over another boy's head. They jumped on him and began pounding him with their fists. Then I saw one of the shadowy figures pull the little boy's clothes off. Terrified, I pulled my covers over my head.

Afterward, I could hear the muffled sobs.

Once, later, they came for me. I screamed when I saw them coming in. Maybe because my cot was beside the hallway; maybe because Someone I had almost forgotten heard my cry; or maybe because . . . I don't know why. They left.

On December 11 I dressed for school. After breakfast, as we filed out, Crow Face grabbed me by my arm. "Get back in here! You're not going to school today. Sit down!" It seemed that every day someone was detained for one reason or another. So I cowered in her small office and waited for what would happen next.

When she returned and busied herself at the desk, I gathered up my courage to ask the reason for my detention. "Ma'am, would you—"

"Shut up!" she yelled, and came over and slapped me. "Don't sass me, you brat! Today you're going to town. You better tell them we treat you real nice or you'll really get it when you get back." Her dark look sent shivers up my spine.

After 15 minutes or so a strange man entered the office, spoke to Crow Face, then gestured to me to follow him. To my amazement, I was ushered into a car filled with my brothers and sisters—all of them! My heart began pounding with fear. Bad things had happened the last time we'd been taken away. What now? As usual, none of us had the slightest idea where we were going. Though we rode in silence, inaudible words flashed from eye to eye. If an army was needed, the silent words said, we'd be armed and ready.

Within a few minutes our driver stopped in front of a huge gray building with tall white pillars. He ushered us out and up the wide stairs and through the wide front doors. My knees were shaking; nothing good could come out of a big building like this! Big buildings like this had big bad people in them, people who put children in jail, or— I was too scared to think.

We were ushered down near the front of a big room, where we sat in a long, straight row of chairs. I wondered whether anyone could hear my heart pounding.

"What's going on?" I whispered to Annie.

Her frightened eyes offered no answer.

We heard a side door open, and in came a large, tall man, wearing, it appeared to us, a black dress. Seven pairs of Wilcox eyes followed his every step up to a seat on a high platform. Then another door opened and in walked—could it be?—our father! He was wearing regular clothes—a white shirt and a tie, black trousers, and black shoes. He didn't look our way. The large building, we later learned, was the Riverside County Courthouse, and the tall man in front was the judge. Was he mad at us? Were we in trouble again? Were we going to be adopted by someone? Whom would we belong to? Anyone?

They called this a second hearing. We had, of course, known nothing of the first. The judge spoke in a firm, deep voice that scared me. But he wasn't speaking to us. He was speaking to Father. At home nobody dared question our father about anything, ever. But this judge, John S. Gabbert, told him to stand, and he stood!

"Mr. Wilcox, today we are here to review the cases of your seven children. Do you understand these proceedings?"

"Yes, sir," Father replied meekly.

The judge gestured, and Father sat in a chair—still without even looking at us. A Mr. Maddox and a Mr. Van Horn stood, one at a time, and described in detail how we had been living in the house next to the farm.

"Sir," said Maddox, "these children were living alone in a rickety old house with no facilities, and they wore rags. They had no food to eat; and they ran through the surrounding hills unattended and unsupervised."

Maddox continued. "The mother is in prison, and the father, Mr.

Wilcox, left them and went to stay with friends in Hollywood. They were alone and abandoned. They did not attend school. We kept them under close surveillance for three weeks. And to make sure that we got all of them, we picked them up at midnight."

The judge sat for a few minutes, sifting through papers. Then he turned to Mr. Van Horn and asked, "What was the state of affairs the day you picked them up?"

"Well, Your Honor, as usual, none of them attended school. They just seemed to wander aimlessly around. I saw them eating chicken feed from the barn, and they went to bed early. They were in a desperate, neglected, and abusive environment. There was no aim or future to their existence, so we picked them up."

We sat, looking straight ahead and waiting for the room to explode with yelling and anger. That's the way it had always gone, and that's the way we thought it would be again.

But it didn't. What we heard knifed through to our souls and cut away the last tiny filament of self-worth that might have been hidden there in one or two of us.

"Mr. Wilcox, please stand." The judge's voice offered no alternative. Mr. Wilcox stood.

"Let me make this perfectly clear for the record," said the judge. "Mr. Wilcox, are you willing to take care of these, your children?"

"No." Father's answer sped to 14 listening ears—his children.

"Mr. Wilcox"—the judge seemed to be carefully picking his words—"are you capable of taking care of these, your children?"

"No." This was a *big* NO. With it went our hopes of getting out of juvenile hall.

"Were you, in fact, taking care of these children?"

"No," answered the man we had called Father. No. No. No.

The judge pointed out that all he had to do to get his children released from juvenile hall was to get a job, get a car, and rent a house. There was no answer.

Finally, as if to cement our fate, and as if to challenge the very essence of fatherhood in this man who stood before him, the judge asked, "Do you refuse to take care of these children?" The judge looked straight at Mr. Wilcox.

"Yes, I refuse."

We were stunned. There was no sound from the authorities present. The judge seemed to sag in his robe, as if he had come hoping for something better. Something more manly; something more fatherly.

The words were forever branded on the hearts of seven children. Seven rejected children. Seven abandoned children. To be sure, he had never taken care of us, as we and a few relatives knew. Now everybody knew. Hearts that had hoped, heard, and knew: He didn't care at all.

There, forever in the court records of Riverside County, California, people could read it: *He didn't care at all.* I had known it; I had experienced it; but my brothers, my sisters, must have had some hope that they were loved. That they mattered; that they were treasured. Something in them died at that hearing. Nothing died in me. My funeral had already taken place.

The judge walked out one door. The man we had called father walked out another. He didn't even turn to look at us. That day we officially became wards of the State of California. We returned to juvenile hall. In one year, we were to be put up for adoption.

Even the approach of Christmas did little to lift my spirits. The Wilcox family had no record of happy family times around a Christmas tree, and I learned that most of the children in the hall had never celebrated Christmas. But when I found that the older boys were putting on a play for us and that the community was sending presents, I got interested. One night I dreamed of candy and toys and happiness.

Maybe I ate too much candy in my dream. For sure, I awakened one morning feeling ill. I hid my condition from the counselors, but that night I started coughing so violently that I pulled a pillow over my head. A trip to the bathroom tripped me up. A hand grabbed me as I passed the office on my way back to bed. "You're hot as hell! How long have you been sick?"

"A while," I mumbled.

A half hour later I was being treated for pneumonia and severe bronchitis at the Riverside General Hospital. Two days before Christmas I returned to juvenile hall and did my best to look well. On Christmas Eve I stepped in line with the other boys and headed for the eating area. In all my time at J.H., I had never seen so many faces full of excitement and rare happiness.

As we passed the office, Crow Face grabbed me and spun me around.

"You're not going anywhere," she said. "You're still sick. Go get back in bed. I'll save your stocking for you until you get better."

From my bed, by straining, I could barely hear happy singing and music. I imagined the stocking hanging on the tree, the Christmas candy being passed out, and maybe even a small plastic car or painted horse being given to the boys. I pulled the covers over my head and cried. It was "Silent Night, Holy Night," all right, but all was not calm and all was not bright. And I had not met that other little boy who was born in a manger some 2,000 years before. I'd like to think that He sat on my bed that night. Whatever. I didn't get a bag of candy. I didn't see the Christmas stockings. I didn't sleep in heavenly peace.

A couple nights later I heard a rustling of sheets as Tom crept out of his bed and made his way over to me. Once in a while we ate together in the cafeteria. Into my silent world that night came Tom's grubby hand. He slid a few pieces of his Christmas candy into mine.

As spring approached, Clara came and talked to me at our walnut tree by the chain-link fence. She was her mother's favorite and was distressed because she had not seen her for six months. "Why hasn't she come to see me?" she asked plaintively. "Couldn't she at least write to me?" Her voice was heavy with pain.

I thought of telling her that mother couldn't write, but Clara was 10, and knew she could. I was really the wrong one to ask. "I don't think she cares for us at all."

Clara started to cry. In all those months we had not received even a note from our mother. Nothing at all. We stood by the walnut trees next to the barbed wire and tried, without success, to find an answer.

One evening Clara was rushed to the hospital, where they removed her tonsils. While recovering from that, she came down with pneumonia. A nurse walked into her room one night and found she was not breathing. She was rushed into the operating room, where a doctor performed a tracheotomy. So critical was her condition that the prison gave my mother a pass. Aunt Jen and my father went to Vista to pick her up. Mother visited Clara, and my older brothers, as well. She never came to see me. Clara recovered, and Mother was released six months early. She moved in with Aunt Jen, only three miles away. It could have been 10,000 miles, as far as I was concerned. The woman called "Mother" never even picked up a phone nor sent a penny postcard to the son named Grover.

Court records say we had another appearance in the county court-house on March 11, six months after the midnight raid. The results were the same. If my father could not have a prestigious position—that meant, in part, that he had to be his own boss—he would do nothing at all. That meant we had no hope at all. Unemployed, he hung around his sister's house, and we hung around the barbed wire. We had heard so many taunts from the counselors about adoption that I began to hope someone would take me. Still, I didn't want to be separated from my brothers and sisters. I saw Tom and others leave during the year. Someday, I hoped, I too would walk through that gate and out into freedom.

But something strange was happening to me. Before juvenile hall my gentle inner self hid among the shadows. However, as spring turned into summer, my soul seemed to split into two parts. The kind and loving child within—the child who had thought there might be a kind and loving God despite what my parents offered as a model—ceased to exist. A tough sur-vivor took his place, a survivor who would battle forces from above or below. The new Grover hid all emotions. He had learned that showing feelings made one vulnerable to attack. No tears, no complaining, no emo-tion for anyone to see. The new warrior hid deep, deep inside. I had at last become truly invisible.

So it was that the Wilcox kids approached the one-year adoption deadline. The counselors were apparently not there to comfort. "They'll not come for you; they don't care!" a skinny counselor jeered at my sister and me as we sat in a room full of kids. "And who would want to adopt you?" It wasn't a question; it was a branding iron applied to our self-es-teem. It spelled "worthless."

On September 10, 1954, Bug Eyes told us we would be leaving, but she didn't say where or with whom. I wandered through the building that had been my home for a year, sat on the bed for a while, and patted the pillow I had pulled over my head that terrible night I had listened to a sex-ually abused boy sobbing. I walked into the dining room and, at last, out to the walnut tree. When I returned, the closet door just off the office stood open. I walked over and gazed at the clothes. Reaching in, I slipped a flannel shirt from a hanger. It had a zipper on the front pocket, and gray and blue patches all around. I put it on. It's all I took from juvenile hall.

I wandered into the TV room, where my sister and I were told to sit and wait. A year—a whole year—had passed! As the afternoon dragged on, I became sleepy. Abruptly I jerked back to alertness as I felt something touching my side. It was Ben. Sad eyes looked at me, eyes full of questions and, maybe, accusations. He brushed away tears. "Do you really have to leave, Grover?"

"I think so, Ben, but you'll be OK. You'll make another friend."

"No, I won't. Never, ever." His chin began to quiver.

"Ben, I don't even know where I'm going." I tried to keep my tears back. *Remember, Grover,* something seemed to say, *you can't be vulnerable!*

"I'll never see you again, Grover," he sobbed.

I reached in my pocket. "Here, Ben, you keep these, and when you play, think of me." I pressed my three rock cars and one twig truck into his hands.

*"What the ——— are you doing in here, Ben! Get outside!"*

It was Fish Eyes. Ben scurried out the door.

Late in the afternoon they were there. I heard a key rattling in the door. It swung open. Framed in the doorway was the woman called Mother. We quietly arose and walked out the door, knowing somehow, as children come to know, that we were simply headed into another prison—a prison of the spirit. Not a word was spoken. We saw a red-and-white Ford station wagon sitting where the police car had sat a year before. We got in—I in the very back with Annie and Clara. There were no greetings. No hugs. No kisses. No explanation. Nothing, nothing but the sound of silence.

I glanced through the side window as we drove away. There, drawing roads in the sand, was Ben. He lifted a grubby hand and waved. *See you, Ben,* my heart said. A half century later, he remains there yet, in my memory. And sometimes when I'm with him, I turn and see a wide-eyed child with his nose pressed through a chain-link fence.

# Four School Days and the Seeds of Rebellion

*School days, school days,*
*Dear old golden rule days;*
*With holes in my shoes*
*And a brothel house,*
*And teachers who called me*
*A Wilcox louse . . .*
— *The Chronicles of Grover, XX, V*

**When I was a schoolteacher** I occasionally drove a group of grade school children to various functions. I can recall asking them to pipe down just so I could determine whether the engine was hitting on all eight cylinders. Sometimes we sang rounds, and sometimes we played word games. Once, after a lecturer said a few things about engagement and marriage that perplexed a junior high school group, they plied me with questions for 50 miles.

Kids, youth, young adults—whatever age, whatever their aspirations—ask questions. They don't sit like stumps. If it's a baseball or basketball team and they've lost, they want to know why. They analyze every play. Did the coach louse things up, or did they ignore instructions? If their team has won, for sure the driver isn't going to be able to hear the engine, and will likely be thoroughly sick of the school song in all its variations. Think of listening to this one for 50 miles:

"A cannibal king on an old May string
Was in love with a Zula maid.
And every night when the moon shown bright,
Across the channel he'd wade
To hug and kiss his dusky miss
Under the old May tree;
And when they met, they sang a duet
That sounded like this to me:

*Katata. Katata, ka ta ta ta*
*Kazula, Kazula, ka za za za*
*Katata Kata, KaZula Kaza,*
*Westport High School, Rah Rah Rah!"*

Actually, after 30 years I've probably messed up a few lines. The "old May string" doesn't sound quite right. I do vividly remember wishing—if not praying—for quiet.

When we seven Wilcoxes, the former inmates of juvenile hall, ranging in age from 6 to 16, got in the two back seats of the Ford station wagon, we were not in the mood for singing; we were in the mood for hearing. Why had we been abandoned? Why had no one come to get us at juvenile hall? Why did our father leave us to become wards of the State of California? Why did our mother virtually ignore us? I can't give you the answers.

There were none.

No "Sorry, kids, let's start over."

No "Hey, we messed up. Let's turn things around."

No "We've missed you so much!"

No hugs. And not one "We love you."

A year before there had been no goodbye. Now there was no hello. What happened in between was treated as if it never happened. The police, jail, courthouses, solitary confinement, prison, cruelty, hospitals—they never happened. That way, our parents didn't have to face their responsibility for what had happened to us. In later years I came to realize that this was our parents' way of reasserting absolute control over us.

Not until the engine in the Ford station wagon began to labor did I have any idea where we were headed. How many times had we lived in the San Bernardino Mountains? And how many times had we come down? One thing, we kids knew, could never be the same. We had changed; whatever our age, childhood was behind us. So was love. We were now a tough bunch of kids—kids with hate and fury in their hearts. In an abusive, dysfunctional family a child's very being is denied in order to keep control in the hands of the parents. I sat, holding Annie's hand. *Maybe,* I thought, *just maybe, there was a little love left in her.*

Just as Liberty Elementary school's name now communicates a wry humor, so does the name of the little town on Highway 18 to which we went. It was the "Valley of Enchantment." The house we moved into was called the "Coyote House." As we walked up the stairs, we encountered a coyote head, snarling at us from the wall. The way it was mounted, it looked as if it had jumped right through the wall. Hanging from a railing on the second floor was a bearskin, complete with head, jaws, and long claws. It was scary to walk past it at night on the way to the bathroom.

We weren't there long. Father quit his job as a used-car salesman in Twin Peaks, came home one day in an old gray Packard, and away we went down the mountain. Before juvie, we lived in West Riverside. This time, after a brief stay at Aunt Jen's house, we moved out into the rolling hills near March Air Force Base. Our house had no electricity, no gas, no heater (except a fireplace with no wood), and, worst of all, no water with which to cook and flush the toilet. We boys broke up an old shed behind the house and used that wood for heat.

The desert had its inhabitants. I was carrying wood to the house one day when Edward hauled off and knocked me flying. As I sat up, he pointed to a black widow spider that had been crawling up my arm. Often Fred and Ned and Edward walked the 10 miles to Riverside, where they looked for work or for coins in the gutters. What we ate—or even whether we ate—depended on what they found.

Soon after our move, we started school. We walked down a long dirt road to the two-lane highway, where we caught the yellow school bus. We had no lunches. My shoes had holes in the bottoms, and the soles flapped noisily. Though my pants and shoes were antiques, I had on a great shirt—the one I had taken from juvenile hall the day I left. We were used to new schools, new looks, new teachers, new questions, registration. Down the hill the bus took us into Riverside. Slowly we crawled through the crowded streets and pulled up to our new school. A large sign above the door of the main building welcomed us to school days.

As we approached the door with the crowd of happy, active kids, I broke out in a cold sweat. My shoes seemed glued to the cement. The school was Liberty Elementary, the same one we had attended while at juvie. I had not recognized it from the front side. I hoped—I prayed—that no one would recognize me.

"Are you new here?" a pleasant voice called out from the office.

I grabbed Annie's hand and walked in. Annie was such a tiny, thin, little thing that I wanted to protect her. The other five offspring of the

Wilcox union went toward another school, Chimawa Junior High.

"Where do you live?" a man who was as huge as Annie was small asked. "What is your address? Where does your father work? Where did you go to school last year?"

This was Annie's first day of school, so I desperately sought to offer suitable answers. "Oh, we live out in the hills. I'm not sure of the address, because we just moved there. My mother is sick today. I'm in the third grade, and"—pointing to Annie—"she's in the first." The final question hung in the air until at last I whispered, "Liberty Elementary."

What I dreaded happened almost as soon as I appeared in class. "Good morning," the teacher said. "Welcome to the third grade. My name is Miss Lowell. When I call your name, say 'present,' and tell us where you went to school last year."

The names droned on, and the alphabet wore away until at last she came to the W's. "Grover Wilcox."

I adjusted my shoes so that the holes in the bottoms would not show. "Here," I whispered, hoping she would go to the next name.

"Where did you—" She was interrupted by a girl down front who was pointing at me.

"Oh, Miss Lowell, I know where he went! He's a juvie kid, and I hate him!"

All eyes turned on me. Every wear and tear in my clothes was examined. I looked at the floor as eternity crawled by. At recess I got into a fight with a boy who wanted to test the "convict." He didn't try again, but others did. Unfortunately, however, an ex-convict can't win without losing. I told myself that I didn't care about anything. I just wanted to disappear.

I made only one friend: books. Lunchtime was hard because we seldom had any lunch, and the kids made fun of how poor we were. So I spent lunchtime fighting or sitting by myself on the swings.

What those kids didn't know was that their hate and taunting were nothing compared to what went on at home. To have your arm twisted behind your back, to be punched where the bruises wouldn't show, to run from your father and hide—these were much worse. But they inflicted a kind of pain that could not be hidden. The embarrassment and shame were worse out in public.

Fred remembers our often going without substantial food for a week.

We boys would go into the orange groves, take off our shirts, and fill them. More than once farmers sought to scare us away by firing a shotgun into the air. We could hear the pellets crashing down through the leaves. But we came back.

What did my father do during this time, other than take any money we made and eat what we collected? I don't really know. He spent a lot of time in a back bedroom with the curtains pulled. With no one working, we were soon evicted. Away we went to a trailer park for a few weeks. Then it was back up the mountain. We would curl up together in the car to sleep. Fred sometimes slept in an abandoned ambulance on a small car lot in the woods.

In the summer of 1955 we moved to a campground at Lake Arrowhead. The camping limit was two weeks, but drawing on the family's expertise gained in moving the tent about on Long Beach when I was 6 months old, we made it through the summer in a small travel trailer. We boys slept on the ground outside. Evening shouting matches must have entertained many campers.

Nearly everyone got some kind of job during that summer, but all the money went straight to Father. Just collecting our money seemed to tire him out. He justified this arrangement by saying that we lived in a Communist home, and it was just too bad if we didn't like it. Everywhere we went, we looked for money. We collected pop bottles for which we got two cents each. We looked for coins under the docks.

One sunny day, having worked in a bit of swimming, my sisters and I headed for the campground. Usually we went around the docks and up a steep hill. This day, however, we thought it would be challenging to take a shortcut by climbing a steep cliff that was more than 400 feet high. We were nearly to the top when I slipped and fell. The bottles I had collected flew out of my pockets and arrived together with me at the foot of the cliff. My sisters scrambled back down and ran to me, fearing I was dead. My right thigh was cut nearly to the bone, from top to bottom, probably by my landing on a broken bottle.

Clara was the first to reach me and tried to stop the bleeding. I asked her if I was going to die. As I lay there, Pam ran home for help. The Lake Arrowhead Regional Medical Center was only a quarter mile away.

When Father arrived, his first words were to Pam. "What in the ———

— happened? I don't have time for this!" After she told him I had fallen down the cliff, he turned to me. "———; how the ——— are we going to pay for this?"

The 400-foot Vista Point cliff I fell down at Lake Arrowhead in 1955.

Pam loaded me into the car. Though Father had no knowledge about such an injury, and the blood loss alone was severe, he drove right past the hospital and around the lake to where my mother was cleaning a house. In some twisted way, he seemed unable to assume responsibility in a crisis. Mother having been consulted, without a word of comfort or inquiry as to my welfare, he drove me back to the hospital, arriving nearly an hour after the accident. The delay could have cost me my life. Many stitches later I was taken to the campground.

I've been to the cliff a few times since. I stand there and wonder how I could have survived the fall. The only answer I've been able to come up with is that an angel slipped a wing under me just before I hit the ground. Why the angel didn't get both wings under me, I don't know. But I believe that someday, as the old hymn says, "I shall understand." My post-fall preoccupation, however, had quite a different orientation; I was battling with guilt for all the pain I had caused my parents.

In September we moved to the tiny mountain town of Running Springs, with a population of maybe 200. It was located at the junction of Highway 30 and the Rim of the World highway. For a time we lived in a one-bedroom cabin. The older boys slept on the small back porch. Pam, Clara, Annie, and I slept in the small loft. Just when the weather cooled to the point where we couldn't stay warm, we were evicted. We moved over the hill into a house that had no heat source other than a fireplace.

A two-story lodge, it had only thin plywood separating the rooms, and there was no insulation. There were eight tiny bedrooms on the second floor. A huge old ivory-colored piano sat in the dining area, which looked big enough for a dance floor. Word had it that it was an old ski lodge; but, in fact, as we were to learn, it had been a brothel. Under some circumstances, its history might have been a source of ribald humor, but to us kids it was a source of

The cabin nine of us called home in Running Springs. A brother says this is where we learned to breathe in unison!

embarrassment. We were likely conditioned to a substantial degree by fear that the sexual abuse in our home would somehow become known. Then

Clara, Annie, and me on a recent visit to the Running Springs "palace." At least it can be said that it was an improvement over a cow pasture.

there was our lack of school lunches, torn clothing, and flapping shoe soles. Enough was enough!

The Wilcox tribe was to live in the ex-brothel in exchange for upkeep. We boys spent many an hour dragging logs from under the snow to be burned in the fireplace. With nothing but an old two-person crosscut saw, keeping the fireplace full was a chore, and even then one had to stand right up to the hearth to feel any warmth. We thought our new quarters must have been a summertime house, unless, of course, the owner had at some time provided another way for guests to warm up.

One aspect of Father's reputation had preceded him to Running Springs: He could, it was said, drink any man on the mountain under the table. It was a reputation he often

The site of the Running Springs "bordello." All that's left today is the remnants of its sign: "Welcome to . . ."

felt the need to prove. Soon he was at it again, using the few dollars his wife and children were able to earn. While he drank and had dinners away from home, we ate our potatoes and oatmeal. Occasionally, that is. My brothers remember our getting a nourishing meal, on the average, once a week. In Running Springs there were no orange groves to raid. Sometimes Aunt Anne visited and brought sacks of groceries.

More often, however, there was nothing, as Annie and I found one day when we rummaged through the kitchen cabinets without finding even a crumb. Not having eaten for three days, we went out and sat on an old oak stump. We knew what we were going to do, but it took time to work up our courage. Finally, stomachs having triumphed over conscience, we headed down the dirt driveway the quarter mile to town. That was our first transgression, for we were forbidden to leave the yard—forbidden even to go across the lane to a friend's house. True, Annie was only 7 and I was 9. But we were a very old 7 and 9. During our year in juvie hall we had witnessed or experienced rioting, beatings, fights, rapes, and scores of lesser abuses. Our stomachs delivered the verdict: "Fie on goodness!" So off we went down a narrow, winding mountain lane appropriately called "Secret Drive." (A half century later it's still there!) Our objective: Gould's Grocery, the only food store in 15 miles up the hill, down the hill, or along the ridge east or west. We weren't anxious to tangle with Mr. Gould, a rotund man of perhaps 50, whose jowls hung so low that kids called him "bulldog." We had been sent there a number of times to charge food. Our bill had gotten so high that we were ordered to tell our parents "No more credit!" Slipping in, we salivated for a minute or two in front of the candy shelf until a paying customer distracted Mr. Jowls. Then two desperately hungry children filched a candy bar apiece. We hurried out with our treasures—a Baby Ruth for me, a Hershey bar for Annie. They were long gone by the time we returned home. In retrospect, I think Jowls must have seen us, only to take pity on two tykes of the tribe Wilcox.

We all hated the life of poverty and abuse that was ours. There were signs that my brothers were beginning to resist our parents' abuse. But the only one with the nerve to speak up was Clara, who was 14 years old. Being my mother's favorite, she must have assumed a backing the rest of us lacked. Clara never said anything the rest of us didn't feel, but we feared the explosions her words ignited.

"You are a lazy no-good!" she would shout at Father. "You don't care that you're killing your wife. Get a job!"

Father would run at her, screaming obscenities, but Clara was too fast for him to catch. We could feel the house shake as he headed back to his room, smashing his fist through the thin plywood walls as he went. One day her tongue sparked the assault we all had feared.

Annie had gone to her room, and I was under the brothel's ivory piano, the usual hiding place for Nobody's Boy. Edward, just home from the hospital, was in the bedroom by the fireplace. A few weeks before, he had been hit by a car. Its rear-view mirror had nearly torn his left arm off. A young doctor, who happened along—if such things "just happen"— wrapped a tourniquet around his arm, and hurried him into surgery, where the arm was repaired. Edward, his arm heavily bandaged, had just stepped out of the bedroom when Clara called Father a no-good bum and told him to get out and get a job to support his family. Enraged, he exploded from his room, cursing her. She ran out the door, and he turned his wrath on the nearest child—Edward. Purple with rage, he grabbed him.

"You no-good! I'm going to kill you!" Jerking Edward's good arm over his knee, he tried to break it. As Edward screamed, Mother came in, plate in hand, and hurled it at Father. It hit the wall behind the piano and fell in pieces within inches of me. I leaped from my hiding place and ran for the door. Father loosened his grip on Edward, grabbed me, and flung me against the wall, face first. Staggering to my feet, I got behind 17-year-old Fred and begged, "Help me; help me, Fred. He's going to kill me!"

Fred stood his ground, eye to eye with Father, who, as if exhausted from his outburst, turned without a word, climbed the stairs to his room, and slammed the door. I slipped up to my room and went to bed, sore-faced and fearful of further repercussions. I didn't go down for dinner; as usual, there was none. At last I slept.

The next morning I pulled on my clothes and tried to arrange my shoes to keep the soles from flapping. It was, after all, to be the first day of the new school year. I crept down the back steps and met Annie and Clara waiting for the school bus.

"Did he really try to break Edward's arm?"

"What are those bruises on your face?"

"What are you going to tell a teacher if they ask?"

Clara didn't get to ask many more questions. Soon after this latest in-cident, Mother sent her away to live with relatives. My brothers were de-lighted to see her go. They blamed her for the outbursts she had provoked and envied her for the better life she had found. Whatever her experience with the relatives, they knew it had to be a substantial improvement over what they endured at home. I personally admired her for her courage in speaking up.

The three-room mountain school had 32 students in grades one through six. Seventh and eighth grades, I found, were to meet in a small meadow by the women's club. This new setup was an improvement over holding class in the back room of a restaurant/nightclub called the Wagon Wheel, which had been the arrangement the year before.

Fourth grade should have offered a clean slate, but it didn't. I looked at the cook, a plump and usually good-natured mother of one of the stu-dents, and an incident from the year before hit me between the eyes. She had gotten fed up with "the Wilcox kids" charging lunches and never pay-ing. The summer months had passed, but her rebuke remained: "Get out of line! You can't charge anymore! Your father is a bum and never pays!" I didn't have to reach in my pocket to be reminded that the Wilcox "for-tunes" (a word alien to the family's vocabulary unless preceded by "poor," "nonexistent," "lousy," etc.) had not improved. Whether empty stomachs pleaded or growled, there would be no free lunches.

Of greater immediacy was another challenge: We were getting a new teacher! What would she be like? What would she think of our clothes? What would she think of—

*The doorknob was turning! The door opened . . . The new teacher wasn't a she!* In stepped a young man who, we found, had just returned from the war in Korea. I couldn't tell you anything about the clothes he was wear-ing, but I'll never forget that he was wearing an ear-to-ear grin! Not that we were to become conversational buddies. He remembers me as the boy who never said a word that whole school year. Still, his constant good humor and transparent joy of living challenged me to believe that some-day I might smile again. I observed a man who never lost his smile. He made our classroom a safe place to be. Day after day I compared the happy order of his classroom with the fearful chaos of my home. His name, be-lieve it or not, was George Jubilee. Could his name have had something to do with the difference? His wonderful smile stirred something deep down in my soul, down where I had buried Nobody's Boy. Could that little boy shed his chains and come out into the sunshine of George Jubilee's smile? No, not yet, but someday. Maybe.

Another thing impressed me. My teacher had only one arm. He had left the other in the hills of Korea during the war. But with that one arm he played with us during recess and at noon. He was the first adult I had ever played with, laughed with, felt safe with. Decades later I looked him up just to tell him, only to be rewarded again with his great smile.

At recess we played tetherball. I put my whole self into each game. My energetic, aggressive, and competitive approach to sports belied my quiet lethargy elsewhere. Playing with Mr. Jubilee constituted my first attempt at communication on any level with an adult, and I loved it! During one hotly contested game, Mr. Jubilee accidentally stuck his finger in my eye. He was so sorry! It was the first time an adult had apologized for hurting me. He could not have guessed my emotion. Here was a badge of honor from my teacher—the first adult in my memory who had touched me without the purpose of causing pain. I wore my eye patch proudly.

George Jubilee and his son. Jubilee's wonderful smile stirred something deep down in my soul where I had buried Nobody's Boy.

I know nothing of Mr. Jubilee's religious beliefs. I know only that he was the first of God's messengers to get through to my soul. He was also the inspiration for my later decision to become a teacher. His smile was to be in my heart every day I stood before my own classes. Each of my students was to become special to me, just as they were to Mr. Jubilee.

The summer of 1956 brought a setback. With a little money on hand, my folks went down the mountain to San Bernardino to shop for clothes for the family. When they returned, all of us gathered in the living room. It was an exciting time, with some semblance of normalcy. Everyone got a needed something. Shoes. A shirt. A dress. I sat expectantly as bag after bag was opened. I got nothing. Not even a trinket. It was the "you're nobody" announcement all over again. In a childhood of pushing things under the rug and denying pain, this one stands out.

You might expect a father to be occasionally insensitive or forgetful, but a *mother?* I've mentioned that when we had some money for groceries she would cook for us. Sometimes on a cold Saturday night she would stand at the stove and make fudge for us. I can recall my impatience as we waited for it to cool in the snow just off the porch. Mother tried, but her life was a nightmare. Mine was a nightmare most of the time, but especially when fresh evidence surfaced that I was just what I feared—Nobody's Boy.

No Mr. Jubilee was present to counter this setback; but there was a whole school full of Baptists, bless their hearts. The Baptist church conducted what they called a Vacation Bible School in the meadow by the Women's Club. Annie and I went. We had a great time doing the crafts, but what really impressed us was the kindness of the teachers. They laughed and talked without their eyes darting around to find someone to punish. They told us they were happy to see us, and they acted like it. We didn't respond with smiles, but somehow our hearts were warmed. We learned songs there that touched our hearts, as they gave us the gift of music. However, they didn't give us the old black church hymnal; Annie and I stole that. We would take it into the woods and sing song after song. We didn't know many of the tunes, and those we improvised seemed to alarm the listening birds and squirrels. I suspect a few hidden angels enjoyed our efforts. We continued our singing excursions into the woods for several years. It must have brought at least a bit of delight to God to see two children from a terribly dysfunctional home sitting on a log deep in the woods, singing "What a Friend We Have in Jesus." Way down inside me, far below where one can hear or see, something—or someone—seemed to be trying to sing with me.

Six weeks after I started fifth grade, I had surgery for a congenital hernia. I was scared to death. During my five-day hospital stay my parents came to visit me only once. I know I had nurses tending me; 40 years later I retrieved my hospital records, and there were their names. Still vivid in my mind is a student of Loma Linda University who worked as an orderly in the hospital. Every day after my surgery he came into my room and talked with me or read to me. A big man with a happy voice, he'd wheel me up and down the halls in a wheelchair. I couldn't believe it—a kind person with a big smile just for me! He read stories from his Bible. After I went home I never saw him again. I'm sure he had no idea of the impact he had on my parched soul. Again, something stirred deep down where Nobody lived.

*One day the King appeared as a funny, one-armed teacher, who sometimes cheated in volleyball. Another time He was a young man in a hospital, wearing a sign in His eyes that said, "You matter to Me. I love you." Yet again He was a whole group of happy Baptists, teaching children to sing, "Jesus loves me, this I know; for the Bible tells me so."*

# Abuse:
# The Twice Killer

*There I stood on graduation day—*
*an honors grad, a mannequin;*
*my emotions and soul imprisoned within.*
—*The Chronicles of Grover,* XX, VIX

**On a warm day in the fall of 1957** Fred, by now a broad-shouldered 17-year-old, quit high school so he could support the family. He promised himself that on his eighteenth birthday he would leave home. In the meantime he worked two jobs, besides helping at home.

At the time, Father was driving a 1941 Cadillac that had developed brake problems. With borrowed tools and the aid of an auto manual, Fred checked the lining, adjusted the brakes, and, as Father told him to do, re-placed the brake fluid with all he had available—transmission fluid. Then he went off to his paying jobs.

Ned and my parents decided to drive down the mountain to Loma Linda, and soon were snaking around the sharp curves that take the trav-eler 6,000 feet to the valley floor. Halfway down the brakes failed. Their choices were not enviable. They could either fly off the road to certain death a thousand feet below, or hit a large boulder that loomed on their right, 50 feet ahead. Father chose the boulder. Within minutes an ambulance, its siren echoing off the canyon walls, reached the crumpled car.

I was working on an arithmetic problem in Running Springs School when the principal, a buxom woman of commanding proportions, entered the classroom. "Grover," she called out, as every head turned toward her, "your parents have been in a serious car accident. Come with me."

I hurried out the door, where Annie, who had also been summoned, joined me. We rushed home, not knowing even to which hospital our par-ents had been taken. Fred joined us there later.

It was nearly dusk when Father drove into the yard in another car. He came in the house and, for some time, simply glared at us. We waited for the explosion. It came, as expected. "Fred, you stupid ———, you nearly killed your mother. You can't do anything right!"

Fred didn't stay to hear anything more. He dashed out the door, hurtled a chain-link fence, and disappeared. That wasn't the usual script in which whoever was the culprit took whatever was dished out without a whimper. Fred walked 15 miles to Lake Arrowhead, and we didn't see him for some time. No question—it was his fault, not that of the father who told him to use transmission fluid. Poor Fred! This tragedy, after he had worked so hard to support the family.

Mother had indeed been severely injured. Her face had smashed against the large chrome radio. Father sustained only bruised ribs from the steering wheel. Ned suffered a concussion from hitting the windshield. Mother was in the hospital for several weeks, but, thanks to well-trained surgeons, had few lasting scars.

The days hurried by until August, and I knew what was coming—the freedom date for Fred, just as it had for Pam. Why did we wait until we were 18 to leave? Our parents had told us that if we left before, they would send the authorities after us. We knew all about authorities—just as our parents knew what it meant to lose a meal ticket. The day after his eighteenth birthday Fred told Mother he was leaving. She angrily ordered him to go upstairs and see his father! I can recall how slowly, how reluctantly, he climbed the stairs to that dark room where depression dwelt. The yelling started there and continued into the living room as Fred walked through, carrying his meager belongings.

"Nothing will ever go right for you in your life, because you're running out on your family!" Mother raved. "You're just thinking of yourself! You're a bad seed, just like your sister and brother!" (I knew who that was.)

With this "blessing" from his loving family, Fred shut the door and was gone. With him went the income from his 80-hour-a-week job. He let the memory of this day and its accusations haunt him for 40 years, though I later urged him repeatedly to place the blame where it really belonged.

Soon the begging renewed, always with the children who, our parents thought, were most likely to elicit a sympathetic response. There was little new terrain to cover, and door after door was slammed in our faces. Halloween, however, brought its blessings. My little sister dressed as an old woman and I as an old man in rags. As ordered, we made several stops at home to leave our take. When we returned from our last trick or treat, all the candy and fruit had been consumed.

Parents without self-respect don't respect anyone or anything. On a school field trip I had bought a small ceramic bull bank with a few coins my teacher had given me. Though worth little, it was my prized possession—in fact, almost my only possession. It held pennies I'd saved from pop bottles I'd found and turned in for two cents apiece. I had told no one about my pennies; however, I returned from school one sad day to find the pieces of my bank on my bed, and my few pennies gone. No explanation. No apology. No respect, no boundaries, no rights. Just keep your mouth shut, don't ask for anything, and hope not to get hit.

That fall Edward, 16, took up the duties of provider in the same restaurant where Fred had worked so hard without thanks. Father hated Edward because of my mother's loyalty to him. Tensions grew—we were never without them; they just changed in intensity. As fall fled the mountains, so did we—again to the desert, where my mother again worked as a server.

During these years God could not be seen, heard, or felt on our premises. But though seldom perceived, He ministered to me through people who touched my life—the hospital orderly, my fifth-grade teacher, and Pete, a fellow student.

Pete and I became friends because we had much in common. We liked cars, the great outdoors, and were pawns in dysfunctional homes. Pete's parents were alcoholics, who regularly relieved their frustrations by beating him and his sister. Because of previous experiences, neither of us complained to the authorities. We knew the rules of secrecy and terror. And teachers never asked, though they must have seen the bruises and the scars on both body and psyche. They must have seen the rags we wore and noticed the missing lunch boxes. Though we never confided in an adult, Pete and I soon were sharing horror stories with each other. The first time I stopped by Pete's cabin I could taste the fear. There is something called "quiet"; and there is something called "too quiet." Pete's house was too quiet.

"Where in the ——— have you been, you no-good ———," a voice boomed from the shadows.

My response was instinctive. I turned and ran, still able, however, to hear the thud of fists on flesh, and Pete's grunts as he absorbed the animal fury of a man punching him and hurling him against the furniture. I felt every blow. I tasted hate. I wanted to hurt, to kill, to destroy, to yell "NO MORE!" But I hid in the woods, shaking, listening, waiting.

"Get the ———— out of my sight! You and your sister ruin my life! Where is she?" the madman bellowed as Pete fled out the front door.

We met in the woods. "Oh, Pete, are you all right?" I whispered. I knew a stupid question when I heard one, even when it came from me. Of course he wasn't all right. Blood was running from his nose and mouth.

"It'll stop; it always does. I just got to sit down. I'm so dizzy." He began to vomit from the punches he had taken to his stomach. There we huddled, two 11-year-old friends, each sharing the other's agony.

"Pete, I hate him! I wish he was dead!"

"So do I, but he always wins. He always finds me. He always beats me. Someday, Grover, I'm going to kill him!"

"No, Pete, I don't mean your dad—I mean *mine*. But I hate both of them! Why can't they just go away? Why can't we run away?"

"I'm glad you understand, Grover. I don't have to explain to you. You're my friend."

"Oh, Pete," I responded. "Let's be friends forever, like Cochise [the famous Apache Indian chief] and Tom Jeffords [the Apache Indian agent]. I'm Cochise!"

He managed a smile through swollen and bleeding lips. "OK, Chief! You got it. Someday we'll get away, and they'll never see us again! But I'm afraid for my sister. He does things to her that make her cry, and I just hold my pillow over my head or run outside. The next day we go to school like nothing happened. Teachers are so dumb. They never know anything. Relatives neither—nobody does."

"Well, one relative does, Pete. She's my aunt—my aunt Anne. My sister lives with her and goes to school and has all she wants to eat. They have a big green house in Riverside that has big windows. My aunt has a 1953 Cadillac Fleetwood that runs. When I go there, we pull weeds in the yard until breakfast. It's real food. Then we get to ride in the car to the farm, where she gets milk and eggs. She keeps her house real clean. And she reads her Bible, and we have a thing she calls "worship." We eat at a table and say prayers, and I get to sleep in a room with a big bed, and nobody else is in there!"

Pete was awed. "You don't mean it! Don't they fight there?"

"No, and I get to sit on a chair in the living room and watch two TV programs before I go to bed. It's wonderful! I always watch what I eat, though, because I could eat everything on the table, the food is so good."

"Wow! It must be neat! When do you go there?"

"Not very often, because it makes my parents so mad when we kids don't want to come home. I don't care, though."

An angry voice called Pete in, and I made quick tracks back to my own hell. But Aunt Anne was on my mind. *If there is a God,* I thought, *He must have put her in this world to give me hope of a better life that is out there somewhere.* I thought that she was a wonderful angel who flew down out of heaven just for that. She was the first Adventist that I knew and loved. My parents went to church occasionally, but the God they modeled before me was not someone I wanted to meet in church or anywhere. Still, would Aunt Anne belong to a church that had the kind of God my parents professed to know? I remembered the Baptist Bible school; surely a good God would love them. Can people be that happy if they're acquainted with the wrong God? What about the Adventists at Loma Linda Hospital who had been so good to me? Who was their God? There was too much turmoil in my soul to sort it out.

Our next move, soon after my visit with Pete, was to Palm Springs. This time we weren't up a rocky canyon 18 miles away, where the coyotes howled at night. Mother got a job as a server (what else!). The little mountain school we had attended for three years had only 21 seventh and eighth graders. In the Palm Springs Nellie N. Coffman Junior High there were 800!

To make things a little tougher, I arrived near the end of November 1958. The office personnel who saw me coming that first morning must have thought, *Here comes a real country bumpkin!* They gave me a printout of my new classes, gave each other a knowing look, and away I went to seventh-grade class. The students were working on two sheets: one was addition, and the other subtraction.

I looked at the material and thought, *They must think I'm an idiot!* I got up, walked out without saying goodbye, and headed for the principal's office. I had brought one thing from that mountain school: I was driven to be the best student in every class. And here they (almost all adults were just "they") were taking away what little identity I had been able to salvage. I marched across the campus and into the office, where I stood at the counter, waiting.

"Were you sent here by your teacher, young man?"

I turned to see who owned the clipped monotone voice. "No," I said to the slim woman who had come in behind me. "I'm here to talk to the principal, please. They made a big mistake."

"You can't just walk in and talk to the principal. Who is your teacher, and why are you out of your class?"

"But I've got to see him! I can't go back there. I'm not who you think I am!"

We were still exchanging can'ts and won'ts when the principal walked in. He called me into his office.

"Well, Mr. Wilcox, what seems to be your problem?"

Disarmed by his caring voice, I plunged right into my speech. "Somebody sent me into an arithmetic class for morons. I did math on that level five years ago. I was the best student in my school in Running Springs."

"Where are your records?" the principal asked. He glanced over his tiny glasses and down his long, thin nose. "We really can't do anything without your records, you know."

I knew what he was thinking. But he had called me "Mr. Wilcox." And he'd invited me into his office. "Well," I said with determination, "records or no records, I'm not going back into that class!"

For an hour I sat in the office waiting room, wondering what would happen. If they tried to send me back to that class, I determined that I wouldn't go to school at all.

Finally the thin woman emerged with a letter in her hand. "Report to Miss Thorax in room 112, and give her this letter."

I started to question her, but she smiled and said I would be pleased. Down the hall and across the campus I hurried, wondering what waited behind door 112.

What I found there was a world I desperately needed. It was one of two advanced classes for the accelerated and gifted student! I've wondered since whether the principal called Running Springs School to check my record. Whatever the answer, I scanned the pampered scions who were scanning me and said to myself, *Get ready, dudes and darlings. I have arrived. Watch out!*

Classes in the rarified atmosphere of the gifted didn't change every 45 minutes, as happened for the lesser mortals. And we stayed with one teacher for all our academic subjects. This room became my refuge, my stage, the one place where Grover Winslow Wilcox could be somebody. I believed that if I got the top grades, nobody would notice my clothes or hair or the holes in my shoes. And they didn't! By the end of the semester, I was the star of the room, a celebrity, with A's in all eight subjects. So what if I looked and smelled like a street kid?

The following year my reputation preceded me into the eighth-grade honors class. And now I added another first to my résumé: I was the best male singer in the eighth grade madrigal singers. We even performed at San Diego State University, where I sang a solo, and with high school and college groups. But at home I was still Nobody's Boy. I never took my report cards home; they couldn't have cared less. I signed them myself.

Grover, with sister Annie, and their niece, Ambre Ann, in 1959.

That year my sister Clara came home and enrolled for her senior year in high school. Her anger at my father had not abated one bit from the day she was sent away at the age of 14. As before, she would yell at him for never working; and, as usual, that would ignite a family fight. She didn't wait for 18; in a couple months she was gone.

I spent my years at Palm Springs High School with one face for the public and another for real. My teachers saw only a student dedicated to excellence, when in truth I was driven to excel to cover my pain. They saw an athlete who loved sports; in reality, I was running wind sprints and shooting baskets into the night to stay out of the house and, thus, out of trouble. There was no radio, no TV—nothing but work. We Wilcox boys always had a job. But because we had to give every dime to our father, I still had no clothes of my own when I was in the tenth grade. I wore Ned's clothes in junior high—he drew the line at lending me his toothbrush. We had become the best of friends. A slim six-footer, Ned was a gifted athlete, with his football prowess drawing the most attention. His blond hair and blue eyes didn't go unnoticed by the young women. We spent many hours walking together in the desert behind our home. He kept me in touch with reality, and I owe him much. When he was drafted into the Army, I was devastated.

Even Ned couldn't have helped me through the excruciatingly humiliating experience I was confronted with one day following our 10:00 a.m. physical education class. We were to read Greek mythology, each student sharing a book with another. Everyone paired off, but no one sat with me, not even a friend. The teacher gestured a student my way, but he blurted out, "I'm not sitting with him. He stinks!" The resulting silence was louder than a passing train. Even the teacher was at a loss for words.

"I'll sit with him," a soft feminine voice called out, and a pretty brunet named Susil sat down by me.

That moment is etched in my mind. I shall be forever thankful for that gracious young woman. After school I went home, took a shower, and scrubbed and scrubbed. For the first time I noticed that the hair under my arms was not dark, as on my head. It appeared coated and white. I took a razor, shaved under my arms, and scrubbed again. The next day I asked a friend what he was spraying under his arms, and I was introduced to deodorant. Here I was, 16 years old, second academically out of 500 sophomores, and I had never learned of deodorant. My friend brought me a toothbrush, and I brushed at school with real toothpaste. I have wondered since, when meeting a former fellow student who says, "Oh, I remember you!" just what he or she remembers me for. I fear it is not always for my academics or my singing.

The last month of my senior year, when I was 18, I was allowed to go on a beach outing with one of my school friends, Richard Koch, the oldest son of a close-knit Mormon family. This experience was a first for me. My other "outings" had all been to make money for the family. When the Kochs drove up in their station wagon, I climbed into the second row of seats with Richard, whose father was driving. He was smiling and teasing the three children behind on the back seat. His wife sat so close to him that one would think they had just been married. Everyone seemed happy; there was much laughter from everyone but me. I couldn't adjust; I knew the joy must soon explode, but it didn't. I searched for the underlying tension that must be there, as it was in our car. Tension was a reality, a constant that I could understand and cling to. I was actually uncomfortable without it. So it is with one much abused. Whenever my "family" went anywhere, we siblings sat in a fossilized tension, the only stance that might result in an outing. Often the car had not left the yard before we were told, "Get out! We're not going!"

This outing with the Koch family was both the most pleasant and the most frustrating experience of my life. Pleasant, because nobody yelled, nobody exploded with anger. Kids were hugged, and hugged back. It was OK to talk. The youngest Koch teased his father. What a picnic! And when they drove me home, they actually thanked me for coming with them!

Still, the outing was frustrating, because I couldn't understand the dynamics of a peaceful outing. Nevertheless, a seed was planted that day somewhere deep in my soul where, unexpectedly, unaccountably, there existed a small plot of fallow ground. Under some rare circumstances, it seemed, there are people who have a peacelike gift. *I'll look for it someday,* I promised myself. I could not yet imagine it could be mine.

Two months later I graduated. In two weeks I would begin my summer's work. Despite my being an honor student, there would be no talk of college. Education had always been a dirty word my parents spat out like juice from chewing tobacco. I knew there was a world out there that opened only for the educated. Not that I felt qualified. Though I knew manual labor from A to Z, I had no social tools. I knew only how to survive. I could not even go into a coffee shop and sit at ease. I felt as if every eye were on me. Even if I appeared to be relaxed, I was testing the atmosphere for the danger that had to be near at hand.

Abuse. The twice killer. First you suffer the experience, then you live evermore with its chain around you, the helpless victim of the large, powerful adult. You suffer the repeated pain of physical violence, incest, or emotional abuse. There is nowhere to turn, nowhere to run, nowhere to hide. You are isolated and taught to keep everything secret. You dare not tell even relatives what is going on; they would not believe you, or would be afraid to cause a family rift by intervening. So they pretend nothing is happening. But they know. They *have* to know! You—the abused—are taught that everyone outside the little family circle of abuse is the enemy.

The hardest part is having to suffer silently because you have no way of fighting back. Even if you were to seek help, you would suffer the consequences behind closed doors. It's as if you live on another planet, with no way to communicate with anyone except family. You develop a hypervigilant attitude, always analyzing the most innocent inducement, second-guessing every invitation. You develop a multitude of defense mechanisms and faces. You can walk from incest or a beating into a public place and appear casual—except for your eyes. You are made to carry the pain, the blame, the shame, the abuse. The adult who molests you feels no remorse or shame, but you do. You feel dirty, feel that you are the cause of the abuse and that to tell would be to destroy the family.

You feel the fear of what is about to happen, what does happen, and the extreme sadness of what did happen. You hide every detail because of the great shame it would bring to be seen for what you are. You are a really bad person—you must be—because bad things, unmentionable things, are happening to you. Bad things happen to bad people. You deserve it. It's your fault; you *made* them do it to you! Over the years you become addicted to the hell—the chaos, the tension; you feel comfortable only in the familiar violence of the family environment. These deeply ingrained messages and reactions take up residence deep in your mind, and they pop up when you try to deal with obstacles later in life. You feel deep hate, fury, anger, and loneliness, all of which propel you toward depression. You are the victim of post-traumatic stress syndrome (I'm tempted to spell that "*sin*drome"). The legacy is passed on, and the victim does any number of things to bury or deny the pain. Among them are workaholism, alcoholism, sexual excess or perversions, crime, and paralyzed dual living.

So there I stood that graduation day, that momentous step toward adulthood—a mannequin whose emotions and soul were imprisoned behind an iron curtain. And the wind blew through my hair, and my eyes were steely. There was no way on earth for the King to reach me, even if He appeared in the sky.

So I thought. But He knew a way that I didn't. And He was willing to wait.

**Six** # A Salute to a Sergeant and a Ring for My Lady

*Where is the Life we have lost in living?*
*Where is the wisdom we have lost in knowledge?*
*Where is the knowledge we have lost in information?*
*The cycles of Heaven in twenty centuries*
*Bring us farther from God and nearer to the Dust.*
—*T. S. Eliot,* Knowledge Without Wisdom

**The day I reached out for my diploma** and the scholastic honors that came with it brought many plaudits from classmates, faculty, and friends. To my parents, however, it brought only worry. Would another meal ticket be leaving home? Most of my fellow graduates had already settled on a college and a course that would expand their world. Despite my achievements, I knew that I was still in elementary school so far as my social graces were concerned. Nevertheless, if someone had asked what I planned for a career, I would likely have said, "Medicine."

Not that I had ever told my parents that it was my dream to become a doctor. One doesn't share dreams with dream-poppers. Those times I had been in a hospital I admired the cool professionalism with which the physicians worked, even when confronted with an emergency in which the stakes were life-or-death. I had observed the way doctors and nurses worked as a team, a concept foreign to the "every man for himself" format that dominated juvenile hall, where I had spent a year. Even among my brothers and sisters, jealousies and rivalries often subverted best intentions. Of course, sometimes it was teamwork or starvation. Medicine, I was to find, is one of the most demanding of all specialties. Demanding physically, mentally, and, as I came to believe, spiritually. It has no place for the student who comes with a burden on his back, as I did. My energies were depleted in keeping the pain, the shame, the hate, and the fury of the abused compartmentalized.

When I told my parents I had decided on a career and was leaving for college, they gave me the usual blessing bestowed on erstwhile defectors.

"So, you're running off to become an educated monkey like your cousin Milton! He's a worthless no-good," said my mother.

My father contributed this blessing: "You'll never be able to hold a job and make a living!" (This from one without a degree but nevertheless an expert on shiftlessness.)

"Don't try to ruin my future!" I replied. "I'll never be without a job." I walked out the door, seething with resentment. They had not provided any of us with the basic needs for growing up: food, shelter, love, affection, happiness, a sense of worth, acceptance, the training to survive life, a work ethic, character, standards, security. Nil! Nothing! Absolutely nothing! Instead they provided physical violence, emotional abuse, sexual abuse, shame, pain, fear, hate, and emptiness.

It was Nobody's Boy who walked out that door.

I carried my parents' final legacy with me—separated children. Abuse works one against the other. With the exception of my relationship with Annie, we children were never close. Just being together brought too many unresolved memories. I headed off to Pacific Union College in Angwin, California, knowing that my leaving was forever.

I soon found, however, that much as I hated to acknowledge it, I carried much of home away with me. It took only one semester of premed to convince me that I had no chance to succeed. I could not concentrate on my studies. I knew that the Vietnam War was chewing up recruits, and that many young men were seeking creative ways to escape the draft, but when the second semester began, I didn't file for a student deferment. It wasn't long until Uncle Sam came calling.

In November I was drafted—one of the few times in my life I could remember being wanted. I didn't care. The farther away from "home" the better. My only sadness was leaving Annie alone with my parents. The "better" in this case proved to be Fort Polk, Louisiana.

Heaven is supposed to be way up there—some say beyond Orion. I've got news. Part of it is in Fort Polk, Louisiana, and part in Fort Sam Houston in San Antonio, Texas. Maybe not for those recruits whose daddies and mamas waved when they left, and wiped away tears. Maybe not for those raised on filet mignon and white wine chasers; or those who sleep in on Sunday morning and play golf all afternoon. But for Grover Winslow Wilcox those camps were heaven!

Absolutely nothing about basic training bothered me. There was great food, great exercise, and a place to live that was better than most of the homes the Wilcoxes had inhabited. Every Sunday morning the would-be soldiers got to go to church. Instead, I practiced running the mile again and again, wearing combat boots. I think that even the drill sergeants began to doubt my sanity. But it paid off. During two and a half months of basic training I grew almost two inches and gained 60 pounds. Food, wonderful food! And blessed exhaustion!

Our days began at 4:30 a.m. Drill Sergeant Antonio Munoz was a stocky bulldog of a man. His jowls drooped low, and his temper climbed high. Stone-tough, he gave every indication of enjoying screaming in our faces. He would march us through the mud in the dark, cold mornings on our way to mess hall for breakfast. We would shovel down our food like so many animals, and then rush back to the barracks to spit-shine our boots.

One frosty morning as we stood stiffly at attention, Sergeant Munoz, his face red and his spittle flying, began screaming. At first I thought his incoherent words were being shared equally with us all, but learned otherwise when he parked his face three inches in front of mine. And suddenly, it seemed it was not Sergeant Munoz shouting at me; it was my father! I saw his twisted features, heard his hateful put-downs. I struggled for control, my fists clenching, my face white, sweat beading my forehead. *Hit him! He's abusing you! Give him what he deserves!* my mind shouted. I almost did. But suddenly something in me said, "Hey, remember all the silent days that made you Nobody's Boy? Remember how you'd disappear behind your brothers, or under the piano in the brothel house? This guy is shouting at you because you *are* somebody. You count. You're worth something. You can be a great soldier!"

It was a close call. I snapped a sharp salute at Sergeant Munoz. I think what startled him most was my smile.

The only downside at Fort Sam Houston was mail call each day. While others got their share of letters, I got two letters in eight weeks, both from my little sister, Annie. I had no girlfriend, as we Wilcox boys were never allowed to date. I had, to be sure, dated a few girls during my five months in college, but knew no one well enough to write to them.

I went home after basic training because that is what everyone did. One evening my father began yelling at Annie, who was leaving for a date with a school friend. "You're nothing but a whore! Why don't you just run off with him!"

Annie was 18 years old. It was only a school friend. My mother said not a word, but I did.

"I hate this place! I hope to go to Vietnam and get killed!" With that I walked out of their house, out of their lives, into the desert, and was gone. I've reviewed my farewell speech a few times since. It seems a bit juvenile. Surely, with my many years of observing a master slammer at work, I should have done better.

Grover, at home in 1966

I returned to Fort Sam Houston, where I went for a three-month stint of training to be a medic. Something funny happened to me on the way. I got nice. Before long, I began pulling KP for fellow soldiers so that they could go to a movie or on a date or just do nothing. Before long I became known as the nicest soldier around. Or, should I say, the nicest soldier on the outside? Within I was still hollow, lonely, and depressed. I found myself thinking of the happy Baptists at vacation Bible school. Of the Mormon family, who had invited me to go along on a weekend picnic. Of the Seventh-day Adventist student orderly at Loma Linda University Hospital (then called the College of Medical Evangelists) who had pushed me around in a wheelchair and read the Bible to me. And then there was the time Annie and I sat in the woods singing from an old hymnal, "Jesus loves me, this I know."

I wanted to be a Christian, but not the kind my folks were. Though I had gone with them the few times they attended the Seventh-day Adventist church, I had no idea what it meant to be a Christian. Their religion, as they "practiced" it, was a set of rules with no love, no kindness, no caring, and, certainly, no God. At least, not the friendly one Annie and I had sung about, even if "the Bible tells me so." I had often heard well-meaning Christians liken God to an earthly father. That did it for me. Period. End of story. End of hope.

I still entertained thoughts of burying my despair in Vietnam. Every month I put in for a transfer there. Could it be that there was at least some kind of God who didn't want me there? *Well,* I thought, *if He wants me here, He'd better hurry.* I hadn't given up on that transfer.

Soon after that I met a fellow trainee who intrigued me. I could not understand how someone could be so contented or so relaxed as Roger Morrisey, a Catholic. He had grown up on a 360-acre farm in southeastern Minnesota, where the family raised corn, soybeans, hay, and cattle. His farm work had given him bulging muscles and an obvious sense of accomplishment and responsibility. Behind his mild blue eyes and ready smile I discerned the gift of contentment. Just as I did, he went out of his way to do things for his fellow soldiers. But he did it from a genuine love of people; I did it from a genuine attempt to escape the bottomless pit within me.

When I accepted Roger's invitation to go home with him on leave, I could not believe the welcome I received. They introduced me to friends as their third son! I was stunned, overwhelmed, and grateful. Just as in high school, I was somebody again. Only this time it wasn't because of something I did; it was because of something God did through Roger. Granted, the crack in my armor wasn't yet a corridor, but it was an opening into an area that had never seen the light of day.

I would have done anything for the Morriseys—and nearly did. I got up at 4:00 a.m. to milk the cows, bail hay, or harvest corn. One day, on my own, I took a broom to the barn and swept nearly every cobweb out of its nooks and crannies. My hosts were amazed by my dedication, but doubled over with laughter because they knew the spiders would rebuild

The peaceful plains of the Morrisey ranch in Minnesota, where a Catholic family made me feel like somebody!

overnight. The harder I worked, the more praise I got, but this time I didn't use it to fill any holes or cure any hurts. The Morriseys got only a glimpse of the healing their kindness produced; I got a lifetime friend in Roger, to whom I shall be eternally grateful.

Not that I suddenly experienced healing. On those warm Minnesota nights I would slip out to the barn and climb into the hayloft. There I would sit and try to make sense out of the nonsense in my soul. I knew it was no use to pretend that nothing had happened to me during my chaotic and abusive childhood. I dug up scene after scene that I had determined to leave forever locked in darkness. Facing them removed some of the terror of the unseen, but left still was the hurt, the pain, the fury of what I now could see all too well.

The Morriseys were aware that a struggle was going on, and they did everything they could for me. But they could not fill the Grand Canyon of my soul, in which every cell was branded and scarred. Still, I owe them much. Often, long gone from their farm, I sought peace of soul in my memories of their kindness.

One day while waiting at the dentist's office, I turned to a self-help column in a religious publication. Some suffering soul was asking how to deal with yesterday's monkey, which was clinging to her back. The answer, written by a teacher, was to the point: "Throw off the past, look away,

Roger Morrisey and two "catches"— catfish, and his soon-to-be wife, Bonnie, in 1969.

think of the future." Then a telling quote: " 'Ain't no future in the past.' "

I found the advice stimulating, but my ambitions were more modest. I determined to seek answers that would help me in the present, for I had concluded that it was necessary to confront repressed emotions. Sources I perused included books on Mormonism and other religious isms, physic writer Edgar Cayce, self-help, and psychology. For the first time I also sought answers in the Bible. I prayed, I analyzed, and at last began to see the size and shape of the burdens I had long struggled unsuccessfully to carry. I fought through the jungle of misinformation and the misunderstood. And this time, as in no other, I took a divine Friend with me. I found that when I faced the pain of the emotions, the hurt, the hate, with Him at my side, something happened. There was not only a reliving, but an understanding and releasing! It's a stunning experience to begin to see the world through eyes He has opened. Soon it had its practical consequences.

Ever since leaving home, I'd sent my paychecks back—$42.50 a month. If I wanted a date, I just took one of the Army WACS to a doings on base. In the fall of 1965 my little sister, Annie, turned 18, and left home in the middle of her senior year. With Annie gone, I decided to no longer send money home. Instead I opened a bank account and began to save. After almost 10 months I withdrew $25 and bought a portable radio, my first gift to myself. I also spent a few dollars to go skiing.

My real recreation (or addiction) was basketball. I played 10 to 12 hours on a weekend. During the week I played basketball with the "brothers," the euphemism for Blacks on the court. They accepted me as one of their own for two reasons: (1) I had a friend who had the keys to the gym; (2) I could play street ball and jump with them. They called me the "Kangaroo Kid," after the 76ers' Billy Cunningham. "Competitive" is too mild a term for how I played. I could not stand to lose. It wasn't fun I played for; it was to win. It wasn't competition that drove me; it was domination. My friends said they knew I was ready to play when my eyes glowed. At last they stopped glowing, not because I lost interest in basketball but because my two-year Army term ended.

I headed back to the University of California, this time as a biology premed major. Then on to Winona State University for a psychology major. At last I thought it would be a wise move to anchor my soul before exploring higher education further.

My "courting" Corvette. Today, in pristine condition, it would bring in excess of $80,000!

One gorgeous spring day I took a recess. I decided it was time to find a wife, a Christian wife, of course. I determined to avoid the mistakes I had seen so many of my buddies making. So as I dated, I asked thousands of questions. The result: a heavy attrition rate in dates. So to get a bit more balance, I cut my list of questions to what I considered the essentials.

Just at this time my sister Clara said she had a friend I should meet. Why not? I jumped into my red Corvette convertible and headed to Palm Desert, a nondescript community across Highway 10 from Palm Springs. Having decided Clara's call could result in a close scrutiny of her big brother, I dressed up (or was it down?): a pair of cast-off Army fatigues, worn tennis shoes, and a UCLA T-shirt. Clara directed me to a nearby swimming pool, where I could find her friend. And there she was, a vision of loveliness, her long brown hair dripping wet, no makeup, and no pretense.

Her name was Edna. She was 18. There we stood and talked until the afternoon fled. As we spent time together, I found she was as beautiful inside as outside. Kind, gentle, caring. But there was a spitfire in there, too! For all her beauty and talents, she wanted to be a housewife. She cooked, she sewed, she did crafts, and loved it all. She was calm, peaceful, and charming. I decided she would fit well in my marriage plans. Telling her about it, however, proved difficult. It was frightening enough to find I could open up and have emotions; describing them in terms that would stimulate a young woman's hormones was another matter. And Edna was a sincere Christian, a Seventh-day Adventist. However, not one like my parents professed to be. She lived what she believed; she never judged anyone; and I often saw her encouraging others to meet Jesus.

Late in the summer of 1971 she moved to Portland, Oregon, to work in a lab. Still in Palm Springs, I wrote 25-page letters that I hoped would fill her heart with love, but that didn't do much for me. Sometimes I beat the mail. I'd take a handful of coins and head for a pay phone. Coins gone, I'd drive to a secluded spot and write another epistle. Letters and phone calls have their place, but you can't put your arms around them.

I got up one morning and called Bill, my boss, and told him I was sick—not the usual flu or fever, to be sure; but I did have a bug, a love bug, and I sure was lovesick! I hopped into my 1966 Impala and headed up Interstate 5 for Portland. There, one beautiful August day, in a park fragrant with roses in the City of Roses, I asked Edna to marry me.

Several days later I headed back to my job in the desert, where Bill and I put sprinklers in the yards of the ultrarich. I planned to save money to prepare for our wedding and life together. But as the miles clicked away, the tears began to fall. Eighty-four miles out they had attained the characteristics of an Oregon rain. Surely the Lord couldn't expect me to jeopardize oncoming traffic! I wiped my eyes, spun my car around, and headed back to the girl I loved.

When I knocked on her apartment door, her eyes said, "Why, Grover! What are you doing back here? Did you forget something?"

(I think she read the answer before I spoke. But here it is, for the record.)

"Yes, Edna, I did. I forgot you, the only woman I've ever loved. The only woman I'll ever love! Get your things; I can't stand to be away from you another minute!"

We were married two weeks later in the living room of Clara's home in Palm Desert. The date: August 19, 1971. My mother, Bill and his wife, Heather, Edna's parents and her brother Clem were among those present. Pastor Varmer Leggett tied the knot. Edna looked radiant in her white gown. She had made her veil, as well as the flowers she held. After our reception we left for a fancy local motel and, for the next few days, explored Big Bear in the San Bernardino Mountains. Then it was back to a Palm Desert apartment and work. On a scale of 1 to 10, if someone had wished to rate our marriage, I thought it was a 12. I ripped open the doors of my soul for Edna as I never had to anyone else.

But along with my love came baggage. The moment we married, I became the King of Responsibility—my wife would never want for anything, she would never even have to ask for anything, she would never suffer anxiety. Unfortunately, what I called responsibility was, in fact, my old addiction, workaholism, come to stifle the carefree days we should have enjoyed together. The irony? I sought to make her life perfect, but in doing so, I cheated her.

Our two daughters, Bonnie Yvette and Julia Marie, in 1977.

August 27, 1972, became the most awesome day of my life. A nurse walked out of a delivery room and placed a little bundle of gurgles and gas pains in my arms. "It's a girl," she said. Julia Marie weighed in at 10 pounds seven ounces. No words can express my delight and pride. This child, I pledged before God, would never know the pain I had known. The past would stay in the past. But already workaholism had shown its head. Edna, too, had grown up in an abusive home; she, too, looked out at life through a cage. Soon we were spending our energies to make sure this and that didn't happen, rather than concentrating on the brighter side of life.

On October 25, 1974, our second daughter, Bonnie Yvette, was born. She and Julia got so many hugs they must have thought their parents had cornered the hug market. Edna created a wonderful home for the girls. She cooked special treats for them, sewed clothes for them, and read to them every day—I remember the *Little House on the Prairie* series. Each evening I gave the girls horseback rides down the hallway to bed. I told them stories before they went to sleep. I called Bonnie "Moose," and each night added a new chapter to the story, Moose of Green Meadows. Edna and I had determined to

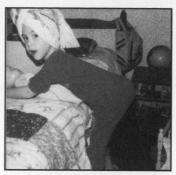

Bonnie: In early childhood but already practicing motherhood with her doll.

have a Christian home; we went to church each week, had family worship, and sang hymns. But even after all the blessings God had showered on us, we found it difficult to think in terms of God the *Father*.

Shortly after our marriage I began having severe migraines and very high blood pressure. Often at work I would have long periods of irregular heartbeats and I feared even to get up and walk. It seemed to be worst after I ate. When the migraines or arrhythmia ended, I would feel as if I had the Hong Kong flu. But I never missed work, ever. I was, after all, the King of Responsibility, and not about to abdicate my throne!

One day, at 26 years of age, I stood in the doctor's office with a blood pressure of 220/110. He gave me a shot and said I'd be dead by 30 if I didn't do something about it. So I began running. Before breakfast I did 10 to 15 miles along the railroad tracks near San Timoteo Canyon. When the pressure stayed up, I went to Loma Linda University Medical Center. Doctors there thought it likely I had a tumor on my pancreas, so they ran tests for three days, during which I was not to eat. Strangely enough, I seemed to feel better when famished.

Finally, on the third day, I was told that if I could run up three flights of stairs and not pass out, I did not have a tumor. The King of Competition was not about to refuse a challenge. The verdict: no tumor. Afterward I sat down and ate a large cheese pizza. The result: a severe migraine. The doctors chalked it up to eating too much too soon, and they arranged for me to go to the downstairs clinic and learn some biofeedback. There I was taught how to control my muscles, reduce my heartbeat, and lower my blood pressure.

I felt that my illness was stress-related, so I escalated my exercise. Sometimes my headaches got so bad that I'd have to stop the car and vomit. But hey, march on, and work, work, work. Workaholics fall into at least three classifications. First, some work hard, rest, and play; others just work hard. Then there is the workaholic whose very life and identity depend on work—any kind of work. Finally, there is the workaholic who is sprinting from pain and depression, unaware of his motivation. Hello! My name is Grover Winslow Wilcox!

When I was 29 I moved my family to Arkansas, which, for some reason, I thought was an ideal place to raise children. We settled 30 miles west of Little Rock, right at the base of the Boston Mountains. There, in the town of Conway, were five colleges, the largest of which was the University of Central Arkansas. With three years eligibility left on my GI bill, which offered the massive sum of $350 a month, I planned to finish college at last. My goal: to become a teacher.

I supplemented my income by working 20-25 hours a week as a plumber. In my spare time I took almost three years of college in 13 months. One semester I took 34 credit hours while teaching at a local junior high school. Each noon I rushed back on campus to take a calculus class. Twelve of my hours were correspondence, which was really time-consuming. One of these was from the University of California at Berkeley. I took the graduate record exam during the semester, though I had none of the prerequisites for the test. I got A's in all 83 credits. My professors were impressed. I acted humble, but inside I gloried in the praise. In fact, if I got a 95 on an Abstract Algebra exam, I was upset— where were the other five points?

Where did I get the energy? As a child I had needed it just to survive. So the challenge of the impossible simply stimulated the hormones that had kept me going then. Further, I convinced myself that God was standing by and admiring each test I took, each A I got. Not so, of course. He does not promote self-glory, even if the seeker is trying to fill emptiness. He had a plan and a place for me all right, but it surely was not what I expected.

So at the time I was a hollow man. I basked in the hollow praise as school after school pursued me. I took a position teaching in an Adventist junior academy in Louisville, Kentucky. I found teaching the perfect career choice for me. I cared for every student and did my dead-level best to make them succeed. I loved every one of them, and they knew it. They became my children, my family, but again an old problem. Teaching gave me opportunity to immerse myself in never-ending work. I did four jobs in one—principal; full-time teacher of grades nine, 10, and occasionally, 11; secretary; and janitor. Again I basked in the praise, but it kept me from seeing myself clearly. Even more important, I couldn't perceive—and thus couldn't seek—God's purpose for me.

Let's get back for a few lines to my purpose in moving to Arkansas. It was the best place, I thought, to raise a family. My motive was great. And I tried with superhuman effort to make my home and myself different from my childhood home. But if you've come out of an abusive environment, you've got baggage with a poisonous snake inside. And no matter your motives, no matter your efforts, you flunk your self-imposed tests. The very stress you incur in seeking a perfect environment bursts forth, and your pent-up past explodes in a flash of red-hot temper. Hello, Dad! Hallow, Mother!

Shocked and mortified, you go to even greater lengths to make life perfect for your family. I picked up every figurative pebble in the path of my family, and smoothed the ground to boot.

By not letting my daughters deal with problems, I failed to teach them how to meet life's inevitable challenges. I would dash home from a 12-hour workday—not stopping even to buy a newspaper—and sweep an already-clean floor. My only friends were at school or work. I sought to fill Edna's needs—her background had its own liabilities—and thus create a Utopia for her and the girls. But smothering a family, however well meant, is simply another form of abuse.

**Celebrating Dad's thirty-fourth birthday.**

During a nine-year stay as principal of Tucson Junior Academy I turned things around—too far. I began to schedule board meetings after hours, help students, visit parents—a sick solution to the hollowness that beset me. My family interpreted my turnaround as emotional abandonment—the very thing I so hated and desperately sought to avoid. My wife and daughters didn't understand my motives, but then, neither did I. Edna begged me to recognize what I was doing and seek a better balance, but I couldn't, though I tried. I felt agonizingly torn between two overwhelming needs.

As it happened, for the next few years I was to be preoccupied with survival. It started in 1986 in a classroom. When you're standing before a class and explaining the formula to solve a quadratic equation, and your heart goes wildly out of rhythm, it's not easy to hide what's going on. But I hid my disquiet for the four hours until the end of the school day, and then headed directly to a nearby heart clinic where the staff did EKGs, sonograms, and stress tests. The irregular rhythm continued for three days, to the alarm of my wife. We didn't share our concern with the girls, but there were no more horseback rides to their bedrooms.

The doctors did a great job of educating me to the dangers of an irregular rhythm, telling me it could lead to blood clots and death. That's not what I wanted to hear. I wanted to know what was wrong and how to right it. The best they could come up with was the assurance that I had the heart of a 17-year-old.

For three years I lived with occasional irregular beats, which sometimes lasted for hours. One day a fellow teacher sat next to me as we watched a baseball game. He asked why I didn't play baseball with the kids; he had seen me playing basketball with them the night before. I told him of my symptoms, of the myriads of doctors, hospitals, and the it's-all-in-your-head comments I'd endured.

He turned to me and said, "I know what's wrong. You, my friend, have food allergies. I am positive. You are experiencing the exact nightmare I had for 25 years. Go see my doctor in Phoenix."

So three days later I did. I was tested for an extensive list of foods and shown to be severely allergic to 41. These included all dairy products, onions, garlic, yeast, and chocolate. I immediately excluded these from my diet, and, after some adjustments, my symptoms disappeared. No more headaches, no flu symptoms, no heart arrhythmia. I could sleep at night. The only one in our family suffering was Edna, who had to learn a whole new way of cooking with a vastly reduced number of foods. She later admitted to having slipped a forbidden product in a couple times, simply to see whether my food-consumption insanity continued. Each time the symptoms returned. I didn't feel she needed forgiveness—rather, applause and appreciation for the culinary miracles she was able to serve up.

In 1993 I took stock of my circumstances. Things looked pretty good. My career as a teacher was such a success that parents and other friends were convinced, as they would tell me, that I could "walk on water." I had a wonderful family, many friends, and, as I saw it, a working relationship with God. After all, didn't we go to church each Sabbath, as God commanded? Didn't we know that people who die don't go right to heaven? And weren't we keeping a lot of kids in the church who might have dropped out had it not been for my teaching?

The truth was that deep inside my soul I was back at square one emotionally and spiritually. In fact, I had perfected a fantastic suit of invisible body armor to protect myself from the nasty little dark memories that crawled out now and then to spread slime over my soul. I was safe inside my armor, because nobody could see in. All they could see was the brilliant and loving teacher. That wasn't, of course, what God saw. He saw the armor, and He saw the cracks in it through which currents of love from Edna and the girls entered, and through which I was able to return love. Someday, at a time of His choosing, the armor would have to come off. I little knew the agonizing trials that I would face. He would almost have to destroy me to save me, to break me back down into clay, to mold me. Someday I hope to walk with Him along the river of life. I can picture us, hand in hand, and He's explaining all my "whys."

# SEVEN

# I Pick Up a "Little Something"

*Down by the Riverside*
*Holding an oar*
*To cross over Jordan*
*Means*
*Forevermore*

—*The Chronicles of Grover, I, XV*

**Why is it that many a man,** however sick, will pass off symptoms with an "I picked up a little something over the weekend" or "It's just a touch of the flu"? Interview a dozen men, and you'll likely be able to add another dozen innovative "touches" of something or another. Edna had a simple explanation for my rationalizations: "Men just hate to go to the doctor." I didn't concede the point, but I had observed that women do seem less reluctant to go. Edna wouldn't let go. She had to tell me that she knew why men just hate to go to the doctor. Men, she said, are afraid they've got something. They're like little boys who've done something bad and don't want to go back into the house.

I really wasn't in the mood to argue. At the moment the principal of Grand Junction's Intermountain Academy was lying on a bed in one of Denver's finest hospitals. At least that's what my family had called it when they advised me to get over there pronto. When you're on your back in an emergency room, looking up, you watch the doctor's eyes. He seemed most concerned about the boils. Until he listened to me breathe. Shortly thereafter a couple orderlies wheeled me down the hall for X-rays.

By the time I got back to the emergency room, I was getting impatient. All this fuss over a little flu! And back at the academy, final exams were at hand. As the principal, I couldn't be late writing them! I had to make them up. "Them" meant all but one of the ninth- and tenth-grade subjects: Bible, 1 and 2; English, 1 and 2; General Math; Algebra, 1 and 2; Geometry; World History; Biology; P.E.; English, 7 and 8; Computers; and Health—now *there* was one for the books. Maybe I could get the doctors to write that test. On the other hand, I wouldn't want them to suggest I should have taken a dose of my own medicine.

Short of the celestial realms, it would be hard to top the school year of 1995-1996. Actually, I had not intended to be there. I had interviewed at several schools and had decided to teach at Sunnydale Academy in Missouri. I went to Colorado in 1994 just to fulfill my word that I would interview there. The school and its proximity to the large gym and church impressed me. But school board chair Nancy Taylor's welcoming smile, and superintendent of schools Jack Milford's uninhibited hug, constituted a welcome to be described only in superlatives. "Jack," as I came to know him, was all of five feet seven and had muscles like a lumberjack and per-suasion to match. In fact, he was so friendly that I forgot the sorry-but-I've-decided-on-another-school speech I'd prepared. The King of Cool was crumbling around the edges. The school board gave me a unanimous endorsement, and I didn't even call Edna to discuss "our" change of plans. The sense of God's presence and purpose was so profound that I could only bow my head, praise His name, shake hands with all my new friends, then go home and pack. I expected great things for the impending school year, and I was not disappointed.

I had a wonderful group of kids in my classroom. We were not sim-ply teacher and classmates, we were family. We rooted for each other; we cared for each other. We exercised the talents God had given us. And we had fun! To us, fun was anything that made life more worthwhile, whether it was laughing, playing, or giving our talents a workout. Our objective was to spread God's love.

The kids were nothing less than fantastic in the way they did it. They were members of Secret of the Cave Club, a group we organized each year. The meaning of the club was not secret: It was the name of a book about two young men in Scotland. Left to fend for themselves in a village while their parents were away, they went about doing good for anyone in need. Everything they did was in secret, hence the name of the book. To belong to our club, a student had to work to his capacity in the classroom and generate plans for secret operations.

Examples: The kids spotted a car parked out front while its owner was tending to affairs in the business office. They sneaked out of class (with ei-ther my approval or help—after all, I was a member too), washed the car, and left a treat on the seat. The class watched the surprised "victim" looking about to discover who had done this good deed. If he, or she, looked in our window, we appeared to be hard at work on our lessons. Other times, upon learning that a family was out of town for a few days, we'd go to their house, mow their lawn, trim their trees, and weed their flower garden. Our joy was twofold: First, in doing something for others while seeking no honor for ourselves; and second, in seeing their joy. We would leave a note that gave no hint as to its author. If some guessed who had done the good deed and came to thank us, we'd deftly sidestepped their "accusation" and gave them a big hug. So what could they do but return the caring to someone else! Our youth also perceived the beauty of love between generations.

We always scheduled weekend blessings. Three come to mind. One day in class a special young woman, Ashleigh Fishell, told us her father had been having headaches. She said he was going to the hospital that day for a CAT scan. Would we pray for him? We did, but we didn't confine our prayer to the classroom. I think the idea popped into four heads at the same time.

"Let's go," I said.

I arranged for a staff member to come to my classroom, we picked up Ashleigh's sister and hurried to the hospital parking lot. Mr. Fishell had just parked his car. We formed a five-person circle around him, prayed for him, and hugged him. There he stood in a state of what I'll call (until a better term comes to mind) bewildered love. The students knew that their arms were God's arms that day.

I recall when all the members of our club—the whole class—went to the home of a special friend, Morris Olson, who had lung cancer. We also visited him by phone and sent notes every day. Morris was hugged and prayed for until his heart felt as if it were bursting with gratitude. He got the message we intended to communicate—God cares, and God loves him. After his death a few months later, his wife told me that the doctors couldn't figure out why he didn't suffer the usual pain of lung cancer. He couldn't; there was no room for it. Our visits had filled him up with love.

The third incident is the kind you never forget. The Secret Cave Club members turned a usually difficult time—school evaluation—into a celebration. Evaluation is an ordeal that occurs every three to five years. A group, usually heavy with educators, looks at every facet of education as interpreted and applied in the school. Usually included among the visitors to our school was the Rocky Mountain Conference superintendent of schools, various educators picked by the conference, and local representatives. Our preparation usually took months and included publishing a detailed self-evaluation by the school staff and the local school board. Nerves are always frayed at these times, even when one's conscience is clear and professionalism is documented.

So what did we club members do? We decided to honor our guests. Weeks before the evaluation we organized committees and learned all we could about every member of the evaluation team. Our goal was to find special things about each person so that we would know how to touch their hearts. Our class artist formed a "bulletin board dream team" that drew cartoons depicting a positive virtue of each evaluator. The lone woman member had a poodle, so the team drew a classy woman walking her pink poodle. They made a cartoon of school superintendent Jack Milford blocking the basketball shot of his assistant, Dave Gilham. Jack was a friend, and spiritual father to our students. I came to cherish him as a Christian brother. During the several days of that visit I believe he got hugged several hundred times! He passed along a precious gift to me. He knew and loved his heavenly Father, and knew that his Father loved him. I, who had suffered so long at the hands of my father, still had trouble thinking of God as my heavenly Father. Jack's gift of love helped. I knew that I loved every student; I knew that no teacher could do more for them than I was doing, both to inspire them to excel scholastically and to love God unreservedly. I too loved Jesus and knew that He loved me enough to die for me. So what was my problem? Why did I still have difficulty with the "Father" concept? And why did I feel so hollow deep inside? I still wore my armor. It had its cracks through which love entered and exited, but little did I perceive what was yet to be.

Our students had planned a special treat for the last evening of the evaluation—a basketball game in honor of our most honored guest, "Papa" Jack. We charged admission and raised enough money to buy a much desired portable and adjustable rim for basketball. It was one of the few times I played with no care about who won. I knew that everyone on the court was a winner. Not that I didn't give it my best, even though I was not at my best. In midweek I had developed a temperature of 103 degrees. It was the flu bug, I was sure, caught from one of my fellow teachers, a sensible soul who had taken the whole week off. Not I! At midweek I began to cough—a deep, wracking cough. As I've hinted, when I did anything I did my best to do it better than anyone else! So Mike had a flu bug and a cough. Well, his was strictly minor league compared with mine. Then toward the end of the week I added a very visible side effect of my flu— quarter-sized boils, one of which was on the right side of my nose. The students giggled and whispered, "Mr. Wilcox has a zit!"

On Saturday night, after a basketball game, Edna and I drove to Denver to see our two daughters, Julia and Bonnie. They had moved away from home a few weeks earlier and now shared an apartment they had dubbed "The Empty Nest." It was there, with only examination week to go, that I slipped into the bathroom to examine my "flu symptoms." I had a few quarter-sized boils with red, volcanic-looking cores. The one on the side of my nose was "small," the size of a dime. A few gentle squeezes revealed what felt like a needle in each. A few days before I'd had an impacted wisdom tooth pulled, and an infection set in because the dentist neglected giving me an antibiotic. The entire left side of my head was numb, and I was still running my "flu" fever. My girls and my wife were worried. However, I resisted their pleas that I go to the hospital for a couple hours until my cough escalated and my joints began to ache. *Wow!* I thought, *this must not be any ordinary flu; this must be the Hong Kong special!* So to pacify the women, I agreed to go to the emergency room in the morning to get an antibiotic. Yeah, right!

**Day 1**

So it was that on Sunday morning a bedraggled nurse called my name. I followed her through a set of double doors and into an emergency room cubicle. Another nurse appeared with a clipboard full of questions. I was surprised at the number of symptoms she wrestled from me. For one, she noticed that I not only had a high fever but was blowing small amounts of blood from my nose. My eyes were bloodshot and had a yellowish tinge. I had begun to shake and feel disoriented. From the expression on the nurse's face, I suspected that my breath was setting some kind of record. For some obscure reason, that pleased me. When you've got the flu, I thought, don't settle for the usual that just anybody can get. Go for it!

The nurse had ceased writing. She got up and left.

When you're on your back looking up, watch the doctor's eyes for signs of trouble. Only now, it wasn't just one doctor but four who descended on me. They circled my bed like Indians had circled covered wagons in days of yore. They had that knowing-yet-not-knowing look in their eyes. They wanted to tell me something, I thought, but they couldn't. They probably really didn't know yet what brand of flu I had. Surely they had a selection of antibiotics. . . Maybe not.

They began to talk in circles and clichés. At first I thought it was because they didn't want to tell me what they thought was wrong. They put the X-rays up to the light and explained that my lungs were half full of some things that appeared to be tumors. I looked, and every defense mechanism from my youth popped up, ready for service. I said nothing. I had shifted into the protective mode that had served me so well when my father beat me. "It looks as if we're going to have to remove your right lung. Those tumors are cancerous. You can live on one lung, you know," a woman doctor was saying. "Lots of people do." She had a strong accent, but I understood her clearly. I also had heard that the tumors were in both the right and left lungs. I didn't have three.

When what seemed a death verdict hit me in the face, I found it difficult to pick anything rational from a multitude of chaotic thoughts. The first emotion I can recall was fear of leaving my wife alone. I thought of our girls, and that I would never walk down the aisle with one on my arm. I would never know grandchildren. The doctors started an IV and told me they were admitting me to the hospital. Lying there, stunned and alone, I realized that no amount of deep gut energy would cause the diagnosis to disappear. And I could not hide it within my armor; the girls would have to know. And what about my school? I had grades to make out, and all the paperwork of closing up for the summer. I was scheduled to conduct the graduation ceremony. Worse than all that was the load of debt we carried. We had held our breath getting our girls through college. For some reason, my memory offered up a cartoon of parents wearing empty barrels to their child's graduation. Now it was done, and we had planned on five years to recover financially. I knew the doctors weren't going to donate their services. Then there would be the hospital bill. And then—how much does a funeral cost? And you have to buy a burial site; and my wife and girls would want a gravestone . . . Two of the doctors returned. One made the preposterous statement that not even Arnold Schwarzenegger could have walked into the emergency room if the spots in my lungs were really cancer. One added that if I had been playing basketball two days before, as I had told them, I was either superhuman, or what the X-rays showed had to be something other than lung cancer in an advanced stage. It all sounded to me like "Maybe we broke the news to him a little too fast; let's toss out some hope."

I lay there on the table, feeling as if I were shrinking in stature and shrinking emotionally. Fear. Uncertainty. So where was God? He must have been in Edna, for sure. She may have fallen to pieces on the inside, as I guessed when she heard the verdict, but on the outside she stayed strong for me. I had always been the iron man, never letting up, and getting stronger as the times got tougher. Now that I was flat on my back, this beautiful and delicate woman responded in a manner that caused me to give her a new name. She became the *real* steel magnolia. She got a doctor to call Julia and explain what they'd found. He put the best spin on it, but Julia had just completed nurses' training and knew the gravity of my situation. Julia passed the news on to Bonnie. From the beginning I had three petitioners besieging the throne of grace. Grace means "unmerited favor." That's just what I needed. When you're stunned because your "flu" turns out to be "bye-bye," you realize as never before that you've got nothing to offer that will tip the scales in your favor. Unmerited favor. My only hope.

The doctors hadn't waited for a revelation from heaven to diagnose my case, and they didn't waste any time trying to fortify their decision. First came the blood woman with her array of needles and tubes. She took blood twice that day. Having learned nothing from it, they decided to do a needle biopsy of my right lung. In this process they put a coil on my chest, slid me into the MRI machine, inserted a needle between my ribs and on into my lung, from which they withdrew tissue they assumed would contain cancer cells.

Then it was over for the day. Edna, Julia, and Bonnie went home for what I knew would be a sleepless night. Adding to my sense of guilt for inflicting pain on them was the realization that Edna and I had planned for a summer vacation that was to start in one week. How silly we humans are. Here I was blaming myself for missing an appointment with my wife when the Grim Reaper had made his own appointment with me. Sleep would not come. I counted the dots on the ceiling tile. I waded through all the things I regretted in my life, such as being a workaholic and missing all those family vacations. The list was long. Then my sense of duty intruded. I made plans to finish my schoolwork—especially those unwritten final exams. So the night passed as I shifted from reality to another planet and back again. I constructed a battle plan: I would fight alone and not let anyone know how I felt. This strategy was hardly new. As a child I had developed the ability to escape fear and violence by retreating into an inner world of my own creation. Whatever happened, whatever needles they poked into me, whatever the final verdict, no one would see anything but a happy warrior. Just at the time I most needed God, just at the time I should have fallen into His loving arms, my past pulled me into its embrace.

As the night hours crawled by, I heard the night noises. My roommate's soft snoring. The quiet passage of nurses. Muffled conversations in the hallway. The beeps and buzzes of monitoring machines. I had been given no sedative because it might interfere with the testing to come.

## Day 2

With morning I put on my armor and prepared to battle an invisible foe. Had I not beaten the food allergies that had besieged me for more than 20 years? That fall off the cliff up by Lake Arrowhead—how many others would have survived that? The many times I had been beaten to a pulp . . . This kid was tough! And so was the man he had grown to be. I determined that no one—the doctors and the nurses, my wife and my children—would see anything but a happy warrior!

Edna arrived just after the needle woman and the nurses finished with me. My fever continued high—the nurses had to change my sweat-soaked bed every few hours. That morning, just as they wheeled me out for another test, Edna collapsed. Her blood pressure shot up so high that she was rushed into ER, in danger, they thought, of having a stroke. By evening, with the help of sedatives, she was able to go back to Julia's. That morning, however, I carried a double burden into another test area—mine and hers.

By midmorning the doctors were back. "Mr. Wilcox, we're going to put this tube down into your lungs. It has a camera on the end. You'll feel like coughing, but when you do, we'll shoot some more medicine into the area." They fed a tube that seemed to have the diameter of a garden hose, down and down and down. (I thought they had said they were headed for my lungs, not my bowels.) Each time I gagged and coughed, the doctor shot more medicine into my lungs. I felt as if I were drowning. The torture seemed to go on forever. It felt like induced drowning. When at last they rolled me back to my room, I had a mental map of the inside of the doctor's nostrils. That was more than they had gained. Two days of torture, and zilch!

With the shock of my death sentence wearing off a bit, I found myself wondering what God was up to. Yes, I loved Him, but all my life I'd had to fight my own battles. There had been no one I could count on. At the moment the best I could do was breathe a prayer of surrender to His will.

That day Edna brought the papers I needed, nurses contributed paper and scotch tape, and with their help I constructed the final examinations in 14 subjects for my students. The nurses faxed the papers to the Nancy Taylor. She became the conduit from my bed to the school. She substituted in my classroom, operated as the principal, and organized the graduation. If heaven gives out medals, there's one up there reserved for her. She told me that students, faculty, parents, and who knows how many others were praying for me. I wished for visits from my colleagues and students, but Inter-Mountain Adventist Academy was 300 miles away.

## Day 3

More tests. The first involved what was called a "breathing lab." I sat in a chair as the technician explained that all I had to do was take a deep breath and hold it until he said to blow out. I found that "blow out" meant "show me a hurricane!" I took a deep breath—and began coughing violently. Another try. Another coughing session. I coughed so long and so violently that I had to hold my sides. It felt as if I were getting a hernia. After I'd tried for 30 minutes without producing anything but coughs, the technician sent me back to my room.

Every hour brought another test. The doctors took cultures and tried to grow them, but no crop. I thought maybe they should call the Morriseys, whom I had visited once on their Minnesota farm. If anyone could grow things, they could.

Later the orderlies transported me to a room where there was a CT machine. I'd been there once before, but this time the doctors had a special treat. I lay on a "table," which moved into a long tubelike structure. The doctors lined up a grid over the worst area of my right lung. They took a needle and deadened the area of skin at the center of the grid. Then they produced a true "horse needle." It was so big that if someone had jabbed a horse in the rear with it, you'd have a Kentucky Derby winner by 50 furlongs. With the gross understatement "This will hurt some," they shoved the needle into my lung and withdrew some tissue. Again, no clue. Again, "We don't know."

## Day 4

With morning came a new symptom. The blood from my nose turned into huge, crusting, scablike lumps that further stumped the doctors. That afternoon a new doctor introduced himself as a physician from Africa. My primary-care physician, he said, had sent him to remove my right lung. He explained the procedure.

Strange, the idea of removing a lung from a man who can't breathe with the two he has; a man with a raging fever who can hardly get out of bed, and who has pneumonia, among other things. I began to feel that the medics were stabbing in the dark for a diagnosis. The doctor explained that they needed to remove the lung to test it because their biopsies were inconclusive. The procedure, he said, would involve splitting my sternum and using spreaders on my ribs to get into my chest. "It's the way we do heart surgery," he said.

My wife beat me to the response: "No way! You're not going to remove his lung!" There was no comma in her response. Just an emphatic period! Discussion ended! NO!

## Days 5-7

The next day I wrote a letter to be read at graduation. It had a simple theme: "I love you, and I'm doing well." I suppose "as well as can be expected" would have been closer to the truth. As for my primary doctor, he chose this day to reveal just how far away from the truth he was, so far as diagnosing my case was concerned. This truth emerged at the end of a three-day battle with him.

On the evening of day 7, while Edna was with me, he came in with his usual we-know-nothing speech, which ended with a startling question:

"Can we test you for AIDS?" This red-flag bit of nonsense brought me back to reality. Now I knew beyond doubt that he and the other doctors on my case were grasping at straws. I felt like a victim tied to a railroad track who could hear the train coming around the bend. Silly us. Edna and I had thought a hospital was a kind of democracy where we could share symptoms and opinions. A doctor friend has since told me that it is a wise doctor indeed who takes time to listen to a patient. They know better what they feel like inside. "Of course," he added, "it is a wise patient who listens to a doctor." But when they're unable to come up with a scientifically defensible diagnosis, it may well be time to look elsewhere. However, we were to find that while it's usually easy to get into a hospital, getting out is often quite another matter.

That evening Edna called the doctor at his home and told him we wanted to seek help elsewhere. He actually told her no. I was stunned. Edna, however, was filled with righteous indignation and more than willing to share it. After what seemed hours of verbal warfare, she told him that if he did not let us go, we would walk out anyway. He used a few choice clichés about what simple fools we were, and then agreed to come to the hospital to fill out the necessary paperwork. A nurse removed my IVs and, at midnight, we were free to go. My arms were full of X-rays, MRIs, and other test results as Edna pushed my wheelchair down the hall. The hospital had insisted that I be moved by ambulance, but out into the night we went, found our car, and headed for another Denver hospital that we hoped would have a doctor able to diagnose my illness. By this time I had abandoned my own diagnosis. Whatever it was, I had to admit wryly, it was not flu. Not even the Hong Kong variety. I was in trouble, and only God knew how deep it was.

During the 10-mile ride to the hospital, demons fought for my soul. Why had Jesus turned His face from me after we had been so close? I had dedicated my life to helping His children; I had given everything I had—physical, mental, and spiritual—to that ministry. I refused to yield to the demons that plagued me; my fevered mind was simply too exhausted to struggle for answers. I would deal with them later.

## Day 8

We arrived at the hospital around 12:30 in the morning. They were expecting me, and took me directly to the ER. I collapsed on the bed, my head spinning. When Edna left, I sat in a chair, coughing. The hours trickled by, interrupted only by a nurse taking blood and a young orderly sticking his head in to ask whether he could do anything for me. I shook my head no, idly wondering in my exhaustion and pain what it would be like if God stuck His head in and asked what He could do for me. What would I ask for? Healing? Did I dare simply ask Him to put His arms around me and—and what? Would I say, "Your will be done"? Or ask Him where He had been when I needed Him? What would He have to say to me? How I wished that my Secret of the Cave Club members would walk in the door and make a prayer circle around me. Where were they when I needed them? Yes, the 300 miles . . . But what excuse did the Lord have? When one is as sick as I was, thoughts are not coherent.

Early the next morning, just as the sun sent its warmth through my window, a doctor slipped in, introduced himself, and said, "We've looked over your records, and we have no idea what you have. So we're going to run more tests. We're going to start by growing some cultures."

I groaned inwardly. I already knew what those seeds would produce. "What about my fever?" I asked. "I'm soaked with sweat."

"We can't give you anything that would affect the test. We have to find what's causing these fevers, along with the pneumonia. I'll be back this evening, but others will be by."

I memorized the look in his eyes. I would compare it with his eyes on other visits and log his reactions as well. Such tactics had served me well during my childhood. My eyes followed him out the door, as they would follow others day after day. Later I was told I would be isolated from other patients; what I had might be contagious.

That morning Edna brought me food. No matter how many times I told the nutritionists of my food allergies, there, on the next plate, would be the offending items. Edna tried her persuasive best to get the word through to the kitchen. A nutritionist came, listened, and made a chart of what I could eat. Edna talked to the doctors. Repeatedly the tray would be brought; repeatedly I had to send it back. Had it not been for my wife's contributions, I would have starved to death—which on some days seemed a blessed option. By now I was so weak that I could hardly stand. But I promised myself that I would never stop moving until I dropped dead. So after my isolation ended, I went for a short walk—down the hallway to the nurses' station, or maybe the main lobby. I shuffled along with whatever tubes from wherever tucked in my hand. Left-right, left-right, just las in the Army. One sunny day I shuffled out the front door, coughing violently and dragging a clanking IV bottle behind me. Rest a minute, and shuffle on. Each day there was another round of tests and another round of I-don't-knows. They still thought, however, that I had cancer.

## Days 9-21

One day I thought, *What difference does it make how I die, as long as I'm going to die anyway?* So out the door and down the street I went, staggering along, sweat fed by my 103-degree fever running off my body, my coughs honking my distress. After so many hours of isolation and fear, I was blessed by the grass and trees. Cars sped by on their way to work, to school, to church, to the store. The world had not stopped. A hundred yards down the road a car pulled up to my side and stopped. I didn't even look; I didn't want to talk to anyone.

"Sir, where are you going?" boomed a commanding voice. I turned so see a police officer.

"I'm just moving along, officer, because if I keep moving I'll be OK," I croaked.

He laughed, and put an arm around my shoulders. "The woman in the green house called and said someone was staggering down the street, dressed in a hospital gown and dragging an IV T-rack. She thought you were running away!"

"Running away? Right." I released a rare smile from my dwindling stock. "I'm heading back now. Thank you for caring, sir."

Here was a soul from nowhere who held out a kind hand to me. Just the kind of person I usually loved to see standing along the highway—busy talking to someone else! On the way back I walked by the administrative offices of the Rocky Mountain Conference of Seventh-day Adventists. I didn't have the energy to cross the street, but I paused to wonder why no one had visited me. Surely someone there knew of my work at the academy, and of my illness. I felt another rug slip out from under me.

My first week at the second hospital dragged on, and each day brought the same song, different verses: "We don't know." "There's another test . . ." I sent a letter to my pastor friend Doug Hardt, telling him I would be home soon and be beating him in basketball. I faxed a letter to Nancy that I wanted read in the church. It was such an emotional moment, she told me, that she read the last page first. No matter; they got the message.

One morning a new doctor came into my room and said he was taking me downstairs to remove two of my boils for testing. I offered him the whole lot. That was before I experienced the pain of the needle and the scissors. As days passed, I longed for something to fight. You can't fight a shadow. Later I was to decide that I had done two things wrong. First, I divorced my mind from my illness. I gave up trying to figure out what was wrong. My mental tape recorder from the old dysfunctional days of beatings and abuse had kicked in, and I treated my illness the way I had dealt with the pains of youth: I accepted whatever came without question and adjusted to it. My method of surviving abuse was to accept and adjust. This process makes one a mindless victim of the whims of others. I thought it made me a pretty tough customer who never whimpered, no matter what. As a result, I never questioned any procedure. I did no research, asked no questions.

On my twenty-first day in the hospital I was in worse shape than when I went in. My white blood count was near 20,000 (10,000 being the norm). My platelet count was 1,200 (140-400 was normal). My sedimentation rate was 29 and rising (0-9 was normal). My fever continued in the 103- to 104-degree range. Sometimes I would hallucinate, especially if I dozed. The real alarm went off when my kidneys began to bleed. I had lost 40 pounds. During my stay at the two hospitals I gave enough blood, I concluded, to supply a fair-sized blood bank.

Edna got me through the days. She would trudge in with oatmeal or a plate of food, covered with aluminum foil. Each evening she would return to our daughters' apartment and suffer in silence. At least I had the partial anesthetic of pain; she had nothing. She got neither comfort nor answers from the doctors. At night I often played a basketball game in my mind against the world's best. With the game on the line, I would launch a 65-foot shot that would drop through as the clock reached zero. So I would daydream, sometimes turning to see the smiling faces of my wife and daughters. On other nights, however, I stood at a riverbank. . . .

"And so beside the silent sea, I wait the muffled oar. . . ."

That line by Whittier was, as I recalled, once reputed to be the most famous in American poetry. A figure I could not identify would be in the canoe waiting for me. I would hear someone calling my name from behind and turn to see Edna, Julia, and Bonnie. Should I go back? Who was that in the canoe? God? The devil? Who wanted me in it, and why?

I would create another basketball game and launch another winner.

# Wegener's Granulomatosis

*"Grover, row your boat ashore; hallelujah:*
*Grover, row your boat ashore . . ."*

**Days 22-29**

    **Nights in a hospital differ** from those you experience at home. In the hospital, when things get desperate, you realize that the real night is much deeper than the home night. It takes on a life of its own, softly flowing over and engulfing everything. It is this deep sleep that sweeps one into a dream world. It is from this sleep that some choose not to awaken; and others, as the ancient Job describes it, sleep all the days of their appointed time, until their "change come" (see Job 14:10-15; 1 Cor. 15:51-54).

    I sit in my stiff-backed chair, knowing that is my only chance to sleep. But sitting up takes energy, so I struggle between exhaustion and desperation. The room is dark except for pin lights from the beeping and whirling machines that reach down onto the beds and into the forms sleeping there. They watch over the pained and the unconscious, a safeguard against their slipping away into the deep sleep we call death. Their rhythmic beeping adds to the hypnotic mood of the world of the unconscious. Now and then a nurse slips past the door as she answers a patient's call for help.

    In my nearly 600 hours in a hospital chair since being admitted, I've become sensitized to every noise, breath, heartbeat. Two rooms over, an elderly woman moans; I've heard her begging God to release her from her agony. I add my prayer to hers. For nearly four weeks I've maintained my daily facade of heroic humor, soliciting smiles from downtrodden patients and overworked staff. But at night the mask is off; I see the river. I see the canoe.

    I pull the blankets around me to quell the chills that wrack me. I'm at the river's edge again. The Jordan . . . The river that separates mortals from the Promised Land. The water laps gently, invitingly. "Come," it seems to say. "Come to a land where your weary soul can find rest at last." Sweat pours from my body, as a 104-degree fever shakes me. Still, I feel a strange calmness on the water. Songs of the long ago speak softly:

"There's a land that is fairer than day,
And by faith we can see it afar;
For the Father waits over the way,
To prepare us a dwelling place there."

Sometimes my soul sings as the softly flowing, deeper night caresses it:

"Grover, row your boat ashore; hallelujah;
"Grover, row your boat ashore . . ."

Yes, the name was "Michael" in the original version. But now it's Grover who's doing the rowing. (If Michael stops by, give Him my regards!) Right now I'm wondering whether God is telling me not to let go, that He wants me here for a while. I'm back to the land of pseudo sleep, and I cough myself awake in the hospital room. My coughs become explosive, convulsive. The oxygen tube in my nose flies out. Desperately I throw the blankets aside and stagger toward the bathroom. I'm now coughing so hard that it seems to be coming from my toes. I begin to vomit. I claw for life as my IV bottle rattles and jerks behind me. The whole ICU comes awake; lights flash on in the hall. In the bathroom at last, I stand shaking over the tiny sink, coughing, gasping, vomiting. I draw mini-sips of air into my diseased lungs. *Dear God, what are those things in my lungs, my throat, my head—everywhere in me?*

A gentle hand touches my shoulder. "Are you all right?"

Of course I'm not! I don't answer. I *can't* answer. I just cough. But slowly I come to life again. Tears flow. The nurse checks my IV and changes me into a new hospital gown, the kind that should come equipped with a rearview mirror. I'm shivering. My teeth chatter. I creep back to my bed. "Dear God," I beg, "help me; I want to lie down so badly, Lord. Just help me not to let my head tilt again." I adjust everything just so.

Gradually I drift back to the river. At the river there is no pretense, no defense mechanisms, no inhibitions. There, in the semi-world, no one can intrude—not doctors, not medical tests, nothing. The few who reach the river and return are forever changed, their perspective of what's important, *really* important, forever changed. They know what counts: God's love. I'm on the riverbank again when the dreaded cough intrudes. Blood flows from my sinuses. How can I keep doing this day after day and have any blood left in me? Another hospital gown, another dry blanket, another pat on the shoulder. But fear of the unknown waters grips me this dark night.

The clock on the wall whispers 4:00 a.m., but it does not whisper that all is well. For a month now I've spent my nights calling up pleasant memories—my wife, my daughters, my students I've taught and loved, brothers and sisters, some of whom I've not seen since (could it be?) just a few years after juvenile hall. What of friends? Jack comes to mind. I'm sure he has not the slightest idea where I am or how I appreciate fellowship with a man who doesn't even know the meaning of self-glory. To be with him is to feel the presence of God. *My friend, my friend; where are you this night? Do you know that I am dying?*

With Jack in mind, however, I can't think sad. I walked from the river to the swimming pool where he shouted his war cry, "Canadian rules!" He jumped into the pool, grabbed me in a bear hug, and pulled me under. I chuckle as I remember stealing the basketball from this alleged Charles Barkley and sprinting up court for two more points—66 total! "Short and Chubby"—another pet name he gave himself—flicked out a paw, grabbed my jersey, and stretched it to what seemed to be 10 feet. I chuckle as I recall that this happy warrior scored his career high of four points that day. *Oh, Jack, I need you!*

Wasn't it only hours ago that I was telling God how I needed *Him?* During my hospital stay I've discovered that as you languish on the river bank or in the canoe, you feel your need of a close friend. Someone who cares for you. Someone whose relationship with God is so intimate that just being with him will put you into answered-prayer territory. My thoughts wander. I'm the hurting, pained, abandoned, abused child of yesteryear. I stand again at the chain link fence, hands clenched, face pressed against the cold reality of a confined soul. I search for the Comforter, but encounter only disquiet of soul. So I reach out for my next-best friend, Jack. I know he has no idea I'm in the hospital. It has all been so sudden—one day, at school; the next, in the hospital. One day, apparently healthy; the next, facing a bevy of puzzled doctors.

Where is Jack? I've always experienced a blessing in the presence of this man who knows the King. Of course, I could call my wife and daughters, faithful and loving both to God and their dad. But I couldn't let them know that I stood at the Jordan.

I sat and watched the door, hour after hour. Six p.m. Midnight. Four a.m. Nobody. No God, no friend, no one to lean on. Still I stare at the empty door. In my mind I imagine Jack asking for my room in his eastern Canadian accent. Getting in the elevator. Walking down the hall.

Suddenly imagination and reality seem to blend. Framed in the door is Jack's silhouette! He bursts into the room without a word, reaches out two strong arms, encircles my emaciated frame, and hugs me. For the first time in all the days of trial, I sob. I let the pain flow—the pain of wandering in the unknown; of seeing, day after day, the blank look of the puzzled doctors; the pain of assuming God's abandonment; the pain of a lifetime of shadows.

I croak out, "Jack, Jack, I love you, my friend!"

And so we sit occasionally sharing a few words, until at last I sleep. Only when the touch of the needle woman wanting blood awakened me do I realize that I've been dreaming. Jack did come later, when he heard I was seriously ill. I told him how much his visit in Denver had meant to me. I rehearsed the dream, and he chuckled.

My daily donation of blood a matter of record, I sent up a wee prayer that this would be the day they identified the diseases that wracked my body. Or maybe this would be the day I rested at last on the other side of the mighty Jordan. Whatever happened, Jack had made it bearable such was his influence, even through a dream.

The nurse entered to change my bed. I asked about the moaning woman. She smoothed out a few wrinkles before whispering, "She passed on during the night."

I climbed from my canoe, hitched up my pants, and put on a smile. There are always patients who need a visit and a word of cheer.

## Day 30 and On

Four weeks into my hospital stay I no longer visited the river; I lived on the shore. Slowly I had come to realize that I was to occupy a lifelong plot on Jordan's bank. My doctor found me there one day.

"I'm sending you home," he said.

I should have been dancing with my nurse at this news, but something signaled caution. "So what's the diagnosis?" I asked.

A good question. A month and I could hardly walk, fever raged, and my kidneys continued to bleed. So what was new? They were going to give me a prescription for an antibiotic called Bactrim, the doctor said, and I was to come back in a week. Edna looked at me, and I looked at her. Our silent conclusion: It was no use asking questions.

We crept across the Rockies that June day. Interstate 70 peaked at 11,300 feet. I gasped for breath, coughed up blood, and nearly passed out. Home at last, I settled into a living room chair, which I occupied when I wasn't crawling to the bathroom on hands and knees. I ate little, drank little, and endured. It was the worst week yet. Though the doctors had found nothing, a hospital held an implicit promise of emergency aid. I hated to think of what Edna might have to do should my condition worsen suddenly. The burden on her was bad enough as it was. I thought of suggesting we pick out a cemetery plot, but there was still one visit to the doctor to be made.

Later I was to find that taking the antibiotic worsened rather than alleviated my condition. I sat there burning up one minute and violently chilling the next. The nights seemed to stretch into forever for both of us, because any noise I made in the living room awakened and alarmed Edna. Had I been in my right mind I would have headed for a nearby hospital. Whoever invented weeks couldn't have had any idea of how long one could be stretched.

The drive to Denver was an even worse ordeal than the one home had been. I entered the doctor's office 45 pounds lighter than before. I fell into a chair, shaking like aspen leaves in a fall storm.

The doctor entered without a word. He sat for a moment, toying with his pen. "Mr. Wilcox," he said at last, "there is nothing we can do to help you. I suggest that you look elsewhere for a solution." He might as well have used his pen to sign my death warrant. "You do have a positive C-ANCA count," he added, whatever that meant. He said he could give me prednisone, but that wouldn't solve anything. The surgeons wanted to open my chest again, as in open-heart surgery, and remove my right lung, but they didn't because they felt I would not survive.

He got up; we got up. He left; we left. Five weeks! It took them five weeks to arrive at that conclusion! We sat in stunned silence. Another death sentence, and I was in a worse condition than when I had entered the hospital. I wondered what it takes for a doctor—a group of doctors, a troop of doctors—and two hospitals to admit they can't even come up with a diagnosis. Just "Go away. Go die. Just go."

We went. We drove across town to our daughters' apartment. While I coughed up blood, the three women convened a meeting in the living room. Both Julia and Bonnie had worked with hospice patients while in nurses' training. They told their mother that I was dying, but there might be a chance at one of three hospitals—Loma Linda University Medical Center, the Mayo Clinic, or Johns Hopkins. Their vote: Loma Linda.

There was, however, a problem. All of us combined lacked the money to buy even a one-way plane ticket to California. Here we sat, our finances depleted by college bills, doctor bills, and hospital bills—not to mention our missionary projects and other charities. Now we were a charity. Edna called my brothers in California, and they agreed to pay for my ticket. I would go alone, because Edna had to hold on to her job in a beauty shop—it was all we had. I knew it had to be, but how I would miss her! She had stood by my side—a counselor, wife, lover, prayer partner, and fellow sufferer. We said goodbye, knowing it very well could be forever. Edna drove away, over the Rockies, numb with an overload of misery and helplessness. She packed, knowing she would have to find a small apartment. She feared it would never be occupied by two.

Julia, Bonnie, and I headed for the Denver airport. The day was brisk and windy as we sped along the crowded freeway and turned west toward the mountains. A few miles later a billboard informed us that the new airport was 15 miles to the east. We flew off a ramp and, as my students used to say, Julia put the pedal to the metal. With a squeal and a flourish we sped into an airport parking lot. Bonnie and I lumbered along while Julia rushed ahead, beckoning us to hurry. She sprinted down the corridor, her flashing brown eyes signaling slowpokes to get into the slow lane. I felt a surge of pride as I saw heads turn to watch her passage. She was always the compassionate one who cared for the hurting, whether a human or a bird. And now she was making sure her father would get on a flight that might offer him a chance for life. When my legs were about to fail, a cart pulled up. I piled on, and in a minute we were at the gate. Our goodbyes were hurried, but eyes spoke love and hope.

The girls were hardly out of sight when my coughing started, sparked by my rush to the plane. I bent over, gasping. I wondered how I was going to survive the flight with the airsickness that I always got added to the coughing. Had the plane's crew known my condition, they never would have let me board. I prayed for a window seat and a glass of water as I staggered down the aisle, gaunt, pale, and coughing. I got my window seat and huddled there, trying not to breathe. I forgot to pray that no one would sit by me.

A preschool girl slipped into the middle seat, her mother taking the aisle. As we taxied down the runway, I coughed and coughed. By the time we were at altitude, sweat poured from my skin and wet my clothes. I leaned against the window and kept my head turned from the child. I'm sure the mother felt I was going to infect them both with some plague, and perhaps die before their eyes. The more I coughed, the worse my hands shook. Soon the plane echoed with my coughing, and all eyes seemed to search me out. What a journey to hell this flight was! How could I ever last for two hours? I grabbed a vomit bag and flew on.

Peering out the window between fits of coughing, I saw the Rockies pass beneath us and, a couple hundred coughs later, the Grand Canyon. So it was that I flew toward my childhood homes—the hundreds of them— and toward Loma Linda University Medical Center, the site of last resort. What reason had I to believe my experience there would differ from that in the Denver hospitals? As I saw it, there was no difference. Try prayer? I had, repeatedly and profoundly. And others had poured out their hearts on my behalf—Julia, Bonnie, and Edna most of all. *I'll see them again someday,* I thought. *Someday beyond the river.*

Eternity ended as the winged torture chamber touched down in San Diego with its shocked passengers trying not to inhale as they viewed the leper stumbling off the plane. At that moment I would have gladly crossed the Jordan had it run through San Diego. Gladly, that is, so long as I didn't have to row. My brother, Edward, and his wife, Judi, gasped when they saw me. Later Edward told me that I looked just like our brother-in-law had before he died from Hodgkin's disease. Loma Linda, they said between my coughs, was only an hour and a half away. I paid little attention to scenery, speed, or elapsed time. I focused on one thing—survival. I didn't even notice the huge hospital, glistening white in the bright sunlight. I didn't see the medical school right next to the hospital, nor the hundreds of cars either parked or looking for parking. I did know that the hospital was a Seventh-day Adventist institution. I was home with my brothers and sisters. Did a touch of hope brush my soul?

Into the emergency room we sped with all my records and my 103-degree fever—just five and a half weeks after my first X-rays had been taken in Denver.

A young intern—about the age of my daughters, I thought—introduced herself and began to ask questions. Finished, she sat for a few minutes, checking my symptoms. "You know what I think?" she said. "You have all the symptoms of a rare disease called Wegener's granulomatosis."

I'd never heard of it.

She explained that it was an autoimmune disease that attacks the linings of one's blood vessels and destroys them. In the process it destroys lungs, kidneys, the nasal passages, and any other place where there are blood vessels.

I didn't know that after I had gotten on the plane, Edna and my academy teacher friend, Nancy Taylor, had checked out a medical book, looked up my symptoms, and within a half hour had come up with the same diagnosis—Wegener's—one that the Denver doctors hadn't discovered in nearly two months of testing and torture. Nancy had worked for years as a medical transcriber and was familiar with medical diagnosis.

Of course, the Loma Linda intern wasn't the last word. Tests would have to be done, but they would show that she was right. Problem was, not only did no one know what caused Wegener's granulomatosis; they didn't know how to treat it. Half of them didn't even know how to spell it. Bless them! They had given me my first smile of the day. Maybe it came because I was past regrets. Of one thing I was sure: God had brought me to Loma Linda. Perhaps it was just to put an oar in my hands. Then again, maybe it wasn't. For some reason (could it be the prayers being said for me?) I knew that if I was to stand again at the Jordan, One who had crossed it before would be there with me.

**Nine** # The Hill Beautiful

*Thy sea, O God, so great,*
*My boat so small,*
*It cannot be that any happy fate,*
*Will me befall,*
*Save as Thy goodness opens paths for me,*
*Through the consuming vastness of the sea.*
—Winfred Ernest Garrison, *Thy Sea So Great*

**Despite my affection for** the Loma Linda University Adventist Health Sciences Center (where I had been a patient as a child), I knew little about it. In fact, it took a patient to point up my ignorance. A professor at Massachusetts Institute of Technology, he was in Loma Linda for the proton beam treatment of prostate cancer. He told me he had researched every treatment in the United States: surgery, seeds, conventional radiation, and proton beam, the latter of which had, for more than a decade, been unique to Loma Linda—*my* hospital! And that's where this professor of engineering had decided to come. He said that he and his wife had never heard of Seventh-day Adventists until they found themselves in the middle of thousands of them!

One afternoon the two of them invited a friend of mine to their motor home and plied him with questions for several hours: *What do Adventists believe? Why do they go to church on Saturday? Do they think people who aren't Adventists will be saved?* They concluded the conversation by saying that they had never been treated so royally as by the Loma Linda Hospital staff. On their last Sabbath in Loma Linda they dressed up and went to their first church service—in the Loma Linda University church.

There were other things the professor and his wife liked. All proton beam patients and their families are given free access to the Drayson Center, with its weight rooms, swimming pools, and handball, basketball, and tennis courts. "It's part of the medical center's emphasis on total health," he told me.

That's when I decided I had better learn more about my hospital.

First of all, the creation of the Loma Linda University Hospital com-

119

plex, it has been said, "was not so much fraught with the inevitable as with the impossible." That the feat was accomplished at all, says a university publication, was the request of "a rare recipe of faith, works, and struggle, liberally laced with the improbable, the miraculous, and the heroic."

Three factors made LLUH a reality. First, the deplorable status of public health in the middle and late 1800s. Walk through the gates of time into yesterday with me and pick up my 1897 *Sears and Roebuck* catalog. Got a health problem? Wegener's aside, it appears that Sears offered a cure for every affliction known to humanity—and even some that weren't. There was the Heidelberg Alternating Current Belt, offered as a help in kicking the habit and shucking the blues. There were also nerve and brain pills, Siberian Catarrh snuff, Dr. Allen's Asthma Cure, Dr. Roe's Obesity Powders, Dr. Barker's Blood Builder (75 cents for a large bottle), good for everything from cancer to syphilis in all its stages. And you'd find assorted cures for epilepsy, Saint Vitus's dance, canker, cholera, fevers, congestions, piles, indigestion, weak stomach, rheumatism, and brain fag—probably the 1890s' equivalent of today's jet lag. There were also home remedy kits (from 85 cents) that contained belladonna, digitalis, nux vomica, and opium. For 40 cents you could purchase a box of Dr. Rose's French Arsenic Complexion Wafers, highly recommended by the famous Madame La Ferris of Paris.

In your local pharmacy you could find, as of March 1885, cocaine toothache drops, advertising instantaneous cure. A cocaine pile remedy was made in Moundsville, West Virginia. And for the health nuts there was Celerine, a celery-cocaine tonic for both sexual apathy and excess. You've heard of that drink advertised as the "real thing"? Well, in the good old days it was. Until 1903 Coca-Cola was a mixture of water, caffeine, and cocaine. Small wonder that in the mid-1800s people died at an average age of 39.4 years. Nearly one out of every six babies died before their first birthday.

Though in the good old days millions of cars were not spewing carcinogens into the air, each of New York City's 150,000 horses produced 20 to 25 pounds of manure per day that attracted swarms of flies and provided a most unheavenly stench.

The deplorable status of medicine in the 1800s cried out for a medical institution that was sensitive to public health. There was one: the Western Health Reform Institute, founded in 1866 in Battle Creek, Michigan. By the end of the century this institution, known as Battle Creek Medical and Surgical Sanitarium, served 1,000 patients, who knew it as a place where people "learn to stay well." Among them: President Calvin Coolidge, Henry Ford, and Admiral Richard Byrd (who sought advice on a diet for his polar explorers). Battle Creek Sanitarium and Loma Linda University, along with many other medical institutions around the world, share a common heritage: They are all institutions founded by the Seventh-day Adventist Church, which brings me to the second reason LLU was founded: the conviction that the Christian's body is a "temple of the Holy Spirit" (1 Cor. 6:19, NIV).

That vision has sparked a world-wide network of hospitals and clinics. It was the concept of serving the whole being, I believe, that impelled Drs. Steven Stewart and Evert Bruckner to seek not only my physical healing but my spiritual healing as well. They not only questioned me about my physical illness; they prayed with me.

**Loma Linda Sanitarium, circa 1905.**

The third reason for the founding of LLU was Ellen G. White, believed by Seventh-day Adventists to have been a prophet, which is said by the apostle Paul to be one of the major gifts with which God would endow his church: "Follow the way of love and eagerly desire spiritual gifts, especially the gift of prophecy" (1 Cor.14:1, NIV). It was she who urged the establishment of health centers where the "whole" person was to be restored by combining the best in medical science with Christian compassion. How grateful I am for both these aspects of medicine!

As a former academy teacher I regret that many Adventist adolescents get a vision of Ellen White as an elderly woman with a lace collar around her neck and condemnations for youth and others that begin: "My dear [brother or sister], I have been shown . . ." They don't see her for what she was—a spokesperson for God, for justice, for mercy. They don't realize that she took on the medical association of her day and staunchly condemned its approach to healing. They don't know that she wanted

Adventist colleges to be centers of training for the unemployed. They don't know that she often condemned "conservatism" in the cause of God. Now, *there* is the portrait of a prophetic reformer that youth could get excited about! And at a time when most medical doctors were treating only the physical ailments, she said Adventist doctors must treat the whole being—physical, mental, and spiritual. That concept was decades ahead of the medical science of her day, which brings me back to Loma Linda University Medical Center and how it came to be.

The property on which LLU now stands was owned by a group of investors who wished to make it the site of one of the finest health resorts in southern California. It was they who changed the name of the site from Mound City to Loma Linda, the Spanish term for "hill beautiful." When this venture failed, the investors offered the property for $110,000, far more than the fledgling Adventist Church could afford. By early summer the stockholders ordered the property sold for $40,000. Though the local church conference said it could not take on even this sum, Mrs. White wired instructions to secure an option.

Loma Linda University Medical Center today. The mountains in the background are where my family lived for much of my early life.

On August 26, 1905, the sanitarium was incorporated. Six weeks later the first two patients were admitted. But the institution was far from achieving the goal Ellen White envisioned. In April 1906 she spoke at the dedicatory service of the newly named Loma Linda College of Medical Evangelists. "Loma Linda," she said, "is to be not only a sanitarium, but an educational center. . . . A school is to be established here for the training of gospel medical missionary evangelists. . . . The securing of this property, is a miracle that should open the eyes . . . our of understanding."

As I walk the halls of today's LLU School of Medicine, I'm aware that more than 3,500 students are enrolled in six schools. Every state and about 80 countries are represented in the student body. Some 35,000 alumni have earned degrees, and most have served, or are serving, humanity in some corner of the world, if not here in the States. I have to push my gait to the limit to visit all the schools in a forenoon. Here's the list: the University Adventist Health Sciences Center, the Proton Treatment Center, Cancer Institute; Center for Joint Replacement; International Heart Institute, Children's Hospital; Transplantation Institute; Outpatient Surgery Center; Rehabilitation Institute;

Loma Linda University Children's Hospital today

Community Medical Center; Center for Neuroimmunology; Neurosurgery Center; Behavioral Medicine Center; University Health Care; School of Allied Health Professions; School of Dentistry; School of Medicine; School of Nursing; School of Public Health; Graduate School; School of Pharmacy; Center for Health Promotion; and Loma Linda University. All are important; but a few remaining departments emphasize the gospel foundation of the institution: Faculty of Religion; Center for Christian Bioethics; Center for Spiritual Life and Wholeness; Students for International Mission Service.

If you were to walk into the hospital and ask about its mission you'd likely be given a paper titled, "Our Mission." Its message? "The mission of Loma Linda University Medical Center is to continue the healing ministry of Jesus Christ, 'to make man whole,' in a setting of advancing medical science and to provide a stimulating clinical and research environment for the education of physicians, and other health professionals.

Schools of Allied Health Professions and Public Health

"Our first responsibility is to our patients, who must receive timely, appropriate medical care with consideration for their privacy, dignity, and informed consent.

"We uphold the values of the Seventh-day Adventist Church and its

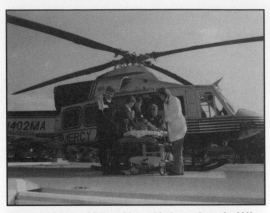

Day and night, residents of Loma Linda can hear the LLU Medical Center helicopter heading out on an emergency run or bringing in patients, often to and from the scene of an automobile accident.

rich traditions by caring for the sick, promoting healthful living, awakening inquiry, and spreading the gospel of Jesus Christ.

"We honor our God, the Father, the 'Son, and the Holy Spirit by demonstrating Divine compassion and kindness through our care of the sick and by respecting and encouraging spiritual values."

Do I love this medical/teaching center? You bet! If it were not for this institution you'd be seeing "Grover Winslow Wilcox" on a gravestone somewhere.

During my ordeal in Denver I had complained to the Lord about the doctors' failure to diagnose my disease, the one that a Loma Linda intern, after a short conversation with me, correctly believed to be Wegener's granulomatosis. Not that Wegener's is to be coveted. A medical book I perused said it would be "fatal within months." Fatal, that is, if patients were left on their own. If I had been correctly diagnosed in the first Denver hospital and treated there with prednisone alone, the usual treatment at the time for this unusual disease, I would not have lived to reach the second. Had I been diagnosed and treated in the second Denver hospital, I would not have lived to reach the Loma Linda University Hospital. In 1996 only a few medical centers nationwide were using chemotherapy with prednisone, a combination that has prolonged the life of Wegener's victims. Loma Linda was one.

An interview with a woman doctor on my second day at the medical center was interesting, to say the least. Sit in with me:

Doctor: "Are you aware, Mr. Wilcox, that you had a positive C-ANCA count on a test taken at your last hospital?"

Wilcox: "No. I don't even know what a C-ANCA is."

Doctor: "A C-ANCA shows the presence of antibodies your body has produced to attack itself. This test is 90 percent for

Wegener's. It doesn't make sense that your hospital never pursued this. They should have taken and tested tissue samples."

Wilcox: "They did, but they showed nothing."

Doctor: "No, I mean they should have taken a lung biopsy."

Wilcox: "A lung biopsy? Oh, they wanted to spread my sternum, as in open-heart surgery, and remove my right lung. They said that would tell them something."

Doctor: "Take your *lung?* They told you *that?*"

Wilcox: "Yes; look in the records."

She left to do so and returned a few minutes later.

Doctor: "The record amazes me. That's all I'll say. You would not have survived losing your lung."

Wilcox: "You should have heard what my wife said when they suggested taking it. She used every version of an emphatic NO that's in the dictionary—and a few that aren't. What made their intention to take my lung even more absurd is that I had pneumonia in both lungs, and they had diagnosed cancer in both! I pointed out that I didn't have three lungs. That's when we moved to the second hospital."

I had hardly reached my hospital room when a pulmonary specialist, Dr. Phillip Gold, introduced himself. His early interest in my case lifted my spirits, and in fact he probably saved my life. Then, as I should have anticipated, I met the "blood woman." She had a bite like a mosquito that had been mated to a very hungry crocodile! According to my calculations, I had in the past two months donated a bathtubful of blood to medical research. I suggested to the blood woman that they install a faucet in my arm.

That evening I sat watching a California sunset between coughs when a gentle voice called my name. "Are you Mr. Wilcox?"

"Yes, I am; come on in. You must be the chaplain, judging from the way you're dressed."

"Yes, I'm the pastor. I'm getting in some training. How are you?"

"I'm fine. I just wish they would find out what's wrong and do something about it."

"How long have you been here?"

"This is my first day, but I've been in hospitals since May 17."

The would-be chaplain shifted into high gear, and in the next few minutes shared a list of clichés that would have done credit to a collector:

"Everything works out for your good."

"Somehow the Lord knows you need this."

"It could be worse."

"You'll only be allowed to suffer what you can handle."

"God knows best."

"Hang in there."

"Someday you'll look back and laugh."

After a short prayer he was gone. Thank *God* he was gone! In my mind's eye I could see him walking down the hall placing an X by my name on some list. I'm willing to concede his sincerity, but unfortunately he personified what had been all too prominent in my search for medical professionalism—clichés.

Early the next morning three doctors entered my room to examine me and ask questions. Their most notable observation: "Your kidneys are bleeding, but we're keeping a close eye on developments." Later that day they sent me to the basement to have a sonogram, which could reveal damage to internal organs. Two doctors—one tall and thin, the other short and chubby—put some sort of cold cream on me and asked me to try not to cough. By now my coughs must have become a conditioned reflex: Put me on a table, tell me not to cough, and plug your ears. Twenty minutes and one more doctor later I was back in my room.

Soon after, a young man, fidgeting with his stethoscope (I could see him talking with two women doctors), nodded his head and came toward my room. He began mumbling something about the sonogram, cleared his throat, and examined his shoes with all the interest of a "sole" doctor. I knew something unusual was coming, but what? Were the doctors about to give Wegener's the boot in favor of something worse? But that couldn't be; there was nothing worse. I decided to try an encouraging smile. That did it.

"Ah, Mr. Wilcox, what we really need is a viewing."

I didn't know whether to laugh or cry. A viewing? The doctors in three hospitals had taken CT scans, MRIs, biopsies, blood tests, X-rays, and contemplated surgeries. They had looked at and through every cell of my body at least 10 times. They'd viewed sonograms, cultures, and growths—but a viewing? *Viewings,* in my lexicon, were what come before a burial. Oh, unhappy thought! Surely not so soon!

"What do you mean by 'a viewing'?" I ventured.

"Well, do you have children?"

"Yes, I have two daughters," I answered, more puzzled than ever.

"And they're your daughters, not adopted or from a previous marriage of your wife's?"

"They're mine, all mine!" Where in the world was this line of questioning going?

"Well, ah, ah, have you ever had a kidney removed?"

"No; there would be a scar if I had."

"Well, we can't find a kidney on the left side."

*OK,* I thought. *So I've gone through life up to now with one kidney.* Were they planning to offer another? Or to tell me that my only one was shutting down? But what would that have to do with a "viewing"? Time would tell. The doctor couldn't examine his shoes forever.

He shuffled his feet, looked up, and took a deep breath. "Well, ah, sometimes when a person has only one kidney, his genitals do not develop correctly, so I, ah, I need to look."

I had the best laugh since I'd held Jack to four points in our academy year-ending basketball game. Doctors of both sexes had seen everything else. Why not? What was it Caesar is quoted as saying—"I came, I saw, I conquered"? I slowly elevated my hospital gown. The doctor saw. "I hope I measured up to your expectations," I said to his retreating form. You can't live forever on humor. But that one got me through a couple days.

Since coughing kept me from lying on my bed, I used it as a table, neatly stacking items according to priority. Nearest was my Bible. Next were two stacks—one for *Hot Rod* magazine, the other for *Classic Cars.* Often when doctors came in, they would pick up one or the other of the magazines and look at the pictures. My roommate, Gerald, who had severe diabetes and was losing his leg, also enjoyed the magazines.

One afternoon a new nurse named Tom introduced himself and went to work on my roommate. A nurse? I thought this guy looked more like a football player. But his eyes looked as if they should belong to a choirboy. They lifted my soul. Tom, I learned, operated heavy equipment. He was married, had two small daughters, and owned a Camaro almost like mine. But the most intriguing information by far was that he had endured a sentence in Riverside juvenile hall—and for the same reason that my brothers, sisters, and I had been there: His parents had abandoned him and his sister! How could it be that after 43 years we would meet in a hospital room at the Loma Linda University Medical Center! Coincidence? Tell that to someone who doesn't have much above the ears. I knew beyond doubt that God had arranged our meeting. After all, we were soul brothers. That night I slept like a baby—sitting up, to be sure, but God's baby.

Two weeks after I entered the hospital, the doctors agreed that I must have Wegener's, though no test had confirmed this diagnosis. They would, nevertheless, schedule (in their terminology) a "conclusive" test—a nasal biopsy. Oh, no, not *that!* I remembered one in Denver all too vividly. I walked to a window looking out over Loma Linda. The lights were on in the houses on the hillside. Were there really people in them doing ordinary things such as watching TV or eating dinner? Did they realize the privilege of simply walking across the room and hugging their children? Did they ever look out their windows and think of the nameless faces so nearby and yet so far away; faces that might never see another dawn? *My* face. I adjusted my chair and settled in, praying for a coughless night. *Not for healing, Lord. Not for a big miracle; just a little one, Lord. A coughless night.*

"Wake up; wake up, Mr. Wilcox." A gentle arm nudged my shoulder. "Why aren't you in bed?"

Two new faces. How many departments were there in this hospital? How many people whom I'd not met?

"Because I can't sleep lying down," I said. "I go into spasms if I do."

"Well, we are the doctors of joy, and we've been sent here to do a nasal biopsy. We usually put a patient under, but we're going to let you stay awake."

I understood what he *wasn't* saying. They knew of my raging fever and cloudy lungs. They were afraid to put me under. I climbed onto the bed, tucked two pillows against the headboard, and sat up. They put a tray next to my bed with implements on it that would have struck terror in a medieval torture chamber. Prominent was an assortment of needles long enough to reach high into my sinus area. Then there was a strange device that had little snippers on the end.

I didn't examine the tray further; I had gone into my out-of-body mode in which I pretend the torture tools are going to be used on someone else. My mind was present and accounted for, but nearly detached from my body.

The doctor said he was going to put cocaine up my nose. Oh, if my academy students were here to see this! Their teacher snorting cocaine! The doctor probably wondered what I was laughing about. The doctors produced a long cotton tube soaked with cocaine. The medication was supposed to deaden the nerve endings in my nose so that they could inject the real deadening medicine with their needles. *Needles?* They looked more like the spears medieval knights are pictured with. I would have felt comfortable facing a charging rhino with one of them. People had told me that when one faces death, every sense—ears, eyes, nose, whatever—operates at maximum efficiency. In my experience it seemed more like it was every nerve that became sensitized, ready at the touch of a feather to shout, "Watch out!"

The cocaine surely didn't seem to deaden anything; rather it caused my heart to race wildly. I found myself wishing my legs were racing down the hall and out the door. Telling me not to cough was like telling a cat not to snarl when you step on its tail. I told the doctor—the one with the big nose—that he, rather than I, should be having this treatment.

I thought that I had experienced everything during the past two months, but when Big Nose stuck the rhino-killer snippers up my nose and began to clip pieces of flesh from up behind my eyeball, I poured out a 16-ounce glassful of tears. I counted 13 snips, and felt every one. With each I would tell myself *It's the last test; it's the last test; it's the last test; it's the last test.*"

That evening I sat in my chair, a worn-out lump of humanity, hardly able to focus my thoughts. When a cheerful, articulate doctor strode in and introduced himself as Dr. Libanati, I wondered what he had ingested that day.

"Mr. Wilcox," he said, "we're sending you home tomorrow!"

It didn't register. Sending me to a *funeral* home, had he said? Was this the real "viewing" coming up? I had found the staff at Loma Linda University Hospital to be a happy bunch, but surely they wouldn't be making fun of a dying man. Still, hadn't that doctor in Denver told me he was sending me home because they couldn't do anything for me?

"We expect the test to confirm Wegener's," Dr. Libanati was saying.

"But now we've got a few things to deal with it. You're going home!"

I sat alone. No, not alone. There must have been a dozen excited angels in the room, every one bringing a precious memory. One reminded me of Roger Morrisey, who had invited me to visit his parents' Minnesota farm, where God had shown me that He cares for everyone, not just the privileged. Another angel reminded me of the Loma Linda University Hospital orderly who had shared love with me, then a 10-year-old stranger. There was George Jubilee, who showed me how to lift the spirits of others. Another angel reminded me of my caring aunt Anne, and of Tom, who had lifted me to a God who loves humility and compassion. A shy angel whispered of Jack, who blesses others without a thought of reward for self. And there was my brother Edward, who had let me see that God would do anything for anybody, just as he had done for me. Another angel whispered memories of Edna and Julia and Bonnie.

Dear God! Oh, *dear* God! I was thrilled, stunned, amazed, and happy all at once. I sat and wept, sobbing out words I had feared were gone forever from my lips: "I'm going home. I'm going home. I'm going home." I laid down the oars on the bank of the Jordan and turned away. I called Edna, and we wept together. She sobbed out a question or two about Wegener's, but all I could say was "Sweetie, I'm coming home." I hardly slept that night. I sat thanking God for a chance—at last.

So it was that in early July of 1996 a nurse took out the IV, the last of 18 I had counted. Dr. Libanati came by to explain that Wegener's granulomatosis was a catastrophic, deadly disease that attacks every organ in the body. There was no known cause, no known cure, and no known successful treatment. However, they were having some success with a few of the new medicines. I would be on chemotherapy every day for three or four years. They would have to regulate me with monthly blood tests, which would mean frequent visits to the hospital. My brother wheeled me into the hospital pharmacy. I would be carrying my life home in a sack.

An orderly wheeled me down the hall to an elevator and out the front door. There I asked my brother Edward and his wife, Judi, to go get the car. I needed a moment alone. When they disappeared, I stood, leaned against the hospital wall, and sobbed again and again, "I'm alive! I'm alive! I'm alive!"

# TEN Bills, Chills, and Walking Free

*Thy winds, O God, so strong,*
*So slight my sail.*
*How could I curb and bit them on the long*
*And salty trail,*
*Unless Thy love were mightier than the wrath*
*Of all the tempests that beset my path?*
—Winfred Ernest Garrison, *Thy Sea So Great*

**So I left the hospital for home** one spring day with a disease that the finest of doctors could not explain. It had a name, but they didn't know how it gets started, and they didn't know how to stop it. They knew that Wegnener's granulomatosis attacked the arteries and veins from within. At Loma Linda University Hospital and a few other leading medical centers, doctors had learned that a certain combination of medicines, including chemotherapy, could extend a victim's life expectancy from a few months to—nobody knew. In 1996, when I left Loma Linda, one victim was known to have survived 10 years. I had no reason to expect to match that figure. My wife told me later that she had already faced the harshest reality—she had come to terms with my impending death.

A couple days after arriving in Grand Junction, I went into one of our basement rooms and got out my few belongings. I set up little stations for each time segment of my illness and, with music playing in the background, revisited each and every memory. Even with the prednisone and the chemo flowing through my veins, it was good to be alive.

But during the nights my dreams were less sanguine, taking me back to the abusive scenes of my childhood. In one I confronted my parents. All nine of us were in the living room when my mother yelled into my face that we children were the cause of our father's condition. We were responsible for our abuse! In the dream I did what I never did in real life—I told my mother the truth to her face. When I awoke, I would write out my dreams. My euphoric state of mind lasted for nearly a month.

During this period, daily, and sometimes hourly, I fervently thanked my heavenly Father for bringing me home to my family. I would recall the nights I'd tiptoed into my daughters' room to brush a kiss across a cheek and gently tuck a curl back into place; the nights that Edna and I had slipped gently to sleep with our arms around each other. I would ask God to someday bring my brothers and sisters together again. I would ask Him to look at His hand, where, He had said, He had my name "engraved" (see Isa. 49). I would lift my hand and hope that I might actually feel His hand grasping mine. I wondered how anyone could go through the pain this planet inflicts without reaching out to God.

From another perspective, however, I wondered how God could reach a soul who had been beaten and choked as a mere baby; neglected, rejected, and abandoned; and a con by the age of 7. A soul who, as an adult, was plagued by migraines and allergies, afflicted by a fatal disease, haunted still by the abuse of his early years, and who sometimes questioned the purpose—if not the existence—of God. What in the world could He see in me that was worthy of His love? The answer, as I've learned, is the image of His Son. That's what he saw in me. Defaced to be sure; but through His grace and initiative at Calvary, restorable.

One day during my fourth week home, reality kicked in, and depression followed. I decided to go through the mail that had accumulated. Mistake! Bills, bills, bills! Day after day I would crawl out of bed after Edna left for work, sit at the kitchen table, and sort through stacks of medical bills. How could I pay them? Surely not on Edna's salary as a hairdresser; that hardly covered living expenses. I was afraid that the extra hours she was working would jeopardize her health. I'd sit for a while, then head for the bathroom and vomit, or lie down in nausea and pain. Chemotherapy imposes its own price on users. Then, back to the bills.

My denominational employer had coverage that paid many of the bills. Then they would deduct my portion from my paycheck, which often didn't leave much. One month I received $100. Many people think the worst pain a sick person suffers is imposed by the illness itself, and it may be. But often, I believe, it is the unanticipated side effects that are the most devastating. More than two months in three hospitals, the services of hundreds of doctors and anesthesiologists, tests and more tests—all make for a bankruptcy-sized debt. Depression often has an irrational component, as demonstrated when I picked up every bill I could find, put them in a box, and headed for the dumpster. Edna intervened with her gentle humor and good sense, saving the bills.

But there was no disguising my mental state. In subsequent days, with the exception of a box of keepsakes I had from my daughters, I threw away everything I owned—even some furniture I didn't like. I gave away my car tools, gardening tools, lawn mower, and clothing—shirts, shoes, pants—keeping only what I was wearing. Out went my teaching material and notes from 20 years. I even gave away my treasured 1976 Cadillac Seville. Some psychiatrists say that such an orgy of giving may follow a near-death experience.

Four months after leaving Loma Linda, I resumed teaching. My students were solicitous of my health. Of course, neither they nor their parents knew just what my problem was. Well, neither did the doctors! We resurrected the Secret of the Cave Club and were soon delighting not only the "strangers within thy gates," as Scripture exhorts, but strangers without as well. Despite my students' grace, life became a daily battle. Seeking to regain some health and strength, I began to walk a shortcut to school. Often, as I passed through a nearby park, I would slip behind some bushes to vomit. Though often nauseated in the classroom, I acted the part of the impervious, unstoppable, and unflappable "teach." Whether it was because I was too successful as an actor, or because they feared they would get what I had got, my colleagues did little to lighten my burden.

The sun was in a good humor that Tuesday in the Colorado Rockies as I drove Edna to work in Fruita, a small town 10 miles from our house. On the way home I contemplated stopping and letting Sol play his benevolent rays on my too-white torso before heading for the classroom. I was hardly on the road, however, when waves of nausea swept over me. I sped up, hoping to get home where I could hide my condition behind closed doors. I made only three miles before I swung the car to the roadside, flung open the door, and vomited. Another two miles, and I didn't even have time to open the door. I could imagine what people in passing cars were saying: "Another poor drunk who can't hold his liquor!" "Isn't it disgusting the way some people are!" Our car, a 1978 Camaro, must have been half horse, because somehow it found its way home.

In the house at last, I collapsed on the floor, going immediately into survival mode. I laid perfectly still, as in a coma, willing my cells to barely function—no movement, no breathing, just total concentration on being only a tiny step above dead. Edna rushed in (I had called her) and hurried for a pan. I knew what to expect—four additional attacks over a two-hour period. When the next hit, I curled into a fetal position and tried not to move even a fingertip. I prayed that no birds would chirp—the slightest noise worsened the episode. No one but Edna knew the details—no friends, no family, nobody. Each attack precipitated a struggle for survival between me and the cells lining my stomach. I begin to shake violently with chills. Edna piled blankets on me. When this failed, she crawled under the blankets and sought to warm me. When I began to vomit blood, she tried to get some Mountain Dew down me. Sip after sip, until I began to feel some relief. Maybe I would live. Slowly I warmed up to near the level of "weak as a rag." Mathematician to the core, I figured I had vomited more than 100 times. It was not a record.

A few days later the doctor at Denver's Jewish Hospital, whom I saw each month, sighed and said, "Look, Wilcox, either you're going to have to quit teaching or you'll be carried out on a stretcher." I knew what he meant. What was that word a doctor at Loma Linda had used? Oh, yes—a "viewing." Find a laugh where you can, Wilcox.

I knew Edna had saved my life several times. Perhaps it was only fair that I saved hers. As usual, it had been a tiring day for both of us, so we retired early. Sometime after midnight I began to flip-flop and dreamed I was sick to my stomach. As I often did when sick, I told myself it was a dream even while I was dreaming, and tried to sleep even deeper.

During my illness Edna had often lain awake in the middle of the night, listening to the sound of my rattling lungs. Or she would awaken and try to figure out how we were going to survive. When the grandfather clock in the living room struck 2:00 a.m., I got up and staggered to the bathroom, falling against the wall several times on the way.

"Edna, Edna," I called. "I need your help."

Finally I heard her voice. "What do you want?"

"I need you, please." I seldom called for help in the night for any reason. Alarmed, she dragged herself into the bathroom and stood by me so I could lean on her. But to my dismay she collapsed, semiconscious. To my numbed mind, everything seemed to be happening in slow motion. And then I too slumped to the floor.

Suddenly I knew! I reached out and slapped her face. *"Edna!"* She opened her eyes. "Breathe next to the floor while I crawl to the front door."

I pulled the door open and crawled back to her. We made it to the front porch, where we lay gasping. We were suffering, I realized, from carbon-monoxide poisoning. There had been a gas leak in the kitchen stove. When I had recovered enough to walk, I turned off the gas and opened windows. It had been a close call for both of us. As I lay in bed the next morning, the sweet feeling of survival flooded my soul. Edna and I had made it through the night, God was in His heaven, and all was right with the world.

A month later I awakened with the same sense of survival. I had made it through the school year, and I had missed only *two days* of school! I lay in bed thinking about recruiting students. Teaching was my life, and my life was teaching. I didn't hear the phone ring.

Edna poked her head around the doorway and told me that I had a call from the superintendent of education. Two mothers had called him, he told me, with some concerns about the school. They were upset because I gave the kids nicknames and had not revealed how sick I really was. They feared it might be communicable. There were a few other matters, he added, but nothing of major importance. They wanted to meet with him the next night. He told me to be there.

I was stunned. My relationship with parents had been great. And the kids loved the nicknames I gave them. Here it was summer vacation, time to recover and relax.

I slept little that night. The next morning I awoke with a major nosebleed and other out-of-control symptoms. There could be no more self-deception. I had to agree with the doctor: Be carried out, or drive out. So it was that one day in early June 1997 we began packing for a move to California. My brother Edward had a sprinkler business in Palm Springs. He said I could work part-time for him. We found a small but beautiful stucco house with a pool near the Palm Springs High School—*my* high school, where I had learned what deodorant is. How grateful I had been for the lovely young woman who had offered to sit with me when I stunk! Why did *that* have to come to mind? How I wished I might go back and relive those years. Could I have done anything that would have kept me from getting Wegener's? Who knows?

Our life in Palm Springs wasn't particularly complex. I would get up, take my medicines, fight nausea, go to work in the clear desert air, and have an afternoon nap—every day the same. At least, I thought, it would be harder in the Palm Springs desert to visualize myself stepping into a boat headed across the Jordan than it had been in Grand Junction, or even Loma Linda.

Still, having to abandon my career as a teacher had been a stunning blow. I thought of the students I had trained not only to love God but to share His love with others. And now, on a good day, I picked up a few dollars putting in lawn sprinklers. It was, of course, an honorable occupation, and I was grateful to my brother for the job. But it was very hard to be grateful to God for this new assignment. I prayed, but only for others. With increasing frequency I recognized the worthless little boy of juvenile hall creeping into my dreams. I didn't have the heart to send him packing, and in a detached sort of way I knew that the healing of my spirit was involved in meeting him. But wasn't it enough that I had met—and barely survived—someone named Wegener? What was there to be gained by looking over a chain-link fence at an abused child? Had not God sought to distance me from him? Was it not somehow my proximity to him that had led me to throw away all my religious books? Doing so had not been a conscious decision. Rather, it was a deep need, an urging I could not explain. It didn't just happen; it *had* to happen. My soul demanded freedom to walk the paths long closed to it, to visit places we were not allowed to discuss, to entertain emotions long denied.

I had no idea whether it was searing pain or magnificent joy that awaited me. My memory had been both friend and enemy. Even from the age of 3 I could remember minute details of places and events. I once drew the "floor plan" of the trailer park and bus we lived in when I was 3. Some memories I kept hidden within, where they could be covered, or even denied. On the rational level I could see the inconsistency in my thinking: Nothing was to be gained by meeting my abused self; on the other hand, everything depended on it.

Memory can offer up scenes and events that we would wish long dead; events, moreover, that burn and sear our inner being and ultimately affect how we live. Letting them out, I came to feel, was the key. To do this, however, requires a fantastic journey. Having danced with death, my soul said that there was no longer a memory to be feared. "You have looked across the Jordan, and it has been revealed to you that death is not the terror of terrors, that not really having lived is the worst terror." So said my soul, and it set me on a journey that memory decreed must begin—and in some way end—in California.

So it was that one bright winter morning Edna and I went to visit my aunt Anne in Riverside. She was the same aunt we had stayed with in New York City when I was 2 years old. A brilliant and interesting woman, she knew more of our history than anyone inside or outside the family. Hers was the only home I had been in as a youth that could be called normal. Ironically, its very normality was what made it seem to me, as a child, abnormal.

She had aged well. At 80-plus her face was nearly seamless, her golden hair coiffed, her gentle hands folded in a manner that

**Aunt Anne had aged well. At 80 her face was nearly seamless, her golden hair coiffed, her gentle hands folded in a manner that comes naturally to the aristocracy.**

comes natural to the aristocracy. She sat poised in a French provincial chair; we on a white sofa, that seemed to welcome us with a hug. I was like a detective questioning the only witness to a murder. "Where were you when . . . ? Did you know that Father . . . ? What did you think when you saw the bruises? Did you know that yours was the only meal we had that week? What did you think when you learned . . . ?" I questioned and wrote for hours, until Edna said I was wearing Aunt Anne out. With her usual charm, Aunt Anne cheerfully denied exhaustion, but a practiced eye (and my eyes had had a lot of practice) confirmed my wife's observation. I sauntered toward the phone desk on my way to get a drink. Judges and juries often wrestle with the question of whether an act is premeditated. My reach for the phone book, I believe, was unpremeditated. I flipped it open to "Government Agencies." And there was a name I had tried to convince myself had come from another planet, a name that had

I asked a thousand questions, and everything went well until I encountered a name in her phone book, a name that had haunted a million thoughts.

haunted a million thoughts and a thousand dreams: "Riverside County juvenile hall."

"Hey, look at this, you two! I'm sure it can't be the same one—they must have closed it years ago." I spoke half to them and half to myself, but my hand had reached out and dialed the number.

"Riverside County juvenile hall," a woman's voice said.

It seemed a strange little-boy voice that responded. "You probably won't believe this, but I lived in juvenile hall for a year when I was 7, as an abandoned child. We called ourselves the 'throwaway kids.'"

"We called you 'foundlings,'" she said.

I told her we wanted to come by to see the compound we had called "prison." She turned to someone in the office and bellowed, "You won't believe this, but a man who lived here 45 years ago wants to come by." She gave me the directions.

I sat, stupefied.

We left my aunt's house for, I told myself, a "drive-by" on our way home. We headed down Magnolia, the street we lived on when the police came for us at midnight. We passed Riverside General Hospital, where I was born and where I was a patient in the 1970s.

Then—there it was!

I parked and got out. Edna followed a deferential few steps behind. I touched the chain-link fence that marked the boundary of my prison. My home. My nightmare! I approached the stainless-steel lettering on the brick front of the building, reached out, touched, traced, trembled:

"Riverside County juvenile hall."

Over there—that's where the police car stopped. Here—the front door, large, glass with wire enmeshed in it. I beckon to Edna, push a buzzer, and the door opens. As we enter, the door closes behind us. A small window opens in a glass wall, and a woman looks at us.

"Hey," she calls to an unseen fellow worker, "it's him! It's the guy who was here in 1953!"

A man, who appears to be in his early 50s, joins us. He is to be our guide. "Juvenile hall," he says, "is now a prison for 14- to 18-year-old criminals." He shows us past metal detectors and speaks of high security.

I can't tell you how it happens, but I do know when. I go around a corner and see a crib against the wall, a crib that had held a terrified child who had just been separated from his brothers and sisters. And suddenly my perspective changes to about the eye level of a 7-year-old. And with that change come changed perceptions, changed emotions. . . .

I'm walking back into my soul, deeper and deeper into myself. My parents, who abandoned us at juvenile hall, had forbidden us even to mention the name. That was supposed to erase the memory, even deny it ever happened. Even after our parents' deaths we children seldom mentioned our imprisonment. Some claim it is better that way, better to forget and move on. But here I am, grabbing the monster memory by the throat and looking it straight in the eye. I have the right; juvenile hall is part of me, and I am part of it.

*As I enter, I see him—7-year-old Grover Wilcox! I stop, stunned. Our guide directs our attention here and there, but my eyes follow a child. I hear the echoes of the past; I hear the mumble of voices that they do not. I see a crib and hear a clock ticking on the wall, where they see nothing. I hear a baby cry, see the sad face of a little friend. Twenty feet from my bed is where Sybil sleeps; I hear her cry out. I step into the bathroom to be deloused. Across the hall stands the clothes closet— empty, Edna tells me later. But she didn't see it as I did. She knew that I had left that child there in juvenile hall for 45 years, left him walking the halls and grounds, ever searching for self, for meaning.*

*I reach down and take him by the hand. As he reaches up to me, I read his number: 10114. I tell myself that juvenile hall can no longer harm me or hold me. I give it back its fear, its hate, its hurt, its pain, its abuse, and its dark shadows. The door clicks shut. We're outside, free to walk away. I stand in silence. The weight of the years rolls off. I throw my shoulders back and walk free.*

A week later, in some strange way changed by the visit to juvenile hall, I went to the Riverside County Courthouse. There, a young woman produced data she didn't think she could—copies of my juvenile hall records and past court records, all of which, she said, should have been destroyed years before. They contained the address of the house from which we children had been taken.

I drove to Magnolia Avenue. The old house was gone, but I found the farm. Then, on an old chain-link fence, I saw a foot-square orange-painted piece of plywood with large black numerals—12710. I walked to what I thought to be the site of our bedroom; I retraced the route and experienced again the events of that sad night. Down the stairs, out into the dust, and into the car, I went. We were driven away, the seven of us, at midnight, down the street and across the railroad tracks that paralleled the palm-lined street. Three miles, it was, to juvenile hall. I drove into its parking lot, and there I sat and wept.

And suddenly, through tears, I saw him grasping the barbed-wire fence, his face tight against it, looking imploringly at me. I opened the door, walked to the

**With my chemo buddy at juvenile hall, now a prison for 14- to 18-year-old criminals.**

fence, and opened my arms to him. I don't know how he slipped through, but I clutched him tightly and told him I would never let him go. And in some strange manner only God could explain, we two seemed to become one. I had lived 45 years split into two beings; standing there, we blended our tears and our souls.

I left that day feeling whole.

# The Enemy Attacks

*Thy world, O God, so fierce,*
*And I so frail.*
*Yet, though its arrows threaten oft to pierce*
*My fragile Mail,*
*Cities of refuge rise where dangers cease,*
*Sweet silences abound, and all is peace.*
—Winfred Ernest Garrison, *Thy Sea So Great*

**When you've crossed the Jordan** and returned, what is left to fear? When you've faced the horrors of an abusive childhood and retained your sanity, what more can be asked of you? I was about to find out.

I spent the three months following my return to Riverside County juvenile hall visiting old schools I had attended and places we had lived. The number of our dwellings, as I mentioned earlier, exceeded 100 by the time I had finished the fourth grade. I use "dwellings" to emphasize that wherever and in whatever we lived, it was not a "home." I talked to many people who had known my family, and I wrote letters and gathered documents. All this was in God's design. He not only knew how much I hurt, but also that despite my introspective triumphs at juvenile hall, I had further victories to gain. In His wisdom He sent a messenger to me, a man who loved Him and loved me. So it was that I heard from my buddy of academy basketball days, Jack Milford. He was the only one, besides Edna, who had met the abused little boy inside me. How eager I was to tell him of my victories!

Edna and I met his plane in Los Angeles. From the number of people who stopped to watch our greeting, I knew not many had friends like Jack. When I let him go, Edna took over. We laughed when he told us he was wearing his glasses because he was sure that if he left them in his pocket they would be crushed by our hugs.

We knew he would be with us for only 29 hours and that we must let him nap for a portion of that. I'm sure we set some kind of record for communication during the 60-mile drive to our home. And he had brought a gift. "I went through my things, Grover, and brought you one of my closest friends." He handed me the book *The Desire of Ages*. I was familiar with this well-known work on the life of Jesus, but since I had discarded all my books that day in Colorado, I had little spiritual reading material. Jack's book had the best recommendation a book can give. It had been so read and was so underlined that it was in immanent danger of falling apart.

After a great dinner in one of Palm Springs' finest restaurants, Jack and I headed for a basketball court at a nearby high school. Now about our basketball: As we played it, first man to 100 with a four-point lead would win. I am six feet two and lean; Jack is built like a hockey goalie who doesn't need pads. Yet for some reason this otherwise rational being actually said he was going to beat me! Of course, I had played him one on one 27 times and won only once. I should explain, however, that he was 2,000 miles away and I (generously) shot for both him and me.

On this day, I never had a chance. Not with his guardian angel tipping in his shots. No way would they have gone in otherwise. If you had been there, you would have seen Jack grab the ball, run down the floor, and make two baskets while I watched. Then he declared himself the winner, 4-0. I hadn't laughed so hard since the last time we played on the academy courts in Colorado.

Afterward, as we walked along enjoying the midday sunshine, I prepared to unload a few questions I'd been saving for my special friend. Now, there are questions and there are questions. Mine were the kind you ask only of a trusted friend. Anyone else might question your endorsement of the 27 doctrines or think you're really stupid. My opening volley, delivered in a parking lot, came right from my heart.

"Why is it, Jack, that some people seem only to suffer, while others seem to have clear sailing? What is God really trying to tell me through this Wegener's disease? Am I a bad person? A "bad seed," as my mother used to call me? How can one know—really know—that God loves them?"

Then came what the French call the pièce de résistance. I spun the ball on my finger and asked, "Jack, how do you know God *really* loves *you?*"

He didn't hesitate. Turning to me with a huge smile, he said, "Because I'm His boy!"

As I considered his response, my questions seemed so shallow, so inconsequential. His answer left me with one incandescent goal—*I must become God's Boy!*

"When God loves you," Jack continued, "He breaks you so that He can remold you in the image of Jesus."

I bounced the basketball and pondered. No question—God had sent these words to me via airmail! All the pain I had experienced had a reason; it was part of His plan. Jack said he didn't have all the answers. He just trusted his Father, who did. For the first time, the word "Father," delivered by a trusted friend, overrode my antipathy toward the father who had so brutalized me. "You have a Daddy who loves you, Grover."

We walked on, bouncing the basketball.

The next morning Edna hugged Jack before going to work. I took him to the airport. All too soon I was waving goodbye through tears as he disappeared into his plane. Just 29 hours together but 29 hours with God's Boy. No, it was more, for we had explored a lifetime. And that, I was convinced, was in God's design, also. Sometimes He sends angels on a mission of mercy. They must at times appear in human form, for the Scripture speaks of humans who have "entertained angels without knowing it" (Heb. 13:2, NIV). But often, I have found, God uses His human subjects as His messengers to love us, to lead us, and to show us who He is. That is the wonderful objective of our mission on earth as His children. *The Desire of Ages,* the book Jack gave me, says it well: "There are souls perplexed with doubts, burdened with infirmities, weak in faith, and unable to grasp the Unseen; but a friend [such as Jack was to me] whom they can see, coming to them in Christ's stead, can be a connecting link to fasten their trembling faith upon Christ" (p. 297).

It finally penetrated: Jesus was painting a picture of God for me through the messengers He kept sending me. My teacher, George Jubilee, showed me the childlike kindness that is a mark of heaven's dwellers. My aunt Anne showed me God's caring nature. Roger Morrisey demonstrated God's nonjudgmental kindness and friendship. The Loma Linda Hospital orderly of my childhood reached into my soul on a dark night and was there for me like God is. And then there was Jack to model God's love. For me, words about God tend to bounce off; I need to see Him at work through His children—children who reflect His character. I was about to meet two of them.

Each month I went to my doctor for blood tests and checkups. This time I told him that I was having trouble lifting my left arm above my shoulder. He seemed to feel that any problem there was inconsequential when compared to my Wegener's complications. On my own, I went to see an orthopedic surgeon. His examination showed what doctors call an "encapsulated shoulder," known to laymen as a "frozen shoulder." It required surgery. Though not major, nothing is minor to a Wegener's patient. I went home, determined to keep the bad news from Edna as long as possible.

A day later she came home from her yearly checkup. The doctors, she said, had found a minor problem. She would need a needle biopsy. So off we went to Loma Linda University Hospital. The lab report showed that she had a precancerous condition that would have to be addressed immediately. We went home feeling like punch-drunk boxers who have been hit too hard for too long. My Edna was everything I had ever looked for in a woman—honest, kind, sweet; always putting others first, even at a great cost to herself. She shared that magic possessed by so few; she could make my heart race just by walking across a room. She was my woman, my lover, my spiritual inspiration, my soul's delight. And now she was in trouble.

We went home that night with the doctor's words inscribed on my eardrums: "You take it easy, Grover; you need to avoid excess stress." *Excess stress?* Is there any other lifestyle? And what about Edna? By morning I had decided to have my shoulder surgery immediately so I could care for Edna when she came home. I was thinking of her in the pre-op room when my lights went out.

Ten days later it was Edna's turn. The surgery was to take between six and eight hours. Nine surgeons would be involved. Wow! A *minor* problem?

I waited for an hour while Edna was prepped for surgery. It was 7:30 a.m. when I gave her a kiss and waved as she was wheeled into the operating room. I adjusted my arm in its sling, grabbed up my reading materials, and headed for the hospital lobby. I checked my watch—Edna was to be back in her room between 2:00 and 3:00 in the afternoon. By the time I got settled, Bonnie walked in. She had been detained by one of southern California's infamous freeway traffic jams and was distraught because she had been unable to see her mother before surgery. Actually, her daddy needed her rare God-given gift for soothing a soul during trials.

For many years I had thought of Bonnie as my baby. As I looked at her in the waiting room, I realized our little girl had grown up. She was a beauty with her ivory skin, black hair, almond eyes, and sculpted frame. Inside she was even more beautiful, with her kind and understanding soul. Her nurse's training seemed to provide a logical outlet for her compassion. More recently, however, her brilliance and artistic nature had pointed her toward interior design and architecture. Whatever, I knew she was a daughter of the King.

"Grover Wilcox; Grover Wilcox . . ." The woman at the courtesy desk held out the phone. It was Julia, distraught because she couldn't be with us. "Dad, keep me posted," she pleaded.

*Funny how children differ,* I thought. Julia loved books and writing. At 2 years of age she began repeating the storybooks Edna read to her. Early on, she wanted to be a teacher. *She'd make a good one,* I thought, *with her gift of understanding and kindness on the one hand, and her gift of gab on the other.* At a slim five-foot-nine, with red-tinted black hair that fell nearly to her waist, eyes usually sparkling with mischief, and a winning smile, she didn't walk into a room unnoticed.

Despite the knockout punches of the past days, Bonnie and I were not in a funeral mode. Rather we were in high spirits as we exchanged observations on what a character her mother was.

I noticed that our humor was not shared by many of the more than 50 people in the lobby. The fellow reading *Sports Illustrated* didn't look worried, but stress and worry characterized most faces. I imagined the surgeries taking place. Maybe an appendectomy, I theorized. And then there was Edna's surgery. I pictured her asleep on an operating table, her soul in the hands of her loving Creator. My mind slipped back and forth between the lobby and her operating room.

### Four hours

Maybe only three to go. A doctor would pop in with a progress report; people left, others came.

"Family of Wilcox," a voice boomed out of a speaker. "The oncologist has finished the procedure and all is going well."

I went to the phone and updated Julia.

### Eight hours

It was time to talk to my "Dad." I went to the chapel, just steps from the lobby, and slipped into a pew. Before me was a large stained-glass picture of Jesus. I shared my fears and praise with the Great Healer. Then I let my soul sing. I lost track of the time, and my fears were drifting away when a young man, pushing a baby stroller, entered the chapel. He went up a few pews, arranged the baby carefully, popped a bottle into her mouth, and whispered to her soothingly. He had just crossed himself and was preparing to kneel. When you've had a catastrophic illness, you can sense when people need help. I could feel the pain in his eyes.

"That's a precious baby you have, my friend. But you look like things aren't going well. Can I be of help?"

It was as if a dam broke. The young Hispanic father poured out his anguish. There was a twin to the baby with him. She had been in the hospital since birth, four months before. She was dying, and he and his wife came every day to watch her fade away. He spoke of his wife, his job, and his other children. I asked him for a hug. (Often I've found it to be more therapeutic for people who are hurting to be asked for a hug rather than to offer one.) He jumped to his feet and hugged me. I told him how much God loved him, and that He was walking with them through the pain. I prayed for this young father, and he was gone. I stood in the chapel, alone, my heart aglow. Who was I that I should be given the honor of pointing this heartbroken man to his Father?

### Ten hours

When I meandered back to the courtesy desk, I was shocked to find not only an empty waiting area but the desk abandoned. Who was that guy who told me to evade excess stress? Yah!

At 8:00 I recognized people passing through the lobby who had been there as "waiters" earlier in the day. They had gone home, eaten, cleaned up, and were now returning to visit.

I sat. I walked. I sat.

### Thirteen hours

I pictured myself in the operating room with Edna. The exhausted doctors were finishing sewing her up. They were congratulating themselves for the excellent job they had done, when suddenly they realized she had expired hours before.

*Knock it off, you idiot!* I barked at myself. *Get a grip!* "Father, Father, you know what she can take. I know you're in there with them."

### Fifteen hours

"The enemy doesn't fight by Marquess of Queensberry rules. He hits low, he hits from behind, he hits wherever he perceives a seam in the Christian's armor. He has an exhaustive dossier of weaknesses. He probes every wayward synapse of our brain, explores the neuron circuits related to memory in our temporal lobes. Events of which we have no conscious recall are imprinted within our mind—every suspicion harbored, every word spoken, every abuse suffered. Every smallest stroke of virtue or of vice has left its scar. The drunken Rip Van Winkle in Jefferson's play excuses himself for every fresh dereliction by saying, 'I won't count this time!' Well, he may not count it, and a kind heaven may not count it; but it is being counted none the less. Down among his nerve cells and the fibers, the molecules are counting it, registering and storing it up to be used against him when the next temptation comes. Nothing we ever do is, in strict scientific literalness, wiped out" ("Habit," *The Principles of Psychology,* Great Books, vol. 53, p. 83).

During my years of college and teaching I had learned that the battle for the soul is really the battle for the mind. And the contest is fought for the attention, the memory, the nerve cells, the file system of the subconscious, and, ultimately, for the will. When the enemy assaulted me with doubt and fear during Edna's operation, he knew what he was doing. He knew where I was vulnerable. But God knew that, too. And in answer to my prayers, He sent reinforcements racing to the vulnerable intersections of my mind. I pictured my heavenly Father sitting next to me. I held His hand. "I love You," I told Him. "I'm Your boy."

### Seventeen hours—1:00 a.m.

I looked up. There stood Edna's surgeon. His hair was wet, his face looked as if it had barely survived being run over by a steamroller. "Everything's OK." He explained why the operation had taken so long. He said he'd see me in the morning.

We both laughed; it was already morning.

### Eighteen hours—2:00 a.m.

I went upstairs to the eighth-floor ICU to see Edna. At 2:00 a.m. a

task force wheeled her in. They asked me to wait until they got her settled. At 2:30, 19 hours after I'd said goodbye, they gestured me in. The
room was stifling hot, and she had an air mattress type of blanket over her.
It had holes on the underside that let hot air flow onto her to keep the circulation going. I watched her for a half hour, thanking God that He had
sustained her though the ordeal.

Later the plastic surgeon told me that if he had anticipated the complication they ran into, they would have gone another route. I staggered out
of ICU and down the hall to the waiting room. Three times during what
was left of the night I returned to touch a strand of damp hair and to brush
a kiss across her cheek. At 6:30 a.m. I went to a friend's house, cleaned up,
and headed back to her side. Though I remained during the day, she never
really knew I was there.

I found myself reminiscing on hospital visits. It amazes me to see how
people are so intimidated by a friend's pain and illness that they are afraid
to speak, as if there were a magic list of things to say. I've been on my back
enough to know that when you're down, you really need a friend to stand
by you. Nothing more needs to be said than "I love you, and I'm here for
you." There are a couple no-no's to note: Don't tell fallen friends "I know
how you feel." Most of the time you won't. And don't tell them of the
time you had a toenail pulled and— Just care. Give them a gentle hug, or
brush your cheek against theirs. They will talk if they can trust you, and
believe me, they will know; pain has a radar for those who care.

Well, Edna wouldn't have visitors, whatever their philosophy, for a
day or two.

At 3:30 the next afternoon I was in my lobby chair when I saw a familiar wheelchair roll into the room, turn, and face the TV. Here, I
thought, was a man twice hurt. He had someone dear in ICU, and I knew
there must be a sad story about his wheelchair. A large, strong man with a
determined chin, he could have been a linesman for the Chicago Bears. I
slipped into a chair behind him.

"How are you doing?" I ventured.

"I'm OK." His attitude said, "Caution: Dangerous road ahead!"

"Do you have someone in here? Well, I guess that's a stupid question."

"My wife has been here for three months and is still on chemo," he
drawled in a stubborn monotone.

"I want you to know that I'll be praying for you and your wife. What are your names?"

"Just pray for Brian and Carol, if you must."

"Don't you have a last name?"

"Not everyone tells everything they know," he said in clipped tones.

The room that had been a place of caring took on a cold shudder. I walked quietly down the hall and leaned against the wall. Out of the corner of my eye I saw the wheelchair come out of the waiting room and turn up the hallway away from me. I don't know the name of the angel who rapped me on the head and said, "Go! Say it!" I went. "Sir," I said, when I caught up with the wheelchair, "I'm sorry for barging in. I just wanted you to know that I care."

Brian didn't react for a moment. Then the wheelchair wheeled around and into my heart.

"The name is Hopwood, Brian Hopwood," he said.

For the next two hours we shared burdens and hopes. His wife, Carol, a tiny jewel of a woman from Taiwan, had been in ICU for three months and had almost every problem known to modern medical science. Hospitals had misdiagnosed her, and serious complications followed. She had liver cancer and had been in a coma for weeks. I told him of Edna, and our hearts seemed to meld into one as the God of heaven nudged two men closer to understanding His gracious will.

Brian was looking past me. I turned to hear the familiar voice of Edna's doctor. "Mr. Wilcox, I'm sorry, but we are going to have to go back in. Your wife has a blood clot." He turned and headed toward the operating room.

Now it was Brian's turn to minister. The same man who had pushed me away two hours before reached out his hand and clasped mine. That's all. No sermon; no prayer; no comforting words. The handclasp said it all.

My mind was a jumble of pain. "Oh, Brian, I don't think she has the strength to make it." A few well-guarded tears slipped through my vigilance.

"Yes, she will, Grover; I know she will. Remember to lean on the God you've been telling me about." He stayed with me for a while before wheeling off to see his wife.

I called after him, "Remember, Brian, not everyone tells everything."

I hurried to the phone and called Jack, telling him what he didn't want to believe. He reminded me that nothing happens to us that does not pass through our Father's hands first. He prayed for Edna and me. I called my daughters and my brother in Palm Springs. They made further calls, and soon two of my brothers, my nephew, and a sister-in-law joined my daughters and me.

Brian came by in his wheelchair; he was headed home. "I have a surprise for you that I'll bring tomorrow. So hang in there, Grover."

Again the hours ticked by, oh, so slowly. We heard the 10:00 p.m.

**Brian Hopwood and his son, Christian. Brian reminded me to lean on the God I'd been telling him about.**

chimes. At 10:30 the surgeon appeared. He explained that the blood clot had been removed. He was worried, and let out more of his concern than he had intended. When he left, my family followed. I saw Edna again in her room at 11:30, and the tears came. She looked like a sleeping princess; but tubes ran everywhere out of her body. I gently stroked her cheek with the back of my hand. At that critical moment I sensed the presence of God in the room. The lower you sink, the harder the trials, the closer the Master presses. He was still teaching me. Still testing me. Still loving me.

Early, as the morning settled in, Brian rolled up. I had learned that he spent every day, from morning to night, with his coma-bound wife. He educated himself on every procedure and medicine the doctors used on her. The medical staff began referring to him as Dr. Hopwood. His education would go on for another three months.

"I told you I had something for you," he said. He handed me an album that told—and showed—the story of his airplane crash in New Mexico. The plane was shattered, and so was he. His leg had been almost severed, and he had other ghastly injuries. He was slipping across Jordan when a vision of his wife and family challenged him to live. He swung his leg over his shoulder, and tied his belt on it as a tourniquet. Then scrabbling on his belly, slipping in and out of consciousness, he worked his way to his cell phone. He was rescued an hour later and taken to a small hospital where they stitched him up, put in pins, and wrapped him in plaster and bandages. Carol flew in from California to be with him and refused to leave his side. One evening security sought to evict her, but she wrapped her arms in the rungs of the bedside and refused to let go.

So here sat this man who abandoned his wheelchair when he entered his wife's room, enduring great pain in his legs and hips. Though one pin traveled the length of his upper leg, the bone broke one night from the weight he put on it. He took more pain pills and pulled himself to her side on each visit. Evenings he and I started going outside into the parking lot to visit and pray. Sometimes he would vomit from the pain, but there we sat together, loving the Great King and holding each other up. Brian let me take the scrapbook home.

The morning after Edna's second operation, I slipped into her room. She was still unconscious, but when I called her name, she would open her eyes and mouth a word or two before drifting off again. Besides the tubes, she had pressure stockings on her legs that aided circulation. Though she could barely speak, within a day she was mothering the nurses and apologizing for their heated environment and overwork. Things were looking up.

That afternoon Brian and I found ourselves in the same spot we had been the day before—just down the hall from the lobby, facing each other, "telling everything," as we had then. As I chattered away, I saw Brian looking past me. I smiled at his attempt to tease me. Then I heard the familiar voice and turned quickly.

"Mr. Wilcox, I know you won't believe this, but we have to go in again. Your wife has another blood clot."

I turned my face to the wall and wept. I knew she could not make it this time. The doctor spoke a few comforting words, but admitted their hollowness. Edna was beyond exhaustion, and I was beyond hope. Brian said nothing. He just stayed by me.

I went into her room and took her hand. She read the truth in my eyes: we were saying goodbye. As the staff rolled her away down the hall, she raised her head, and we threw each other a kiss. I turned around, and there sat Brian. How can you meet someone, a total stranger, and in 48 hours be friends for a thousand years! We prayed again, and I went to the phone—again. I called Michigan. "Jack, you won't believe this, but they just took Edna into OR again. Oh, Jack, I don't think she's going to make it!"

"Close your eyes, Grover; let's talk to our Father."

There on the phone two of God's boys poured out their souls to their

Daddy. Then I called my daughters and saw that the family was notified. I went to the chapel and walked to the edge of the Jordan. It was cool and clear at the river's edge, and there I visited with Carol. As we talked, I saw Brian get into the canoe and pick up the oars. "How could he be here?" I wondered. "Visitors never accompany anyone across the river." But here he was, the incarnation of the wedding vow "Until death do us part." I spent three hours in the chapel, too wounded to pray, too exhausted to cry, expecting every moment that someone would enter with the word that Edna, my Edna, had crossed over.

At 10:30 that evening I returned to the ICU floor and hurried into the room. There she was, sound asleep. Not however, the sleep from which none shall awake until that bright morning when the "trumpet" shall sound, and the dead in Christ rise from their graves (see 1 Thess. 2; 1 Cor. 5). She looked so pale and fragile. I was asleep on my feet, but could not make myself leave.

Finally the charge doctor came in. "Grover, you better get home and get into bed. Your Wegener's and your surgery are real reasons for worry. If you want to be around to help your wife in the next few weeks, don't tarry."

I didn't. God's Boy went to sleep, secure in the love of friends He had sent to me.

*"Jesus, Jesus, how I trust Him; How I've proved Him o'er and o'er. Jesus, Jesus; precious Jesus! O for grace to trust Him more."*

# TWELVE | The King of Care

*At the heart of the cyclone tearing the sky*
*And flinging the clouds and the towers by,*
*Is a place of eternal calm;*
*So here in the roar of mortal things,*
*I have a place where my spirit sings,*
*In the hollow of God's palm.*

—Edwin Markham, *The Place of Peace*

**Early the next morning** I rushed back to the hospital and up to ICU, room 9. Edna appeared to be so tiny against the white sheets. I just stood and looked and prayed. She opened her eyes for a moment, as if sensing my presence and my love. Unfortunately, others sensed my presence and kicked me out so that they could proceed with their "procedures." Now, that's a word that can cover a multitude of sins! Procedures may be both inviolate and violated, depending on circumstance and station. I was weighed and found wanting.

That afternoon Edna emerged from her drug-induced haze—or was it from a miracle? We thought so. For the next few hours she was a sparrow barely hanging on to the branch on which she perched. I had to tell her what had happened to her while she was standing on the bank of the Jordan, waiting for the ferry. We were interrupted. Another procedure.

It was midafternoon when I returned to Edna's room. "You have a visitor," the nurse whispered. As I entered, I saw a tall, distinguished man standing at the foot of her bed. Perhaps a chaplain, I thought, giving my attention to Edna, who was crying, but not, it appeared, under duress. Rather, she was releasing anguish of sorts. Between sobs Edna managed to introduce the visitor.

It was Don Schneider, president of the Lake Union Conference of Seventh-day Adventists. I knew immediately that Jack had asked him to stop by. I found that he was attending a hospital board meeting. I was still kind of new to my mission of ministry to the hurting. What would be an appropriate greeting, I wondered, for a church leader taking time out to comfort us? Well, hugs had seemed to work on almost everybody. Why not? *Is that what you have in mind, Lord? Use my own judgment? Fair enough.*

I stepped to the foot of the bed and said, "Give me a hug." And he did. In fact, he seemed a natural—that hug had come right from the heart. Of course, that hug was fortified with both Jack's love and that of our mutual Father. Edna told me that the caring he shared with her before I came in had broken through a great dam inside her, a dam that held back not only her own pain and anxiety, but that from dealing with my illness during the past three years.

Imagine it: A busy executive steps into a hospital room to greet strangers who are battling a multitude of hurts. He comes a stranger; he leaves a friend for life. After he prayed for us, Edna took his hand, kissed it, and held it against her cheek.

I turned to him and said, "Don Schneider, do you know who you are?" I picked up *The Desire of Ages* Jack had given me, turned to page 297, and read: " 'There are souls perplexed with doubt, burdened with infirmities, weak in faith, and unable to grasp the Unseen; but a friend whom they can see, coming to them in Christ's stead, can be a connecting link to fasten their trembling faith upon Christ.' You are God's Boy, Don Schneider, and God's messenger."

(Yes, I know I used this quote from *The Desire of Ages* earlier. And if I can find another reason to do so before the end of the book, I'll use it again. I hope you memorize it and, above all, practice it. Remember, it is even more powerful if after having quoted it, you ask for a hug!)

**Don Schneider and wife, Marty. He's an executive who meets needs from the heart more often than from the policy book.**

After leaving Edna's room, I sang hymns all the way home. Just before going to sleep, I remembered that Pastor Schneider had brought me a note from Jack. I found it in my trouser pocket. It read: "Dear Grover, I'm sending you the 'King of Care,' but he's not much into hugging." *Oh, really? You could have fooled me, I* thought. The last I remember, I was laughing.

A few days later Edna was moved into what was called the "step-down unit" on 8200. The care given her was fantastic. They said she could go home in two weeks, if I could transform myself into a nurse/housewife. I had my medics' training in the Army to fall back on. Each day I had to measure the drainage from the six tubes flowing from her and clean the containers they drained into. My cooking was another matter. Though she was less than charmed by my rubber eggs, she began to heal. Her greatest incentive to healing was to get me out of her kitchen.. Six weeks later she was her old self—or would she prefer that I say her young self?

★ ★ ★

No trials and sorrows I observed at Loma Linda University Hospital struck deeper into my heart than those of Brian and Carol. For almost a year Brian fought and prayed for his wife's life. Day after day he sat beside her in ICU, never rewarded with a smile or a touch. I spent many hours with them after he honored me with an invitation to enter their sanctuary. It was a mutual ministry as we shared stories of God's grace and love. Each evening we met in the parking lot. Those late-night vigils linked our hearts for eternity. Brian would wheel up in his Jeep, and try to settle his stomach (not always successfully—and how well I knew that result!). He would work his way back into the Jeep's driver's seat, and I would lean on the door or sit on a portable three-legged canvas stool he carried.

It was during one of those sessions that he told me of the brutal beatings he received from his father. Often such a background results in drugs, alcohol, depression, and even suicide. After we shared prayers and pain and praise, he would drive home, praying all the way. I would drive home singing all the way—hymns, of course. Not that I expected green pastures and prosperity. Job's pain had ended in healing and prosperity, but many humans must wait for a world made new before receiving an eternal reward. I had come to the place in my experience where I could say, "It's OK, Father, whatever. Just hold me in Your arms."

Brian and I did find one thing hard to endure: To listen to a lecture or sermon, or read a book on trials by someone whose greatest trial had been a broken leg. When great pain—emotional, physical, mental—strikes and strikes and strikes, you never need or want the painless isn't-life-a-breeze, cliché-toting Pollyannas to flit by to tell you, "This too shall pass, and blue skies will reign again." The sufferer's greatest need is for the deep, abiding, and sustaining love of a God who cares for each cell of one's being. From fellow humans the sufferer needs someone who will walk deeply into their forest of pain and stand as a mirror of the love from above. In comforting the suffering, don't try to be profound or wise; just be. I can still feel the warmth of Brian's handclasp as Edna was wheeled in for her third operation.

★ ★ ★

One evening outside the ICU I saw a man of about 40 leaning against the wall. He was an open book of anxiety, aloneness, hurting, and waiting as he fidgeted with his sweater, turning often to look toward the adjacent elevator. I suspected that suffering was new to him; he had little experience to help him put odds on the good or the bad.

I left my place on the wall and approached him. "I know you're in great pain, and I want you to know that God loves you and so do I." I was about to hug him—in fact, I tried to—but he threw his arms around me like a drowning man clinging to a lifeguard.

"Oh, you're a Christian and you know my Father!" Keeping up with his talk was challenging; he fired words at me with the speed of an auctioneer. He spoke of his father, who had an aneurysm while visiting a brother in Oklahoma. He was to arrive in a few minutes on the hospital's helicopter. He didn't know whether his father would make it. I stayed with him until the helicopter arrived.

The next day he and his brothers were eating in the cafeteria when Brian and I walked by. "Grover, come over here!" Turning to his brothers, he said, "This is the man I was telling you about—the one who was here for me when I needed him. He knows the King!"

And yes, he got up and hugged me. I was aware, as the song has it, of "Not I, but Christ." When you suffer and submit your will to the King, His supreme love flows over and through everything in your life—all is a blessing. When you look to self, the enemy is there to whisper that God doesn't care. That is what I listened to and believed for many years as I depended on my strength and gut determination to get me by.

Sometimes I think God sends an angel to tap a needy soul on the shoulder and say, "Look over there; He will help you!" He does this because He knows they won't see me, but the Father they need. Sometimes

He sends an angel to tap me on the shoulder and say, "Look over there; there's someone who needs help!"

So it was one day as I walked by the Palm Springs Mall bouncing my basketball. A burly man walked out of the Rite-Aid Store and down the sidewalk in front of me. His feet caught my attention because he was very pigeon-toed. I surely don't make a habit of commenting on something that could embarrass a person, and I can't suggest that the Lord does. All I can say in self-defense is that an angel told me to do it. I said, "I have never seen anyone who is so pigeon-toed. Do you know what that means?"

Taking another lick on his ice cream, he replied, "No; what does that mean?"

"That means you can run like the wind. You see, all great sprinters are pigeon-toed."

That did it. He stopped, turned to me, and for 45 minutes poured out the story of his life. He spoke of having a major heart attack four years before that changed his life. He had lost his job, friends, money, self-respect—everything but his wife.

When he finished, I said, "Wayne, I want to share a wonderful secret: You are God's Boy. If you look closely you'll see the Great King walking by your side, carrying you over rough ground, because He loves you. He knows about your heart, your hurts, and your soul. And you know what else, Wayne?"

"No; what?"

"You are my brother, and I love you." I got his address, and as we parted, he said, "Thank you, sir; you made my day and gave me hope."

"Remember who you are, Wayne—God's Boy."

★ ★ ★

Could it be that believing yourself to be God's Boy has its own challenges—pride, for example? When I was a teacher, I began to believe some of the plaudits showered on me for my scholarship and my teaching skills. It's nice to be told you can walk on water. I struggled greatly, because this pride had insulated me from the inferior feelings that had plagued my youth. As long as others thought me to be a superstar, they had no reason to know that I was an ambulatory bundle of chaos. But God knew both what I was and what I needed. He gave me what He had given the apostle Paul—a thorn in the flesh. My thorn was called Wegener's, and it didn't take it long to correct my self-image. Paul explores and explains the whats and whys so well that I'll let him speak for me:

"To keep me from becoming conceited because of these surpassingly great revelations, there was given me a thorn in my flesh, a messenger of Satan, to torment me. Three times I pleaded with the Lord to take it away from me. But he said to me, 'My grace is sufficient for you, for my power is made perfect in weakness.' Therefore I will boast all the more gladly about my weaknesses, to that Christ's power may rest on me. That is why, for Christ's sake, I delight in weaknesses, in insults, in hardships, in persecutions, in difficulties. For when I am weak, then I am strong" (2 Cor. 12:7-10, NIV).

**THIRTEEN**

# Lessons From
# Mr. Squirrel

*Who fathoms the Eternal Thought?*
*Who talks of scheme and plan?*
*The Lord is God! He needeth not*
*The poor device of man.*

—John Greenleaf Whittier, *The Eternal Goodness*

**The wind had been howling** for three days, and the temperature hovered in the low 20s. Not unusual for October in the Sierra Nevadas of California. Edna and I love to go there, though it resurrects unhappy memories from my youth. So in 1999 we went to Lake Arrowhead. Near it I could see the 400-foot cliff I had tumbled over in 1955, though not the angel who had spread wings under me. And over there . . . the Lake Arrowhead Regional Medical Center, where I was taken for treatment almost too late. At that time we lived in a small trailer; this time we were to stay with the elite in Point Hamitare, a gated community. Not in our house, to be sure, and not without some effort. We were to be caretakers of a luxury home. (Candor compels me to reveal that our quarters were above the garage.) My responsibility was to keep the yard up and two speedboats clean. For 20 years I had taught Bible, among other things, to teenagers, been a church elder, and counseled parents. I'd preached, conducted school board meetings, worships, and even a funeral. And all this without knowing who my Father really was. So He set out to show me, to overwhelm me, to electrify me, to love me. How? With, of all things, a squirrel; a genus *Sciurus,* to be specific.

New-fallen pine needles blanketed the forest floor, and now and then a whirl of oak leaves blew past. It seemed hopeless, but I battled the wind and continued to rake needles from the driveway. Finished at last, I leaned on the garage door and scanned my handiwork. That's when I saw the half-grown gray squirrel appraising me from 30 feet away. There we were, staring at each other. Most of the time they don't stay around long enough to encourage a conversation. But I tried: "Say, little one, you better run up a tree and find a warm place out of the wind or you'll freeze." Still he made no move. My mind flashed to an article that suggested that even the animals of the field were happier because of the presence of Jesus. I decided to see what would happen if Mr. Squirrel heard love and kindness in my voice.

"Mr. Squirrel," I said, "Jesus loves you, and so do I." I didn't have to wait long. He calmly sauntered toward me as if he were on a Sunday stroll. My mouth fell open so far Mr. Gray seemed to be examining my teeth. He walked right up to my left tennis shoe and placed his tiny foot on mine. I had the feeling that he was going to go back to his family and brag, "You should have seen his face when I put my paw on his shoe!" I talked on, and he seemed to ready himself for a leap up my leg. It so shocked me that I jumped back. He looked at me as if to say, "What's wrong with you? I just wanted to examine you close up." He shrugged and said what I thought I would say in like circumstances: "These humans are a strange species!" Then he turned and sauntered off into the woods. I studied the scars on his back from confrontations with fellow squirrels. There I stood, absorbing this miracle of a wild creature taking his marching orders from his Creator!

I'm not sure the homeowner believed me that evening when I told him what had happened. But the next morning, after my wee prayer for a repeat performance, Mr. Squirrel marched up the driveway, meditated a moment, and stepped up on my shoe (the right one this time). Skeptic was on the porch, talking on his cell phone. I heard him yell, "You are not going to believe what is happening!" I could understand his amazement. I spent several days trying to figure out why this God of ours would cause a little creature of the field to feel comfortable in my presence. Yes, I had prayed that he would. I found myself wondering whether I shouldn't be more careful what I pray for. Surely the God who keeps the planets in orbit and the stars on their course shouldn't be bothered with a request that He tame a squirrel. Or does He want us to know that He'll make the decisions about what's important and what's not? That He loves us so much that His ear is open to the most humble, the most misguided, request? That if He answers it, you can count on it being the answer of His loving heart? The point?

*If He loves us that much, how can we neglect reaching out to His children—*

*those often in pain, those who've not met their heavenly Father, those He sent His Son to save?*

\* \* \*

I can't recall the day when I first understood something wonderful about God: He reaches us not by threats and fear of damnation, but by showering love and kindness on us until we respond by coming to Him across the barriers of sin. You see, it took the "kindness" of the cross to reach us after sin introduced chaos into a peaceful universe and separated heaven from earth. The kindness of the Son who paid the penalty for our sins; the kindness of the grieving Father who could have reached down and taken His Son from the cross, but didn't. His kindness doesn't force us to accept Him; He says only "Whosoever will may come."

This gift of kindness was what He had sought to show me all my life, but I've seen it clearly for only four years. Kindness—that is the secret the squirrel whispered to me. After living on Jordan's bank most of my life, waiting to cross, I've finally learned to fully trust my Father. I talk to Him during every waking hour. I commit myself to Him before closing my eyes in sleep. And I shall do so when He beckons me home. As the hymn writer has it: "I'm but a stranger here; heaven is my home." No chemo served up there; I'll satisfy my thirst at the river of life. No sickness there, no death; I'll live forever and never get bored. No hate. No jealousy. Just eternal love and kindness. Not that I have no questions, but I expect that someday my Daddy will walk with me, hand in hand, beside the river of life, and there explain all that has perplexed me here.

I suppose everyone knows someone who stands out for his or her kindness. In a medical institution nurses are often mentioned. But when it comes to doctors, the most complimentary terms are usually *efficient, good, great*—maybe even *personable* or *professional*. There is a "professional" reason a doctor is most often defined in these terms. Conventional medical and educational wisdom says the doctor must not get personally involved with patients' spiritual and emotional support. Medics call this "professional distance." The irony is that *a number of diseases not only yield to these needs, but cannot be cured without them!*

During my hundreds of visits to hospitals, clinics, and doctors' offices, I've met many doctors who do involve themselves with the physical, mental, and spiritual needs of patients. In fact, I have met several who not only treated my symptoms but prayed for me.

Two stand out not only for their medical expertise but for their kindness. Strangely, I found the first one in what I call "the House of Pain"—the urology office behind the reception area in Loma Linda University Hospital. Five busy doctors work there, doctors who daily face the frightened and concerned eyes of patients who expect them, whatever the case, to work a miracle. Often a patient sees the physician's office as the last station, the last refuge, of hope. As a result, some doctors put on armor: They become remote, plastic, aloof—shielding themselves against the unattainable hopes of their patients. As one who has a disease for which there is neither a known cause nor a cure, I can understand why a doctor might wish to show me the door.

Dr. Steven C. Stewart didn't. However, as a veteran of physicians' offices, I entered his waiting room with a measure of apprehension. There sat the usual row of petrified faces, seeking refuge behind the bland and obsolete waiting room magazines. I had a different subterfuge—I wrote letters. When my name was called, I knew it didn't mean instant service, but rather a further sit in what is fittingly called a waiting room. Within minutes, however, there was a gentle *tap-tap-tap* at the door. I was not used to such a respectful entrance. At my invitation in walked a husky, barrel-chested man with a face that left you thinking he was smiling even when he wasn't. His grayish hair was slightly balding, a dimple distinguishing one cheek. The name tag on his white smock introduced Steven C. Stewart, M.D. I had done my homework, so I knew he was the best. He had spent four years as a chemistry major in La Sierra College, four years in medical school at Loma Linda University, four years as a resident doctor, and then 33 years as a surgeon. Even more important, one look and I knew he was God's Boy. He had what the Irish call "smiling eyes," rather than "clinical eyes," which are disinterested and coldly objective.

"How may I help you?" he asked.

Wow! If he only knew how much help I needed! In my mind, whatever I had now was something I was sure physicians had never heard of. To my surprise and subsequent relief, he had not only heard of the disease but assured me it could be treated, though it might take as long as a year and a half to gain control of it. Although he talked of injections and surgery, at least he didn't leave me waiting for a diagnosis. I knew God had put me in the hands of another of His boys. In the silence of my soul I heard my Father's gentle whisper: "Sit still, my boy; just sit still, and you shall see My kindness." This time, I was aware, it was to come through Dr. Stewart, a man I soon found to be of steel and velvet. He had the steel to deal with patients in great pain and facing death. He needed the steel to do intricate surgery, hour after hour; to teach in the medical school; to give speeches at international conventions. He had the velvet to inject a series of seven to 10 excruciating shots on each visit with such compassion that he seemed to will me through the ordeal. The subsequent surgery offered still more pain, but again he was there, caring that I hurt. Even more important to me, he began to share his life, his challenges, even his soul. We became not only friends but brothers in Christ.

For a year and a half he prodded, poked, injected, bruised, battered, and cut on me—all to get me well. Each step of the way, just when pain and frustration were about to overwhelm me, he was there with a smile, a pat on the shoulder, a joke, a prayer, a touch on my soul to lift me. He did the things every patient longs for. Though he didn't oversee my Wegener's care, any time I needed a boost, I would  stop by, and he would work me in. I studied him to determine how he could give so much to patients who wanted only to take, take, take. I confirmed my first intuition: Dr. Steve was God's Boy, and in that I found the reason he defied the conventional. He works for a different Boss; and his Boss says, "Lean on me, and I will give you not only kindness, but also the energy to share with my pain-filled children."

**Dr. Steven C. Stewart: another one of God's Boys.**

With Dr. Steve there is no striving for fame, notoriety, praise, or honor.

★ ★ ★

Dr. Evert Bruckner came to me at the end of a long search. I had decided I must find a physician who could at least stabilize my Wegener's. In the preceding year, 1998, I had gone to nearly 100 doctors' appointments. In the previous two months alone I was in doctors' offices 23 times. I learned some valuable lessons along the way. Patients facing a catastrophic illness should become as knowledgeable as they can about their disease and treatment. Quicky visits and such answers as "Let's add more chemo" or "No, let's not" are hardly helpful.

For example, I read that patients on an extended period of daily chemotherapy should have their dosages regulated by their weight, and their white blood counts should not sink below 3,000, because chemo attacks the bone marrow and diminishes its ability to produce white and red blood cells. Further, it lowers the hemoglobin. When I discovered this information, I had been through three years of blood tests. In checking them, I found that my white blood counts had run around 2,000, and even dipped as low as 1,800. The chemo dosage administered ran a third higher than my weight indicated. The result was permanent damage to my bone marrow, which could no longer raise my blood count above 3,000. So I was subjected to a bone marrow biopsy to check for suspected bone marrow cancer. Negative, thank the Lord!

In fairness to my doctors, even today nothing is known about how one gets Wegener's or how to cure it. Further, I saw scores of doctors for problems other than Wegener's, though a number resulted from it, including bloody noses, chest pains, and coughs. I put my plea before Dr. Stewart in terms I hoped would touch a father's heart. "Dr. Stewart, if I were your son, what would you do to help me? Who would you recommend?"

He asked for a few days to think before recommending an oncologist, Dr. Evert Bruckner, associate professor of internal medicine at the Loma Linda Veterans' Hospital. Bruckner, he said, was an excellent doctor who loved challenges and was a caring person.

Bruckner had impressive credentials both as a doctor and as a man of God. Not only was he a graduate of Stanford University Medical School; he was an evangelical Christian who had been a missionary in Honduras for 10 years. On my first visit with him Bruckner spent two and a half hours listening and questioning. Though of average height, he communicated the aura of a giant of great inner strength. His eyes were compassionate, kind. That day he learned all he could about me as a person—a physical person, an ill person, a spiritual person. He gave me more caring than I'd experienced in the first 20 years of my life. Here was a Christian gentleman unafraid to talk about, and to share, his love of God. Here was a loving father and husband who made you feel as if you were part of his family—his wife, Joanne, and two boys, Luke and Daniel. He openly admitted that he didn't know much about Wegener's, but said he would search and research. God glowed through him in a way that caused me to confide in him. I told him all my fears and hopes, things I never had the chance or the courage to share with any doctor other than Dr. Stewart. Before I left, Dr. Bruckner prayed for me. And when I left I knew I had been in the presence of one of God's chosen.

Over the next several weeks I gathered records from four hospitals and arranged them in two huge black notebooks, each six inches thick. There were X-rays, CAT scans, MRIs, and other reports. Bruckner studied them and visited with me. One day he said something that I cherish still, and that he had no idea would lift me so. I had spent a lifetime hiding pain, never asking for help, no matter how serious my illness. So there I sat and told him I didn't know the meaning of moderation.

He replied, "I think I need to take a rope and tie you up and take you home and put you in my closet to keep you safe and warm"—his way of

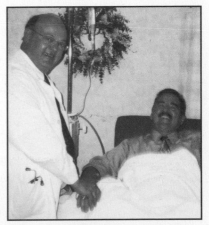

Dr. Evert Bruckner: a Christian gentleman who's unafraid of sharing his love for God.

saying that he understood some of the deep-down things in my soul, and that he would minister to those needs. I found myself wishing I could have been introduced to my Father in heaven in such a home. How could homes be so different, loves so diverse? I found it difficult even to imagine living in a home like his.

One day I was surveying my fellow sufferers in Dr. Bruckner's waiting room. A receptionist and two nurses were at the check-in desk. Eight of us sat facing each other about four feet apart. I knew that everyone there had faced the other-worldly feeling of a death sentence. They knew the depression and the feeling of not being fully human. They had experienced friends shying away from them as though they had leprosy. They had experienced daily chemo battles, nausea, body cramps, fatigue, pain. They knew the methods of survival, how to quiet cells against nausea, and how to rearrange their life physically. They knew the pain of career and job changes. They had experienced loss of sexual intimacy.

In the VA you wait for hours to get into your appointment and hours to check out. We sat, fidgeting, until I decided to shatter the silence. I turned to one of two men in biker outfits. "Hey, you look like you aren't enjoying your visit."

His brother replied, "He's not. He's just out of the hospital, where they found two brain tumors. He's here for his first treatment."

The tumor man sat there while chemo tales swept the room. They stopped momentarily as the door to the chemo room opened, and a man, sick to his stomach and shaking, almost crawled to the empty seat across from the nervous biker. Then down the hall came the wheelchair man. "You must be a visitor here," he said to me. "Are you a drug salesman?"

*What!* It took me a few moments to collect my thoughts. *"Me?* Oh, no! I'm a visitor." I told him of being on chemo for two years and seven months and of having two hospitals give up on me as hopeless.

"But you look so healthy," he responded, "so healthy and happy. Nobody would know you're sick."

My soul soared. Maybe what he saw was the Master alive in my life. Maybe he saw the reflection of His love for me and my love for Him. The testimonials resumed, everyone sharing freely for two reasons: There was nothing to lose, and all needed the comfort of fellow sufferers. If I were asked to name the phenomenon, I'd call it the kindness syndrome.

This day brought an unusual victim.

"I'm Dr. Jones, and I need that form right away."

I turned to see a middle-aged man at the check-in desk. When he didn't get a quick response, he said, "An hour ago I was diagnosed with prostate cancer, and I need that form to avoid jury duty."

The C word drew all eyes, but no one spoke. When he sat down next to me, I put my arm around his shoulder. "I can understand your pain and fear, and I want you to know that God cares about you, and so do I."

He told me that as a physician he had diagnosed many cancers, but this was his first experience as a victim. All of us in that room understood. Few understand, however, how God relates to human suffering. Does He exhibit less kindness than we? Even worse, does He bring the diseases and disasters on us?

One day while walking in the woods near Lake Arrowhead (my squirrel friend's habitat), I got to thinking about the many earthlings who have a jaundiced concept of God's character. Often He is blamed for religions and their followers who profess to know Him but whose acts are those of the father of lies. Even more often, He is blamed for the disasters—tornados, floods, and earthquakes—that kill innocents. "If He's God, why doesn't He do something!" Few understand that a cosmic war between evil and good is being waged. Even fewer perceive that the conflict is nearing its end. So they ask, "Where is God when we need Him?" If anyone has the right to ask that question, it is Grover Wilcox. As I walked the woods of my childhood, my Father directed my thoughts to an ancient story, likely the oldest story in the Bible. It offers not only a fantastic glimpse of the combatants and the issues involved in the cosmic war, but also the part human beings play.

The story opens with a meeting involving the United Nations of the universe. Representatives of many worlds are there. They're all God's children. He is the chairman. Then in walks an uninvited angel named Lucifer, who asserts his right to represent Earth, the one dark blot in all of God's creation. Lucifer has gained the allegiance, he says, of all Earth's inhabitants.

At that meeting of long ago, with the whole universe looking on, Evil One did his usual taunting about how the wickedness of all the earth proves that God is unfair, unjust, and a liar. Then it was that the King scanned the planet. Was there someone, somewhere, who loved Him— who would care to be—a witness for the accused? He must have smiled as He said it:

"Have you, Satan, seen that one called Job? He is over there, in that dusty valley. He loves Me; he is Mine; he will stick by Me, no matter what! He's my boy!"

I can imagine that the eyes of all the universal empire—maybe by some means even better than our telescopes and satellite TV—focused on one tiny man on one tiny planet in one tiny valley sitting on one tiny rock—Job, God's Boy. And Job said, "Yes, I'll vouch for the King, no matter what!"

"Does Job fear God for nothing?" Lucifer sneers. "Have You not put a hedge around him and his household and everything he has? You've blessed the work of his hands so that his flocks and herds are spread throughout the land. But stretch out Your hand and strike everything he has, and he will surely curse You to Your face."

The Lord has confidence in Job. He responds, "Very well, then, everything he has is in your hands, but on the man himself do not lay your finger!"

The story is well known. Movies have been made of it, and college literature classes study it. If they do so carefully, they start by noting that Job is an honest man whose belief in God shapes his life. It is evident, too, that his prosperity is not uniquely of his making; God, Lucifer admits, has blessed Job's work and investments. Less noticed is the fact that it is Lucifer's hand that causes all of Job's subsequent troubles, including loss of prosperity, his children, and his health. (From his symptoms, I wouldn't be surprised that we have here the first recorded instance of Wegener's!)

There's a very important point here for one who has suffered as I have. The story tells me that evil comes from the evil one; blessings come from the Blessed One, God Himself. Yes, God permits the test of loyalty, but He does not create the havoc. At the root of all humanity's problem is sin. Most of us don't have to look up the word in the Bible to know its meaning. Something in us—we usually call it conscience—tells us what is sin, what is good, and what is bad. In essence, sin is rebellion against what God is. The opposite of sin is obedience to what God is, as revealed to us preeminently through that One who walked among us to say, "I and the Father are one; he that has seen Me has seen the Father." How did He relate to us? He healed the sick. There were whole villages in perfect health after He had passed through.

He graciously forgave sin. When the self-righteous of the neighborhood tossed a woman at His feet and said she had been caught in the act of adultery and should be stoned, what did He say? "Let him that is without sin throw the first stone." And when the last of the would-be prosecutors had slunk away, He told the woman to "go and sin no more." Talk about kindness! That's the kind of person I'm comfortable with.

Move on to the principle of love, which underlies all true obedience and relationships, both to God and to His creation. The book of Job tells us that God is not holed up in some celestial ivory tower, watching humanity struggle and suffer at the hands of the enemy. He's with us in every trial; He loves us through every kindness, through every act of mercy and compassion and love. The story of Job would hardly fill three pages of a metropolitan newspaper. You can read it for yourself in any version of the Bible.

Still, there is one big WHY: WHY didn't God just wipe Satan out when he first revolted?

*Come on; tell us, Grover! If He'd done that, you wouldn't be suffering from Wegener's.*

No, but the whole universe would be suffering from fear of a cosmic bully—God! Fear would be the dominant element in an apprehensive universe. Remember the school bully—big, tough, and mean? After a beating or two—or sometimes after nothing more than a threat—we went along with his "program." So it would have been in God's universe: The Big Bully had beaten up on an angel who wanted nothing more than to let everyone do his own thing.

That option would never have produced a peaceful universe. God could not win the allegiance of His creation by acting the part of a heavyweight fighter beating up on a flyweight angel. "So You beat up on me, God, not because You're right, but because You're bigger than I am." As one theologian has pointed out, Satan and his allies would have charged God with "being ambitious, proud, selfish; of using lies, deceit, violence, anger, hatred, prejudice, racism, and terrorism." God couldn't—and, of course, wouldn't—use such means. As the Creator, He knew the psyche of the creatures of His hand. Satan's rival kingdom, consisting of fellow angels he had brainwashed and, later, earthlings who were likewise deceived, could be overcome only by love, truth, justice, freedom, and order.

But did God have to let Satan harm Job? Did He have to let him afflict me with a disease that crawls through my vascular system, seeking to destroy my blood vessels from within? Of course, I've wished to be healed, prayed to be healed. I can hear Satan demanding the right to torture me, and the Lord responding "Very well, then, everything he has is in your hands" (Job 1:12, NIV). That's hard for us to take. We'd all like to see a world without murders, rapes, plane and car crashes, divorces, child abuse, wars . . .

One day we will, and it won't be long. But for now we must understand that *Satan could be defeated only by someone who was weaker than he.* And that was done through what theologians call the Incarnation, wherein God Himself became one of His own creation, demonstrating what Godlike love looks like when it walks among us on two human feet, and then, permitting the real bully of the universe, Satan, to pound nails through His hands and into a cross. It is that sacrifice that has won the allegiance of millions through the ages, many of whom have given up their own life rather than yield to the epitome of evil—that one who is usually called Satan or Lucifer or the devil.★

These were the thoughts that God put in my mind that day as I walked through the woods. He revealed to me as never before the part God's faithful boys and girls play in upholding His honor, in demonstrating His kindness, in putting issues of right and wrong and guilty and innocent in proper perspective. We're all Jobs, in a sense, for all of us suffer, and the stakes involved in how we suffer, in how we answer the charges against God, are no less momentous than on that day of long ago when the United Nations of the universe met in conference. I can imagine that each day the Lord scans the planet and wonders, "Who will love Me today? Who will stand up for Me today? Who will be My boy, My girl, today?"

Then over there, in Loma Linda! Oh, joy! Look! Look over there! And out there—beyond the spiraling nebulas and flaming galaxies, on worlds that have not fallen to the blandishments of Lucifer—are beings that look like us and some that don't. And God says, "Do you see My boy, Dr. Steve, serving broken bodies and battered minds? And over there, in the Veterans' Hospital, see My boy, Dr. Evert, praying with his patient? And look, over there and there. . . ."

If we were on a satellite circling earth, and had the perception of heaven, we'd see bright pinpricks of light glowing here and there around the world. They're God's boys and girls keeping alive the hopes of the coming kingdom of kindness! Fittingly, Dr. Steve is known as God's Oklahoma Firefly! He offers the three gifts every patient longs for—the gifts of understanding, of caring, and of hope. The hope may be for healing, or it may be the gentle, loving hand in yours as you journey to the bank of the Jordan. When I'm in the hospital, all it takes to cheer me are their smiling faces, looking down at me. Sometimes we visit in the parking lot for fellowship and prayer after hours. Their kindness is one of the reasons I have the courage to carry on. They're everything a doctor should be.

*Oh, look! There's Mr. Squirrel again, moved by the One who answers prayer to come fearlessly to my feet. If God loves us enough to answer such a wee request as I made, how can we neglect reaching out in prayer on behalf of His children—*

*those in pain; those who've not met their heavenly Father; those He sent to His Son to save?*

---

\* For the insights in the above four paragraphs I am indebted to Jiri Moskala, professor in the Old Testament Department at the Seventh-day Adventist Theological Seminary in Berrien Springs, Michigan. His thoughts appeared in "Winning Through Weakness," "The President's Page," *Perspective Digest,* Nov. 3, 2003, pp. 10-12.

# Fourteen

# Bryan the Lion and Other Tales

*He cannot heal who has not suffered much,*
*For only a sufferer sorrow understands;*
*They will not come for healing at our touch*
*Who have not seen the scars upon our hands.*
—Edwin McNeill Poteat, *Stigmata*

**He is one tough, rough, character:** a blue beret with a chest full of ribbons and medals—Legion of Merit, Distinguished Service Cross, Bronze Star, Air Medal, Purple Heart. He has seen it all—Grenada, Guatemala, Honduras, Panama, Beirut, and more. As leader of a special operations team, he had 164 confirmed kills. His name is Bryan Gulley. If you've been in the Loma Linda VA Hospital, you may have seen him rolling along in his wheelchair. How I came to call him Bryan the Blessed is quite a story. But then he is the most extraordinary person I've ever met. And early on I discovered that our canoes were tied to the same tree on Jordan's shore.

Bryan's life was a backlash of a childhood so hauntingly familiar that it stunned me. He too was a nobody's boy in an abusive home, beaten by both his mother and father. He particularly recalls the day his mother used an electric cord that severely cut his forehead. One brother suffered from birth with severe birth defects and would spend his life in an institution. His parents differed from mine in two respects: they were not poor, and they both held steady jobs in a Swiss embassy. The guards, Bryan told me, would seek to soothe his anguish by giving him candy; but this only made him feel worse, because he knew why they were doing it.

Finally his family moved to North Dakota, where his parents divorced. Though his mother was a nurse with a good income, she sent all but one child to live with relatives. Bryan, at 7 years of age, was sent to a military school. He cried so hard and long when his mother drove away that he became known as "Cryin' Bryan." Soon, however, having experienced the realities of the harsh life there, he became embroiled in so many fights that his name was changed to "Bryan the Lion." As I did, he became an overachiever, determined to excel. In sports he earned 12 high school letters. He was brilliant in his studies, graduating from high school in three years. At 17 he joined the Air Force and continued his education at San Diego State, where he earned a degree in chemical engineering.

So here I am, trying to fulfill the Lord's mission assignment of reaching out in His name, with His kindness, to those in pain and perplexity. And that sure includes Bryan. But how do you reach a man who is sprinting away from even the mention of God? A man who is, moreover, a supreme killing machine? I didn't know, but I knew that my Daddy knew. And He told me, "Tell Bryan that I love him." Didn't God know what this guy had done? Of course He did! And if God loved him, who was I to keep that information to myself? I didn't know, however, that Brian the Lion was already God's Boy. Of course, he didn't know it either. We were to find out together. Still, in my wildest dreams I didn't anticipate the ministry Bryan would extend to me. I had not only seen my Father perform miracles; I had experienced His miracles. But I'll admit that I thought one that would embrace Bryan would have to be the granddaddy of all whoppers!

When Bryan invited me to visit him in his home near Loma Linda, I didn't hesitate. He beckoned me to a seat near his wheelchair. In a few moments I was flying with him in a helicopter above the jungle canopy of Nicaragua. He was keeping an eye out for the enemy below.

The missile that hit the chopper came from a hand-launched grenade. It blew a hole in the bottom of the cabin and flipped the chopper over. Shrapnel killed all but two of those on board. It crashed upside down, high in the jungle canopy. Bryan hung out of the helicopter, his nearly severed left leg useless. Having used his belt as a tourniquet, he struggled out of the wreckage and dropped to the ground. Using his rifle as a brace for the leg, he and the only surviving crewman evaded the guerrillas while waiting for rescue. Sadly, his companion bled to death in his arms. An hour later Bryan was airlifted out and taken to a hospital, where his leg was stitched back together and a plastic knee installed. Recovered, he returned to Central America. Subsequently, he and squad members were exposed to nuclear radiation in an incident that is still classified. He was the only survivor.

Bryan told me that he and his wife, Heidi—who later divorced him—had two boys. His youngest son, Neal, was born with a multitude of birth defects, attributed to the radiation to which his father had been exposed.

Soon after, Bryan noticed a lump on his testicles, which subsequently was diagnosed as testicular cancer. It was surgically removed, and he was sent to Loma Linda University Hospital, which at that time had the only proton-beam accelerator in the United States. In addition, he endured chemotherapy treatments three times a week for four months.

In addition, he developed lymphoma and had three lymph nodes removed, followed by more chemotherapy. When the lymphoma recurred, doctors removed two more lymph nodes. There followed more chemotherapy. He began to vomit so violently that it tore his esophagus, leaving him impelled to vomit whenever he was on his feet for more than three hours.

The doctors then found a tumor on his neck so close to his carotid artery that an operation would be life-threatening. Surgeons in the Los Angeles City of Hope did the delicate bypass surgery and removed the tumor. More chemo. His jaw had to be rebuilt after another cancerous lump there was removed. Doctors then cut out a lump behind his nose, which had to be rebuilt. He developed 13 skin cancer lesions on his body. A further complication brought seizures, for which he takes medication. On a recent visit to his modest home in Yucaipa, I asked him for a list of the medications that keep him alive. Here it is, as compiled (and served up each day) by his wife, Paula. Yes, I said *each day!*

Trazodone—100 mg. (2½ pills)

Vicodin—500 mg. (8 pills)

Hydrochlorothiazide—25 mg. (1 pill)

Gabapentin—300 mg. (8 pills)

Gemfibrozil—60 mg. (2 pills)

Niacin—500 mg. (2 pills)

Oxybutynin—5 mg. (3 pills)

Metoclopramide—10 mg. (4 pills)

Felodipine—10 mg. (2 pills)

Lisinipril—40 mg. (½ pill)

Sertraline HCL—100 mg. (2 pills)

Venlafaxine—37.5 mg. (1 pill)

Prochlorperazine maleate—10 mg. (4 pills)

Loratadine—10 mg. (1 pill)

Ibuprofen—800 mg. (3 pills)

Lansoprazole—30 mg. (2 pills)

Metformin—500 mg. (2 pills)

Baclofen—10 mg. (4 pills)

Chlorpheniramine—4 mg. (3 pills)

Aspirin—325 mg. (2 pills)

**MONTHLY INJECTIONS**

Coumadin—1

Testosterone—1

Alprostadil—20 mg. (as needed)

Bacteriostatic—1 (as needed)

Sildenafil citrate—100 mg. (4)

Spinal injections—100 mg. (6)

**Daily Totals:** Pills—between 55½ and 60½. (Three are "sniffs.")

I'm sorry to tell you that Bryan's daily doses and mine are similar. I can just hear a reader (maybe you) saying, "No wonder you're sick! Toss it all and depend on the Lord!" How nice that would be! If Bryan did so, he would be dead within 24 hours. I might live a few days longer. If you think you have the faith to do so, I'll be glad to donate the disease. I'd suggest you put your affairs in order and leave your loved ones with the motto you'd like to have on your gravestone. I've been much impressed by the motto near the graves of my parents: "If love could have saved him, he would have lived forever." I've rested my case and Bryan's in the hands of One who is love.

Ultimately, say Bryan's doctors, his organs will fail. Currently another lymph node has become infected and needs to be removed. But because of its location, doctors fear removal will perforate the bowl and cause serious infection. Bryan waits for surgery to repair his esophagus and knees. Meanwhile, doctors treat him for post-traumatic stress syndrome.

Can you imagine the mutual awe of one of the few Wegener's survivors, and Bryan, as we exchange diagnoses, symptoms, and expectations? Could there be two sorrier specimens of homo sapiens in all the world? Two less likely to be featured on the cover of *Vibrant Health* magazine? Two more in need of paying up the balance on their cemetery plots? Two more in need of a free ticket to that forever land across the Jordan? The Lord knew what He was doing when He put us together. Whatever vision of God Bryan was fleeing, he saw in me, a fellow sufferer, a vision of God that captured his appreciation and, quickly, his love. Whatever vision of a case-hardened killing machine I saw in Bryan quickly evaporated. In its place I heard the silent cry for someone to care, someone to love, someone to value him—the same longings I carried from childhood.

Bryan and I have no doubt: God brought us together. The King told me, "Love My boy," and I do. Our visits are wonderful! The Lord showers us with blessings. Sometimes I sing hymns to him or read to him. Bryan, on the other hand, lifts my spirits as much as I lift his. One day he hobbled to a bureau, took something out, and handed it to me.

"This is for you because I love you," he said. It was his Silver Wings medal. I often put it on and proudly wear it around my motor home. Not outside, because I didn't earn it. But I shall treasure it until the Lord replaces it with His own version of wings. And I fully expect that Bryan will be there to receive his from the hands of his Father.

As Christmas approached, I saw this courageous man smile, laugh, and cry. One day he was with me, following my doctor's appointment, when I had an allergic reaction to the shot I'd been given. Bryan insisted on walking with me to the car instead of waiting in his wheelchair. When we got to the parking lot, I was so dizzy I couldn't find my car. I turned toward him to tell him of my dilemma, only to see him vomiting in the bushes. When he came back, we looked at each other and doubled over with laughter. What a pair! When we found my car, we faced another dilemma. Who would drive? It may not be legal to drive 40 miles an hour on Highway 10, the busiest freeway in America, but I did. When we got to his trailer, I lay on his bed and watched the room spin. Every few minutes he staggered past on his bad knee to vomit in the bathroom. Can you believe that on his way back he would stop to see if *I* was OK? What a friend!

One would think Bryan carries enough emotional and physical baggage without the haunting memory of his 164 confirmed kills (the total, he says, actually tops 200). But in the night he finds them walking through his dreams. Forgiven, yes, but not forgotten. On Christmas Eve I prayed that God would point me to a way to lighten Bryan's burden. God's answer was swift: Reassure him of his Daddy's love, His gift of salvation, His kindness and compassion.

There was one thing more, and the more I thought about it the happier I got. The next morning I handed him God's gift: a pillowcase with the number 10114 on it. Inside I put 164 tiny cutouts of his Silver Wings, and on each I wrote, "I love you, My boy. Signed, the King." Then I wrote the same thing on the pillowcase with a magic marker and tied the tip with a ribbon. It told him that this gift was for him to carry over his shoulder in place of the huge burden of guilt he had been toting around. He put the pillowcase on his pillow and sleeps on it. Once a day he takes out one wing and throws it away. Now this God's Boy sings hymns with me in the car and goes peacefully asleep each night in his Father's arms.

But I have not spoken enough of the gift God gave me in Bryan, who is a mirror image of myself. Through his experience I can see myself more clearly and thank God for the miracle of grace He has invested in me.

Bryan: Loaded with medals by a grateful government but haunted by 164 confirmed kills. We are likely the two homo sapiens in all the world least likely to be featured on the cover of a health magazine. Among Bryan's medals are the U.S. Air Force Cross, the U.S. Distinguished Service Cross, the Distinguished Service Medal, the Legion of Merit, the U.S. Distinguished Flying Cross, Bronze Star (with silver clasp), Meritorious Service Medal (4 bronze clusters), Purple Heart (3 bronze stars), Air Medal (4 silver clusters), Outstanding Unit Award, Armed Service Survivor Medal, Air Force Commendation (3 silver clusters), the Silver Wings, and 14 more.

Bryan's friendship has helped me perceive the magnitude of my Father's love. It reminds me that when one finds God, one becomes stronger, more courageous, and more childlike. Christians like Bryan are tough as a crocodile, yet possess the gifts of simplicity, self-forgetfulness, and confiding love. What kind of love is this!

I'm reminded of Bonnie, our younger daughter. Edna and I thought she was the most wonderful gift on God's green earth. Maybe it was because she was so loved that she was so secure. Every night when she got her "jammies" on—the kind with the feet—we played ball, read, sang, and told stories. I called her "Moose," or "Bubba." She had such confidence in our love that she would have jumped from a second-story window into our arms. That's confiding love.

A young man in Denver would know. He was in a head-on collision when he returned from college. Feared dead, and in a coma for months, he now is in a wheelchair and totally dependent on his parents. Though barely able to talk, he is one of God's gems. For months I have visited with him on the phone. I tell him that he is God's Boy, and that I love him. For my

Christmas gift he got on the phone and sang "Silent Night." Those words and his voice shall ever ring in my heart.

It's been a long and winding road from my genesis as Nobody's Boy, with choking, punching, loneliness, pain, shame, disease, glass cages, armor, and burdens. And it has been a long road for Bryan, beset with guilt within and horrible diseases within and without. What has been our response? We have given them all to the King. What did He do with them? He disposed of them at Calvary.

★ ★ ★

One day in the fall of 2000 I went into my main doctor's office for my monthly checkup. I had become the patient of one of the kindest, most gentle men on this planet, Dr. Keith Colburn. This brilliant doctor had gone through a bout with cancer, and his is a heart of compassion. My joints ached so badly I could hardly keep from crying out. My nose had been bleeding for two weeks, and my lungs ached with every breath. I didn't have to tell the doctors that I had spots all over my legs. They didn't have to probe far to find 10 of them, as well as other symptoms. So was it chemo again? Wegener's is harder to deal with than cancer. Because it has no cure, no definite treatment, and is full of side effects, every treatment is an experiment in prolonging life.

"Dr. Colburn," I said, "do you have any other patients with Wegener's granulomatosis?" There are so few that I didn't expect his answer.

"Yes, I have two, and they are both in ICU with relapses."

I was stunned. In my years with Wegener's I had never met anyone else who had it. He, of course, could not tell me who they were. I left his office with the burning desire to find at least one, but where to start? I headed across the street to the Loma Linda University Medical Center. I knew many of the hospital staff, but they too, for legal and ethical reasons, could not help me. My final stop was the ICU unit on the top floor. I asked the receptionist whether anyone with WG was there. The best she could do was recommend that I leave a note that a nurse "might deliver" to a family.

Downcast, I walked to the elevators down the hall and reached out to punch the button. Then it was that my Father said, "Go to the ICU waiting room." I knew the voice, and I knew the reliability of the source. I went. I stood in the doorway a moment and then called out, "I have Wegener's granulomatosis, and I know there is someone in this hospital with it, and I need to find them."

People in ICU don't ignore pleas. They know duress and pain, and they cling together in little family groups. They regarded me with blank yet caring eyes. Then, over in the corner of the room, a woman jumped up, waved her arms, and called, "It's my husband!"

Of all the experiences I've had as God's ambassador to those of His children in pain, this one was the most unusual and, in a sense, the most touching. "My husband's name is Richard," she told me. Her name was Marie. Her husband had been sick since 1996, the same year I became ill. He had been looking for a person with WG to talk to for four years. Now he lay in ICU where that very day she was signing papers to have his life support discontinued. And here I was, dropped into their life by One who knows the needs of every one of His children. Soon we were sharing heartaches like old friends. I sought to console her with hope and spoke of my Daddy in heaven who must have sent me, because Richard was His Boy.

"Could I see him?" I asked.

"Oh, yes; but he has been in a coma for a week."

As we entered his room, I saw a chubby man lying on the bed, hooked up to a myriad of tubes, including a respirator.

"Richard," Marie said, "there's a man here who has Wegener's, and who has come to see you."

I stepped close to the bed. To our astonishment, this gentle man flicked his eyes open and tried to focus on me. His right eye succeeded; the other drifted about the room. Though shocked by his response, I bent close to his face and said, "God loves you, Richard, and so do I."

A tear trickled from his focused eye and fled down his cheek. I tracked it with my finger and brushed it away. He lipped the words "I love you, too" through his respirator.

Marie and I stood there, stunned. God's loving-kindness flooded my soul for the next 15 minutes as I whispered assurances of God's love. "He's sent me to you, Richard, to assure you that He knows you by name and is waiting to welcome you to your real home. There's no Wegener's there, no pain, and the King is preparing a wonderful reception party where Marie and you will never be parted again."

He drifted in and out of consciousness as I stroked his forehead, and several times he squeezed my hand, something he had not done in a week. As he drifted closer to the hands of his loving Creator, I whispered, "Wait for me, Richard." Marie and I stood in silent awe. Returning to the waiting room, we spoke of the miracle God had granted us. After four years of searching I had 20 minutes with a fellow Wegener's patient.

"I'll pray for you," Marie promised.

Two days later I went to see Dr. Colburn. Usually I put on my best face when visiting a doctor, and I minimize symptoms. This time I not only told my friend how rotten I felt, but I couldn't stop tears from cascading down my cheeks. He sent me for blood tests after giving me a shot of cortisone, and I returned home.

At 11:00 that night my phone rang. It was Dr. Colburn. *What a wonderful man,* I thought, *calling this late to see how I'm doing!* He was indeed wonderful, but his reason for calling was disquieting: "Get to the nearest ER as fast as you can!" he said. They had found that I was not only in kidney failure, but my potassium count showed me ready to go into cardiac arrest. Needles flew, and lines were hooked up. Worst of all, Wegener's was back in full force. Plans were made to begin dialysis for my only kidney, but after three days it began to function, although slowly, on its own. During my crisis Drs. Stewart, Bruckner, and Colburn all stopped to see me. They were, of course, more than doctors; they were my buddies.

On the fourth day I learned that Richard had died. Services were to be held at 2:00 Monday in the nearby chapel. I had lost track of even the day of the week and the time of day. I glanced at the clock—it was Monday. It was 2:00. I grabbed the bedside phone and called the chapel. At 2:10 I managed to get the funeral director. He told me the services had already started. I dictated a short note to Marie and asked him to deliver it. In it I told her to give Richard a kiss on the forehead and to tell him that I would see him soon, because I was in the hospital with kidney failure. Ironic, I thought: God had directed me to Richard just before he died, and now I was about to join him at the river, where the dead in Christ shall rest until that glorious morning when they shall rise together "to meet the Lord in the air"! (see 1 Thess. 4:16-18 and 1 Cor. 15).

Suddenly it was as if someone were shaking me. I opened my eyes on the most surprising event of my life. There, all dressed in black, stood

Marie, her daughter, and the minister who was conducting Richard's funeral. It was not over, I learned. When Marie read the note I sent, she stood up and simply called "time out." She told the 300 friends there that she and her daughter had an errand to run and would be back shortly. I was dumbfounded. How could this be? They stayed and talked for some time before returning to finish the funeral. What does one say? What does one think? Was my Father wearing a smile? They came to see me, yes, but what they really came for was to hear a bit more of the Father's great love for their beloved Richard. And that they did hear! And they came to pray for me! During Richard's funeral service! Tell me

**Marie and her husband, Richard: She called "time out" during his funeral and, with her daughter, came to my room to pray for me!**

anything. Tell me that the ocean is pink. Tell me that water is intoxicating. Tell me anything, and I'll believe it.

For the next three nights I had to call the doctors in the middle of the night because of complications. The third night I was coughing up straight blood. Again, the ER. When I arrived I was in atrial fibrillation. I had a hemoglobin of 7.3 and an oxygen rate of 83. I was bleeding in my kidney, my lungs, and my sinuses. After three days, with the help of treatments, my heart returned to normal rhythm.

Everyone seemed to have heard of Richard and the funeral, and it seemed that no hour went by that someone did not come to hear of the King of kings. On an early morning I lay there looking my Daddy straight in the face. "I'm Your boy, Daddy," I repeated again and again. It seemed that I had hit rock bottom and would soon be sleeping with Richard. I began to sink. And suddenly, while talking to my Father, I saw Him slowly turn His back on me—just when I needed Him most. It took only moments, but they seemed to stretch into eternity. How could this be happening?

"NO!" my soul shouted. Without forethought I leaped through the air and onto my Daddy's back. I clutched Him by the neck from behind. In my mind's eye the tubes and the IVs and the bedsheets and the monitors all went flying, and this man child clung to his Father. Incredibly, in that moment I sensed a great smile spread across His face. "I will never leave you or forsake you," a voice I knew well whispered. He had tested me, and I had clung to Him. For the remainder of the week I was suffused with peace and joy. It was as if I were a child again, but one wrapped in arms of love. In a few days they put me back on chemo, but no matter. I had stood on the bank of the river Jordan, and my Father had gently led me away. I had a work yet to do.

A few weeks later I stood in line at the checkout counter of Stater Brothers Market in Lake Arrowhead. There I witnessed a scene that says it all. As I pushed my cart forward, I noted a tiny boy sitting in the cart ahead of me. His father, a large, husky man, picked him up, and the tot tried to hug him, but his arms reached only a little way around his daddy.

I heard his father ask, "Do you hear it? Can you hear it?"

The child pressed closer, trying to hear his father's heartbeat.

Just that closely are we privileged to clutch our heavenly Father! As a favorite author puts it: "Let your heart break for the longing it has for God, for the living God" (*Christ's Object Lessons,* p. 149). It was with my heart against his heart that I stopped asking the painful questions: "Why are You doing this to me, God? Why do I have to be the one who suffers?" Instead, I now ask, "Father, what can I do for You? What appointments have You made for me today? I await Your wish." When things get tough and He looks to see how I am reacting, I squeeze His hand and watch His heart soar.

I do three things that electrify my soul. Each time I get into a vomiting spell from the chemo, I stop in the middle of it all, look up, and say, "I love You, Father. I love You. I love You anyway!"

I picture Him waking me. He sits on my bed and says, "Will you be sick for Me today? For if you are ill, you can talk to the nine people I shall send to you. They will know you understand their pain, and they will want to hear about Me." And I say, "Oh, yes, Father!" At the end of each day, after all the joys and sorrows and pains, I lie on my bed and say, "Good night, Jesus; good night, Holy Spirit." I then add the names of my children and friends as well. I work my way down the list. Then, best of all, I say, "Good night, Daddy." And I turn my cheek for Him. When I know He has kissed His boy good night, I go to sleep.

## I'd like you to meet some of my friends:

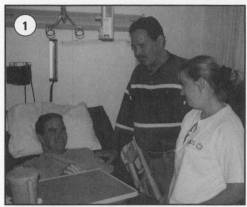

1. Geoff Sanborn broke his neck in a motorcycle accident and is paralyzed from the chest down. His brother-in-law, Chris Brooks, is my dear friend.

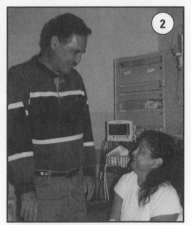

2. Cecelia Garcia is a bone cancer patient. She and I have had many infusions in this room—she for her plymyositis, me for my Wegener's.

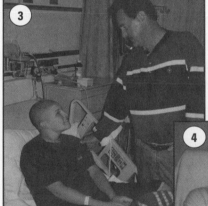

3. Jonas Nyberg was diagnosed with osteosarcoma in October 2002 and has been on chemo ever since.

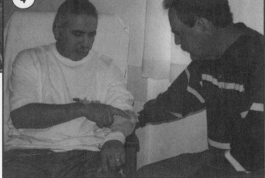

4. Richard Vasquez, suffering from chronic heart failure, has been waiting for a heart transplant since September 4, 2003.

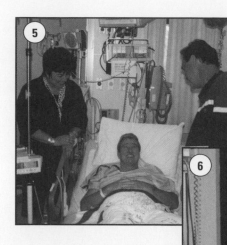

5. Paul Tomko had a heart attack that destroyed 40 percent of his heart. He's waiting for a heart transplant. This retired bank president and founder has a wife and six children.

6. My buddy Alan Gould had a racing heart that led to an ICD defibulator in 2001. After repeated shocks, he was sent to Loma Linda to wait for a heart transplant.

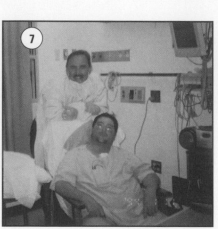

7. Rick Puccio, my good friend, had a heart transplant in 2002 at the age of 36. Because he suffered from a rare heart disease, his old heart is being researched at Johns Hopkins in Baltimore, Maryland, in Italy, and in France.

# What a Real Father Is Like

*There is a peace that cometh after sorrow,*
*Of hope surrendered, not of hope fulfilled;*
*A peace that looketh not upon tomorrow,*
*But calmly on a tempest that is stilled . . .*
*A peace there is, in sacrifice secluded,*
*A life subdued, from will and conflict free;*
*'Tis not the peace which over Eden brooded,*
*But that which triumphed in Gethsemane.*

—Jessie Rose Gates

**What a week! I spent it** in 9100 ICU. The hub is a nurses' station from which the patients' rooms branch out like spokes at the end of a wheel. But 9100 also has a back room in which there are a half dozen beds. Everyone in there is deathly sick. I call the room the "banana skin," because many patients slip quietly away.

During my week in the back room everyone was in a coma, most medically induced. I was fully alert, but had atrial fibrillation (irregular beats of the heart) and recurring renal failure. My Wegener's had leaped on me with the fury of an attacking tiger. I lay there, hearing one code after another, signaling a medical crisis. I heard code red, code blue, and code pink, each color describing a different type of emergency. From my place next to the nurses' desk I overheard each case described in blunt detail.

The nurses kept an eagle eye on me, trying to restore a normal heart rhythm with dioxin. Late in the week a nurse checked my status and yelled out, "He's in rhythm!" and I was soon transferred to the sixth floor.

When it came time for X-rays, a staffer helped me into a wheelchair. I was still weak; my side hurt from an open lung biopsy, and a drainage tube stuck out of my side. As we approached the X-ray room, the carrier rolled me up beside a gurney. On it was a man covered with a sheet up to his chin. I assumed the woman standing beside him was his wife.

My Father said, *Go ahead, child, talk to him*. So I reached out and patted him gently on the knee. "How are you doing?"

There was no response. His wife turned to me and said, "He's paralyzed from the neck down, and they're trying to figure out what to do. He can barely breathe."

I didn't waste any time. "Friend, you are in God's hospital, and I know that He will 'see to it.' He always does." I told him of the love of the Great King. When his wife whispered that his name was Dwayne, I became his buddy:

"Dwayne, your Father knows your pain. Jesus felt all-consuming pain for us. He knows your fear, and that is why He has you in His hospital. He's with you right now. He dearly loves you. Dwayne, you are God's child, His Boy, and He has your image engraved on the palm of His hand. He knows what you need. Hang in there, friend." When they rolled Dwayne into the X-ray room, his wife dragged a chair over and asked many questions about God.

We were interrupted by a technician who rolled me into one of the X-ray rooms. All they needed was a chest shot, but everything seemed to go wrong. I was too wide for one X-ray, so they had to do it over again and take two shots to put together into one. As she pulled on the drainage tube that was sticking out of my side, the technician nearly caused me to faint with pain. I wondered what was happening. Why was it taking so long? At last she put me back in the wheelchair and rolled me out into the hallway. Just as we passed the room Dwayne was in, the Lord said, *Stop, boy. Go back!* So I told the tech to roll me back. I looked in, saw Dwayne lying on the gurney, and hollered, "I love you, Dwayne!"

My mouth fell open in astonishment as Dwayne lifted himself to look at me. The X-ray tech was so astonished that, as she rolled me back to the sixth floor, she told everyone about the "miracle." I went to bed, but not to sleep; the nurses kept coming in and asking what had happened.

"Oh, God lives in this hospital," I replied, "and He's my Daddy, and yours, too."

I had just closed my eyes again when two women rushed into my room. It was Dwayne's wife and sister. "You won't believe it, but Dwayne is free of paralysis from the waist up, and all he can talk about is the God you told him about and that you said you loved him."

For the remainder of my hospital stay I rested, aware of God's approval.

I also understood why I had been delayed in the X-ray room. I had thought that everything had gone wrong. Now I knew that in God's design, everything had gone right. He had delayed me until I could look into Dwayne's room, see him on the gurney, and share God's love with him. That's the way it goes in Loma Linda University Hospital, the workplace of the King

★ ★ ★

## The Proton and the Doctor

It was one of those magnificent weekend days when most southern Californians head for the mountains or out in the desert to Joshua Tree. Many from Loma Linda are among them, but only after going to church. I parked in the hospital lot and walked to the Collegiate church, located just north of the medical school. I sat in my usual place in one of the wooden pews across the back of the church. They're reserved for the deacons, but they know that I'm on chemo and often need to make a quick exit when nausea hits. And it was hitting hard that morning, but somehow I sensed that I was to be in church.

The Sabbath school lesson was half over as I settled into my spot. A kind-looking man at the front of the church was talking about my Father. Maybe it was just me on that Sabbath, but he didn't sound like he really knew Him. I wondered what would happen if I got up and said, "Excuse me, please. Let me tell you about my Daddy. He's so kind and loving that I can't hear the mention of His name, or a hymn about Him, without tears of joy. He knows every cell of every one of us, and if you open your heart wide enough, you'll know He's sitting right in the pew with you."

*If I did,* I thought, *a deacon would come and discreetly usher me to the door.* "O Father," I whispered, "I just wish I had one person to tell about Your love this morning."

As the Sabbath school lecture was nearing its end, I saw a man near the front stand up and head toward the back of the church. He walked past a door leading out, hurried to the back pews, and sat down beside me. Now, I had learned two lessons from my Father: Never be shocked at how He works, and remember that anything can happen. Nevertheless, I was surprised to see this neatly dressed man in a dark suit lean over to me.

"I want you to know," he began, "that God told me to come and sit by you."

"Really?" I said, for once at a loss for words.

"Yes," he went on in a whisper. "I'm a doctor from Dallas. I'm here for the proton treatment for prostate cancer. I need someone to talk to, and God directed me to you. I know this sounds crazy, but nothing like this has ever happened to me before."

God doesn't always send people to me to get a sermon. Sometimes it's just to listen. And that's what I did now. Then, with a smile, I told him about the request I had just sent heavenward for someone I could tell of God's love. "You're the living answer." For 20 minutes we talked about the King we worshiped. My friend became so animated and happy that I expected someone to stand up and whisper, "Will you two shut up back there!"

Finally, his anxieties gone, my friend gave me a sideways hug, stood up, and left the church. I just sat, and my heart said, "O Father, You are too much!" All that Sabbath afternoon I could sense my Father smiling down at me. "See, My child," He seemed to say, "I thank you for being ill for Me today. I need you on the bank of the Jordan River so that you can share the good news with the hurting and the ill."

"The good news?" I questioned. "Oh, You mean the truth that Your love is everything to this dying world!" I was smiling as I dropped off to sleep.

## Donavon, My Friend

The phone kept ringing, and I couldn't answer it—I was in the shower. If it was Jack, he'd call back. If it was one of my daughters, she'd call on the cell phone. But when it began to ring again, I toweled off and dashed the 20 feet to the receiver.

"Hello."

"Is this Grover?"

"Yes."

"We have a patient here with Wegener's, and the family asked to speak to you. Can you come over?"

"I'll be right there."

Each morning, after my Father awakens me, I say, "Good morning, Father; I love You. What do You have in mind for today?"

This day He hadn't even waited for me to get dressed!

Another Wegener's patient . . . I had already lost two friends to Wegener's in just a few months. Perhaps that was why I hurried as I dressed. Sometimes things go fast when your illness starts with the big W. I wondered why they had him in the cardiac unit. Could he have an irregular heartbeat, as I did? I looked in the rearview mirror and added another 20 miles per hour to my speed.

As I raced up the stairs to 4700, the cardiac ICU, I met the unit director. She was looking for me, so I knew it wasn't just bad—it was very bad. I hurried into room 20. Lying on a bed was a man whose name, I learned, was Donavon. He was large, slightly chubby, with thinning hair and big capable hands. His eyes were closed, but I imagined they were blue (I'm not sure why). All he had on was a thin, short hospital gown. He was 52, they said.

I had been 50 when Wegener's slugged me. Every tube, every machine, aroused memories—the heart monitor, the irregular rhythm, the lungs full of granuloma, the blood trickling from sinuses, the renal failure, the open lung biopsy, the high fevers—everything. He was, I saw, in a medically induced coma. I shook off the reminder of my own mortality.

"Hello, Donavon; God loves you, and so do I. I know exactly how you feel, buddy." In my mind he was at the river, and I was climbing into the canoe beside him. I came with the searing love of my Father and with my Wegener's. Once more I said, from the depths of my heart, "I love you, Donavon."

Somehow I knew he heard. I rubbed his shoulders and held his hand, as my tears dripped into his canoe. Across the bed I saw that his sister was holding his other hand.

Later I talked to the rest of the family, who wanted to know everything about Wegener's. I didn't have the heart to tell them. Of course, in me the family saw living evidence that Donavon could survive, for seven years anyway. They observed the care with which the hospital personnel ministered to Donavon, gently touching and turning him, talking to him soothingly. I watched Dr. Gregory Cheek interface with the family and admired his gentleness. Nurse Sandra Letts, one of several nurses who were rotated daily, was an angel of love and care. The respiratory therapists, Mike Dalton and Mike Trenner, talked to him as gently as they would to a brother. "Good morning, Donavon," Dalton said, touching his shoulder. "We're going to check your breathing tube."

When everyone left the room, I sang hymns to this child of God who struggled for life—

"Yes, we'll gather at the river,
      The beautiful, the beautiful river."

We were there together, my friend and I. prayed for him and give him a hug. "I'll see you tomorrow, Donavon. I love you, boy!" I did not try to hide my tears. Oh, how I wanted him to pull through! Each day I stayed with him from morning to late evening. And, little by little, I learned something about him from the family. He was a caring man, good to his wife and daughter, generous in his help to the community. One evening the doctor came to the waiting room where the family and I were talking.

"It doesn't look good," he said, "but let me tell you that he wouldn't have a life worth living if he were to survive." This frank appraisal took a bit of the edge off the family's pain. The doctor didn't know that I had Wegener's, and I didn't feel it was the appropriate time to tell him. It is true that if a "healthy" person has a hundred things in life he or she can do, I have only four—eat, sleep, take medicine, and share my Father's love. These were, I was sure, great reasons to battle on. So I listened as the doctor told the family that he did not expect Donavon to make it through the night.

Donavon did not know I even existed, but I'll be there to meet him in that morning when he comes forth in the bloom of eternal youth.

Later, I went to see him for the last time. "Oh, Donavon, I know I'll see you in the morning, when you come forth in the bloom of eternal youth. I'll be there to meet you, friend."

Strange, isn't it, how the King works. Here were two of His children, one of whom did not even know the other existed. One who spoke words of love into an unhearing ear. And yet, through the grace of God, we were brothers who would spend eternity together. "See you, buddy." I kissed his forehead.

An hour later I got the news. I wept.

The church was packed to bursting at his service. I go down to the cemetery often and sit and tell him about the angels who were with him at the hospital. Then I get after him for leaving me, but I always tell him I love him anyway. I hold my Wegener's support group meetings at Donavon's home. Four more friends are resting now, and someday I'll join them.

## Daddy and Keven

The last drops of the IV dripped slowly into my arm. I glanced at my watch. Six hours. Doctors call the medication amphotericin B, then grin and tell you that its real name is ampho*terrible*. It surely earned its nickname, because the immediate impact is stronger than chemotherapy. I had developed a condition called mucormycosis, a deadly fungus of the sinuses. It is, alas, a close relative of Wegener's, and usually shows up in patients who have not succumbed on schedule to that disease. The doctor came in during my first day in 8300, room 9. She didn't mince words.

"Expect that you'll be in a four- to five-month deadly struggle for your life. Expect that tomorrow morning you will enter surgery to have the right side of your face removed. That means you'll lose your eye, half your nose, your ear, cheek, and even half your teeth."

It takes a while to absorb news like that. But wait! My *right* ear? That's the one my Father usually talks into. The doctor likely wondered why in the world I was chuckling. My second thought was I could wear a Mickey Mouse mask one day, Elvis the next. The visual imagery was too much. I laughed! However, it took only a few seconds for reality to rear its face-eating head. I was about to lose half my face. A leg I could lose. Or an arm. But somehow it seemed to me that you can't cut away half a man's face without cutting away a part of who he is.

That evening as I lay on my bed bidding farewell to my face, a quiet man in a doctor's smock slipped into my room. It was Dr. Steven Stewart. There were no magic words or medical solutions, just kindness washing over me. "No matter what happens, I'm here," he said. "I'll be praying for you, Grover; and I'll be thinking about you." He left me assured that the King walks the hospital halls in many forms.

I silently turned to my Father and hung on.

That afternoon the doctors carved out my sinuses down to the bone. They couldn't get all the deadly fungus, but, thank the Lord, in the operating room they decided to try amphotericin B before resorting to the half-face removing surgery. I had 34 infusions. As the last drop went through the tube in my armpit, I lay there, shaking with the chills.

Enough. I got up. Usually I put on my robe and visit my friends—doctors, nurses, technicians, and patients. This time, profoundly impacted by the near loss of half my face, I headed for the lobby and my chaplain friends. I had faced death many times without a shudder. I'm not a Mr. America, but I am reasonably attractive. It wasn't loss of my looks alone that troubled me. How would patients react to a visit from a man with half a face? Forget the celebrity masks—the reality would be far different.

As I moved toward the open elevator door, a man pushing a teenage boy in a wheelchair collided with me and sent me bouncing into the side paneling. A glance revealed a thirty-something muscular man with a Marine haircut, communicating both vitality and energy. I mentally cataloged him as "the Rock." Quite a contrast to the rubber-legged ampho-man!

It was in an operating room such as this that half my face was to be removed.

Laughing, I grabbed him by his arm and pretended I would sling him out the door. Clint and I became friends on the spot. He introduced his son: "This is my boy, Keven. He's had two heart transplants and is back in the hospital." I rubbed Keven's shoulder and offered a hello.

I never reached my chaplain friends that day.

Over the next several months I became better acquainted with Keven and his parents, Clint and Karen Hooper. One day we met at the information desk.

"Good to see you, Clint. How's Keven?"

"Not too good. In fact, he's in serious shape."

I could read the pain in the father's eyes.

"May I go see him today, Clint?"

"That would be great, Grover. How are you doing?"

"Oh, all right," I replied, not mentioning the vertigo that had the room spinning. I walked with him to the lobby, where we joined his family. They told me that Keven had endured eight open-heart surgeries. At 3½ he had his first heart transplant; at 9, another. He was a tough little trooper. Self-pity never reared its ugly head. He touched hearts with his great smile. He had become his father's shadow.

Strange, but when we converse with others a phrase—a mention—may trigger a memory in us of which they are totally unaware. So it was that their mention of "his father's shadow" sent my memory stumbling back through the years to my own early teens—and to my father. I was still remembering the abuse, the neglect, the brutality, as we headed for 5800, room 4, and a visit with Keven.

Clint's love for his son, and Keven's love for his father and mother, warmed my heart. I could see my heavenly Father in their embrace. The family had been to Loma Linda's Childrens' Hospital hundreds of times and knew many of the staff. They had sung and prayed together for Keven. I knew his doctor, Robert Tan, and his angel nurses, Sandi and Maria, both of whom were on the transplant team.

I could see that Keven's condition had deteriorated. The boy I had first seen in a wheelchair was now lying on the bed with at least 20 machines either pumping fluids into him or monitoring his body processes. There were so many tubes that five or six nestled around his feet. He had IVs in his legs, arms, groin, and chest. His belly ballooned out like that of a woman in the eighth month of pregnancy. Keven was 15, but he looked as if he were 7. Perched above his head was a black-and-orange Pooh Bear that he loved. And, yes, he was his father's shadow.

I stood at the side of his bed and took his hand in mine. I was startled; it felt as if I were holding a baby's hand, so soft and gentle it was. With all my heart I wanted to grab that boy up and squeeze him to my chest. How can you love someone so when you've only just met him? That's what Keven did to visitors. Oh, how I wished that I might touch him and say, "Be thou made whole." Instead, I could see him getting into a canoe on the river Jordan and slowly heading for the other shore. To be sure, his Father would be there to meet him. The Lord must have put the words of the song in my mind:

> "Someday He'll make it plain to me,
> Someday, when I His face shall see,
> Someday from sin I will be free
> And someday I shall understand."

I stepped back and watched Clint as he ever so gently took his son's hand, softly spoke soothing words, and placed his other hand on that swollen stomach.

"Daddy's here, buddy. I love you."

It sounded like soft music. *Is this what a real father is like?* I wondered. I could not hold back the tears as I saw that angel father move his hands to Keven's legs and begin massaging them. Then he was stroking his son's crew cut, so like his own. There was no other sound in the room as the two nurses, the respiratory therapist, and I stood in reverent awe. What love! Never would Keven feel that he was nobody's boy. For 20 minutes I stood, transfixed, as a father showed me both a father's love and a father's broken heart. I knew as never before how much my heavenly Father loves His earthly children.

*But what of my father?* The thought intruded, igniting a memory I had thought long gone. *Oh, my father, where were you when I hurt? Why did you ignore me? Why did you beat me again and again? And then you stood in a court of law and said that you no longer wanted me! You made me Nobody's Boy!*

*Yes, Father, that's in the past. You're sleeping that long night called death. But one question haunts me still: Will I ever be able to forgive you?*

"Grover." The quiet words penetrated my reverie. "Would you pray for my boy?"

How could I speak at all? I saw the pain in Clint's eyes and knew I must. Three nurses, the respiratory therapist, Clint, and I joined hands with Keven there in a hospital dedicated to healing the physical, mental, and spiritual wounds of humanity.

"My Father—" I began.

I don't remember what I said. I can remember feeling those heavenly arms around me that I know so well. When I finished my prayer, I leaned close to God's boy and whispered, "I love you, Keven."

For the next week I sat with Clint, his wife, Karen, and their large extended family and friends. Each evening I had the honor of praying for Keven. I shall never forget the joy of holding his hand. Finally, with cancer

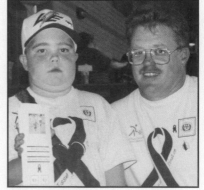

**Clint and Keven Hooper in happier days. In Clint I saw, through tears, what it means to have a father.**

added to his heart problems and chemotherapy failing, Keven, tough little

Keven, could not fight on. Clint and Karen stood at his bedside to say goodbye. Keven's sister Linda came out into the hallway, hugged me, and said, "He's gone, Grover."

More than 1,500 people attended Keven's memorial, a testimony to the precious child who had won so many hearts. I'll see Keven again some-day soon. And "then o'er the bright fields we shall roam, in glory celestial and fair."

Goodbye for now, Keven.

# Sixteen

# Wrestling in the Graveyard

*I do not ask that flowers should always spring*
*Beneath my feet;*
*I know too well the poison and the sting*
*Of things too sweet. . . .*
*I do not ask my cross to understand,*
*My way to see;*
*Better in darkness just to feel Thy hand,*
*And follow Thee.*

　　　　—Adelaide A. Proctor, *"Per Pacem Ad Lucem"*

**Drive west on Barton Road** from Loma Linda, and just past the city limits you'll see the Montecito Memorial Cemetery, tucked below the rolling hills marking the southern flank of the San Bernardino Valley. A scattering of scrub pine, fir, and cherry trees are interspersed among the modest gravestones. Behind you are the hulking San Bernardino Mountains, where my parents moved from house to house as the rent came due. Could the gravestones speak, many stories of heroism and sacrifice would be told of the hospital's pioneer staff who await resurrection morning. Included among them are doctors, nurses, technicians, and others who valiantly battled the angel of death.

Here and there, visitors stand by grave sites. A gray-haired woman in her late 50s is arranging a bouquet of roses. Up the hill a young man embraces a woman who may be his mother. A hundred yards across the way a family of five is standing silently before a gravestone. Some bring flowers; others pause, hatless, for a moment of meditation or prayer.

My parents are buried here. Perhaps it's fitting that they rest at the base of the mountains they wandered over for so many years. Their sites have no gravestones. They have no flowers. They have no visitors.

My heavenly Father has asked many things of me. To bear my Wegener's to His glory. To be His emissary to other sufferers. To endure the loss of position and home. To put my life in His hands. And I've done so, not from a sense of duty, but because I love Him. And then one evening in May 2003 He asked me to forgive my parents—who had beaten me, starved me, ignored me, while never saying "I love you" to a son who wanted nothing more in all the world than to hear that he mattered. Who spent most of his life fighting the demons they implanted in him, and who has gone through hell because of them.

And not I alone. To reveal the consequences of the abuse my brothers and sisters suffered would make another book. I've chosen not to reveal their tribulations, other than to say that they match or exceed my own. Their victories have been few and hard-bought, hard-fought. I've talked to them all in the past month. One for the first time in 28 years, another for the first time in 23 years. They've all been in denial. But now, as I've contacted them and shared the words you read in this book, they're clawing their way out of their own personal hells.

Only two have been to our parents' grave site, and that was at their burial. God has never asked them to go. But now He has asked me—for many years Nobody's Boy because of parental abuse and neglect—to go and to forgive.

The night He asked me to forgive my mother, I formed a brotherhood with Jacob. Jacob, says the Bible, wrestled with God. In fact, he wrestled all night. So did I. But it was a gentle contest. I was more interested in having God go with me than in defying His wish. "Father," I said in submission, "please go with me tomorrow and hold my hand. This boy doesn't think he can handle this assignment alone." My pillow was wet with tears when I fell asleep.

I've lived through many mornings when I was glad just to be alive. The earlier morning came, the better. This Sunday morning, though, came too soon. I sat for a while on the edge of the bed.

"Good morning, Father. I suppose you know it is Mother's Day. That isn't going to make my visit any easier, you know."

He knew. For as long as I've been able to remember, I've known that I had no mother. There was, to be sure, a woman who claimed to be my mother. She lived in our house. She threw things. She had a voice—I had heard her scream and curse and cry. But she never called me "son." She never held me. Never hugged me.

And now my Father wanted me to go to her on Mother's Day to tell her that I forgave her.

He did leave me a little loophole: He hadn't asked me to go and tell her that I loved her. However, that omission really didn't give me much comfort. I had come to know my Father well enough to anticipate, with some accuracy, what was coming.

My breakfast of oatmeal and applesauce seemed to glide down all too quickly. I had the strange sensation of being two persons. One was the warrior, ready to storm ahead, determined and confident of victory. The other, the small child in me, drew back in wide-eyed terror.

The warrior won. He dragged the child in me out of my motor home and into my 1978 Camaro. Never had it started more readily. Never had it hit the speed limit so effortlessly. (Of course, I knew who was pushing.)

Then halfway to the cemetery, a happy thought! I hadn't seen my good friend Donavon, my Wegener's buddy, for a few days. Surely he needed a visit! So I went looking for him. Never had I needed him more! "Where are you, buddy?" I mumbled as I crossed and recrossed the area where we usually met. No go. No Donavon. Then I had a second happy thought: I had a brother-in-law buried somewhere in this graveyard. He had died in 1966. Surely he needed a visit.

My lollygagging was noted and brought to my attention. Yes, Lord, I hear You. It is time.

A few hundred yards into the cemetery I stopped near where I thought my mother's grave site might be and reached for the directions Aunt Anne had given me. I followed them to a steep grassy hillside. I knew her grave was unmarked. I didn't want to find it. I didn't want it to exist, because I didn't even know what a mother was. My sisters had told me that soon after my birth the woman who called herself my mother had placed me in the arms of my sister Pam, and it was she who became my substitute mother.

I walked slowly across the short-cropped grass. The coordinates said her grave must be about here. I kicked at the grass, pulled a screwdriver from my pocket, and began to stab it through the grass into the soil. I wondered what the few nearby visitors thought. Did they think they were viewing some kind of hate crime against earthworms? Or more likely a cemetery employee digging out dandelions?

Why had I come? Why did I care? She certainly hadn't. The child in me got up to leave, but the warrior sat down. The battle was on: Leave, stay, leave, stay . . .

"Father, where are You? I can't do this!" I tore at the unyielding crabgrass.

Anger welled up. "You're here, aren't you? You're dead, and you're still controlling! You're hanging on to the grass roots with both hands. You never gave an inch!"

The memories were raw. I struggled, wet with sweat, hot with anger, grim with determination. After what seemed like forever, I hit a cup in its container. The number on the cup: A 273. My mother, Sarah Thompson, had died on August 20, 1993, of pulmonary fibrosis when she was 72.

After what seemed forever, I hit a cup and its container. Mother's Day or no Mother's Day, I lost it. "Why am I here?" I demanded. "You were no mother!"

Mother's Day or no Mother's Day, I lost it. "Why am I here?" I demanded. "You were no mother! A mother is supposed to be the one person on earth you can depend on absolutely. But I was nothing to you. You called me a 'bad seed,' and left me in limbo." (This was the 7-year-old of juvenile hall speaking.) Didn't you see me clinging to the fence, my heart broken? You never came to see me. You turned your back on me. I tried to be perfect for you, and you never noticed. I needed a hug; I never got even one! *Do you hear me! Not ONE!* You bitch! What do you expect me to say—'Happy Mother's Day'? The only reason you had any of us kids was that you thought that would keep your husband home instead of in another woman's bed. When that didn't work, you hated me! Why couldn't you have at least pretended that I was a person? You made me disappear.

"Didn't you hear our voices when we cried, 'Mom, I'm hungry; Mom, I'm cold'? Didn't you ever notice the little boy with the empty eyes? *Oh, Mom, it would have taken only a few hugs to fill them with tears of joy!* You hated me because you hated your philandering husband, and I looked like him. You called me a no-good brat. But even that was better than the days, the months, the years of cold indifference. So often I wanted to scream out, 'I'm a person. I'm alive. I count. Couldn't you see me? Didn't you hear me?'"

I sat, drenched in sweat and shaking.

Later I found myself wondering whether she had ever had a happy day. Had she ever laughed? How little I knew her, my mother. I was still sitting, exhausted, when my Father, the one who cared, touched a few spots in my brain, and I heard His soft words: "It's all right, boy, you're precious to Me. I love you." It was then that I could speak to her quietly: "I know something of the nightmares you experienced all those years. I can only imagine the pain you felt, knowing your husband was repeatedly unfaithful to you. You must have felt pain for us when you sat in prison, knowing your children were behind barbed wire in juvenile hall. You made a hard choice: To keep your husband, even if it meant the sacrifice of your children. You did not deserve the life of hell that was yours. I understand. I forgive—"

*O Father! I can't.*

*You can, My child.*

I felt my heavenly Father's arms around me—"I forgive you. I forgive you."

I wept.

"I believe you gave your heart to God before you died," I told her. "I want to see you on that great morning when the dead in Christ shall rise. Maybe, maybe, you can begin to love me there, and I'll know you as you were before the nightmares began. Until then I'll think of you as that 16-year-old girl in New York City, where you first met the man who became your husband.

*O God, my Father, give me the grace to love her!*

I went home exhausted and crawled into bed. I got up two days later.

★ ★ ★

I should have expected it. There is, after all, a Father's Day.

It came just four weeks after my visit to my mother's grave. This time I knew what my heavenly Father wanted before He asked.

Again, I had to get the grave site coordinates from Aunt Anne. And again, I had to crawl about in the close-cut grass at the site where my father's grave should have been. I pulled my screwdriver from my pocket and began to plunge it into the soft soil. Suddenly I felt a strange compulsion to plunge it into my father's heart!

"Why were you never a father to me?" I burst out. "How could you beat my tiny body as you did? And for nothing! I was so helpless, so frightened. You were not my father—you were a monster! You never even spoke to me! I hate you! I hate you!" (Not a very good beginning to the forgiveness bit.)

The screwdriver hit metal. I dug with my fingers and brought out a small metal cup. I tore away the grass and soil. There was no marker; just the name "Wilcox" written with a black marker. No one had wanted to remember. It was a 7-year-old's fingers that brushed away the dirt.

I had to get my father's grave site coordinates from Aunt Anne. There was no marker. No one wanted to remember him. It was as if a volcano of pent-up hate erupted. I spoke ugly words. Cutting words. It was a tiny boy who spoke up at last: "Didn't you know I spent 50 years looking for a father?"

Wendon Wilcox was only 54 when he died of a heart attack in April 1970. He has lain, undisturbed, in this unmarked grave for 33 years, a forgotten soul filled with darkness, fury, violence. No flower had ever been placed on his grave to say "I care."

With that realization, forbidden words flowed unchecked.

"You don't know I'm here, do you? I know *you're* here, but you're hiding again. You don't even have a gravestone with your name on it!"

It was as if a volcano of pent-up hate erupted. "Oh, why did you let us starve? Didn't you see our bones and hollow eyes? We wanted you to just go away. Disappear. *Die!* You left us lifetimes of pain and struggle, and the terrifying thought *that we might become like you!* I wanted to grow big and strong so that I could hurt you—throw you against a wall as you threw me! In basic training I pretended I was fighting you! You bastard! You never cared for your children. All you cared for were your women!"

Ugly words. Cutting words. I sat silent, drained.

The adult was done, but then the tiny boy spoke up. "Didn't you know that I spent 50 years looking for a father? I looked around every corner for the father you never were. I can never forget those years. *Never!* You want to hear my memories? No food, no clothes, no home, no safety. And all that is nothing compared to not having a father, for all the years you never knew I existed. And now you don't know I am here."

Somehow the words of the child soothed the man.

"Look, all the memories of all the years, all the neglect, all the pain, all the abuse—I don't want to carry them anymore. I don't want to remember them anymore. Your sons and daughters all suffered terrible wounds, and only now are they facing what happened. And as they do, they're reaching for healing. We're going to get together someday soon. And I hope—I pray—that all of us can come someday and visit you here with our souls free of hatred."

It took the reach of faith, but I said it: "I love you, Dad. I shall stand not as your judge, but as your son, even as I stand as the son of my heavenly Father. I forgive you."

Somehow it didn't seem necessary to recite the litany of abuses for which he should have sought forgiveness. The God who came down and walked among us as one of us forgave His earthly children even for the nails they had pounded through His hands. "Forgive them, Father," he prayed, "for they know not what they do."

I walked back to the car. There I reopened the week-old letter from a psychiatrist who had, at my request, examined my father's medical records. My eyes scanned the page that summarized his conclusion:

"After examining all the records available to me, I believe your father likely suffered from bipolar syndrome. He's got all the indicators. If he had been diagnosed early, I believe he might have been able to live a normal life."

I know that bipolar is mood disorder involving a cycle of depression and mania. I read down the list of textbook symptoms:

Mania, excessive energy, impulsive behavior.

Reckless activities.

Manic episodes.

Inflated self-esteem or grandiosity.

Decreased need for sleep. Talkative. Flights of ideas/aggressive thoughts.

Untreated, can make one nonproductive.

Increases goal directives/active.

Excessive involvement in pleasurable activities that have a high potential for painful consequences.

Sexual indiscretions.

Elevated or expansive irritability.

Impulsive travel.

Hostile and physically threatening to others.

If psychotic, then hostile.

Racing thoughts; ideas fleeting.

It is not known to be hereditary, which might be the case if a higher incidence were observed in the same family.

*Dear God! No road map could have pointed more directly to my father!*

Depression and mania. Yes. "Not necessarily abusive" doesn't mean "never abusive"—especially during manic episodes.

Reckless activities, impulsive behavior, *grandiosity . . . The Cadillacs, the posturing with movie stars.*

Impulsive travel? *Bingo!*

Nonproductive when untreated. *Who was it but my brothers and mother who supported the family for many years?*

Excessive involvement in pleasurable activities that have a high potential for painful consequences and sexual indiscretions. *The names of his sex partners would fill pages! And for one of those pages he hadn't even had to leave the house . . .*

My eyes traveled through the list of 20-plus symptoms—and he had them all. My hands were shaking. But the diagnosis said more than that my father was likely bipolar. It also said that he likely would have been a different man had he received the right medication. He was sick. He did not make himself sick, and neither could he make himself well.

I thought of the death of his father when he was 12; of an overly indulgent mother; of what acquaintances called his "dark side." Had his illness hit early? Was it his illness speaking in the Riverside County Courthouse when he told the judge he didn't want us, his own children? When he tried to break Edward's arm and flung me, face first, into a wall? When he failed to provide his family with the basic needs for growing up—food, shelter, love, affection, happiness, a sense of worth, the training to survive life, character, standards, security?

God only knows. And yet I had tried him before my judgment seat, convicted him, and sentenced him to hell. Had I done the same for my mother? Had she ever—?

*Yes! A memory.*

I could picture her cutting pictures out of a magazine and gluing them onto cardboard for our only Christmas presents. And she had sewed clothes for Clara from cloth she had gotten somewhere.

And what of my father? Yes, he had taken pride in my scholastic achievements. How old was he then—45? 50? I determined I would henceforth probe the recesses of my memory for anything positive. *Oh, dear Lord, I'm going to need help. The pain is so raw, so all-compassing. But is Your love not wider, deeper, higher still?*

For a few moments it seemed as though I was no longer in my car beside my father's grave. Rather, I was standing in 5800, room 4, watching my father bend over *me* and gently touch my swollen belly. It was not Keven but *me* on the bed! My father was tenderly holding my hand, rubbing my shoulder, and saying, "Grover, I love you. I'll see you in the morning."

No, it never happened. But something like it *had* happened the day before in room 4. Was my heavenly Father reminding me that He is the mender of hearts? Maybe my parents really shall learn what love is. Maybe someday. . . .

Whatever the case, their future is in the hands of a just and merciful God.

Putting aside the letter about my father's bipolar condition, I looked back at the grassy hillside where two tormented souls are at last resting in peace. Slowly their silent Nobody's Boy raised a hand that gestured farewell. It was, however, Somebody's Boy who drove away. Somebody's Boy who whispered, "I love you both. I'll see you in the morning."

★ ★ ★

Today I have little left of what the world values. A small motor home that sits on a space in Loma Linda's Mission RV Park. A few changes of clothes. A nice used car that Edward bought me. Lost is my career as a respected and loved teacher. Lost, too, are my home, old friends, money, belongings, health, and, almost, my life. I shall meet future crises as I have met scores of others by putting them in my Father's hands.

There is another sadness with which I live. Unable to understand what, in her view, God had done to me, my wife left me.

Yes, some days I get lonely. And I find myself almost asking, "Why me, Lord? Couldn't you find a more worthy 'Job' than I?" How wonderful it would be to wake up some morning able to say, "Wegener's? What's that?" And that morning shall come, for my Father promises that the "former things"—the miseries of this life—"shall not be remembered" when He creates a new earth (see Isa. 65:17). And then I remember that God says that His strength is made perfect in weakness.

With the poet I pray:

> "Forgive me if too close I lean
> My human heart on Thee!"

But write it in your memory in capital letters: I'M THE HAPPIEST PERSON ON EARTH! It is my joy now to go to the cemetery once a week to visit my parents. I bring flowers, sometimes from a florist, most often from the hillsides. I sit by their grave sites and visit with them, though I know they are sleeping and cannot hear. My hatred and fury have been replaced with sadness for the tragic lives they lived, and hope in the unfathomable love of that God who came down and walked among us as one of us. What a relief it has been to dump the sacks of shame, agony, and hate that I carried for so many years.

On the days I'm too ill to go out or am lying in a hospital bed, I picture my heavenly Father in His throne room. I converse with Him, trust Him, love Him. He has replaced old friends with hundreds of His hurting children—among them brothers and sisters long lost to me, but now, too, finding their way home. I hope that someday they'll be able to join me in writing a book called *The Healing*. My greatest joy is to visit my Father's hurting children. He has commissioned me to bring them a message of love and hope. I walk the corridors of Loma Linda University Hospital as His emissary.

> *I long for household voices gone,*
> *For vanished smiles I long,*
> *But God hath led my dear ones on,*
> *And He can do no wrong.*
>
> *I know not what the future hath*
> *Of marvel or surprise,*
> *Assured alone that life and death*
> *His mercy underlies.*
>
> *And if my heart and flesh are weak*

*To bear an untried pain,*
*The bruised reed He will not break,*
*But strengthen and sustain. . . .*

*And so beside the Silent Sea*
*I wait the muffled oar;*
*No harm from Him can come to me*
*On ocean or on shore.*

*I know not where His islands lift*
*Their fronded palms in air;*
*I only know I cannot drift*
*Beyond His love and care.*

*O brothers! if my faith is vain,*
*If hopes like these betray,*
*Pray for me that my feet may gain*
*The sure and safer way.*

*And Thou, O Lord! by whom are seen*
*Thy creatures as they be,*
*Forgive me if too close I lean*
*My human heart on Thee!*
—John Greenleaf Whittier, "The Eternal Goodness"

I have a name now. If you're ever in the area and would like an introduction to my Father, just ask for God's Boy.

# A Closing Word
# From Jack Milford . . .

*(in conspiracy with Grover's editorial friend, Roland)*

**A few chapters back, my friend** Grover referred to a favorite book I once gave him—*The Desire of Ages,* an account of the life of Christ. The author speaks of Jesus passing through towns and villages "like a vital current, diffusing life and joy wherever He went" (p. 350). So it is with Grover as he shares words of life and hope with the patients of Loma Linda University Hospital. Interview the doctors and nurses, and you will hear of incidents that cannot be credited to medical procedures.

How is this possible? Out of great adversity, Grover has learned to live moment by moment in his Father's presence. When he enters a hospital room to share quiet words of hope and healing with a patient, one senses that he is not alone. His "Daddy" is with him. What a joy to be counted a friend to one who knows who he is—God's Boy—and what he is here for: to reach the heart of the suffering, even as Jesus did.

Some months ago Grover sent me a page titled "What I Have Learned From the Deep Water." In 12 succinct passages he shared the secrets that have enabled him not only to surmount the ravages of Wegener's disease, but to achieve an intimacy with God that, in my estimation, has made him a modern Job. Though beset by the loss of all that humanity holds dear, he daily echoes the words of that ancient believer: "Though he slay me, yet will I trust in him" (Job 13:15).

Here, then, are his insights:

### Deep Water

1. In simple trust, give God your heart. Confide in Him with the innocence of a child. Be His boy or girl, and let Him love you. He is your Daddy.

2. Stay by His side. Walk and talk with Him. By faith, slip into God's throne room and give Him a hug. You'll sense His joy!

3. Let Him hug you! As His arms embrace you day by day, all of self and selfishness will be squeezed out, and all of Jesus will come in. When the pain of remolding engulfs you, "look full in His wonderful face; and the things of earth will grow strangely dim in the light of His glory and grace."

4. Sit quietly by His side, asking nothing. He will teach you the song of His joy in the darkness, that you may sing it in the light.

5. When the deep, dark waters threaten to wash over your head, look into His face and say, "It's OK; it's OK, Father; I trust You." Then smile at Him, and let your soul glow!

6. Know that you are His treasure—His trophy—hard-fought, hard-bought on a cross. Take His hand and stand by Him when multitudes turn away.

7. Let Him hug you so closely that you can hear His heartbeat. Be one with Him, and He shall "see to it"; He will direct you in all your ways.

8. Seek only His approval, His will, His glory, His honor. Let the world's hollowness echo in the corridors of the lost.

9. Permit His deep soul love to reach out to others through you. Fearlessly share the understanding and caring words that He has spoken to you.

10. Ask of your Father that you may give to others—His words burning in your heart and warming cold consciences into a tingling awareness of right and wrong.

11. Daily enjoy sharing your Father's agenda—introducing Him and sharing His mission to humanity.

12. Never compare yourself with others. You are God's child, and He has "tailor-made" the experience you need to enjoy citizenship in His kingdom soon to come.

**APPENDIX** # Protecting Our Children From Abuse and Neglect*

### Caring Adults: What a Child Needs Most

Children depend on many adults as they grow up. Parents, relatives, teachers, and child-care workers all provide children with love, support, and guidance.

No one wants to see children grow up with fear, anger, or neglect. But no one is born knowing how to care for children. Sometimes we make mistakes that hurt them.

Whether you are a parent, a teacher, a relative, or a caregiver, you can make a difference and help the children you love grow up in a caring, loving environment. Adults don't have to be perfect—just willing to listen, learn, grow, and change.

### Why Do Adults Hurt Children?

*Carlos came home from work in a foul mood. Seven-year-old Miguel ran out of the kitchen just as his father walked in, and they ran into each other. Carlos cursed and grabbed his son. He shook Miguel hard while yelling at him, and then shoved him out of the way. The next day Miguel's arms and back had bruises.*

It takes a lot to care for a child. A child needs food, clothing, and shelter as well as love and attention. Parents and caregivers want to provide all those things, but they have other pressures, too. Sometimes adults just can't provide everything their children need.

Adults may not intend to hurt the children they care for. But sometimes adults lose control, and sometimes they hurt children.

### Reasons That Adults Hurt Children

▷ They lose their tempers when they think about their own problems.

▷ They don't know how to discipline a child.

▷ They expect behavior that is unrealistic for a child's age or ability.

▷ They have been abused by a parent or a partner.

▷ They have financial problems.

▷ They lose control when they use alcohol or other drugs.

### What Is Child Abuse?

This is an example of physical child abuse.

*A few minutes after Teresa had changed 18-month-old Dale's dirty diaper he had another messy diaper; this made Teresa angry. She thought that putting him in hot water would punish him for the dirty diaper. When she put him in the tub, he cried loudly. Teresa slapped him to stop the crying and didn't notice the scald marks until after the bath was over.*

### Examples of Physical Child Abuse

▷ Shaking or shoving

▷ Slapping or hitting

▷ Beating with a belt, shoe, or other object

▷ Burning a child with matches or cigarettes

▷ Scalding a child with water that is too hot

▷ Pulling a child's hair out

▷ Breaking a child's arm, leg, or other bones

▷ Not letting a child eat, drink, or use the bathroom

### What Is Sexual Child Abuse?

This is an example of sexual child abuse.

*Nine-year-old Susan's mother works at night. Her stepfather, James, is around when she goes to bed, so many evenings James lies down beside Susan. As she goes to sleep, he rubs her breasts and genital area.*

### Examples of Sexual Child Abuse

▶ Fondling a child's genitals
▶ Having intercourse with a child
▶ Having oral sex with a child
▶ Having sex in front of a child
▶ Having a child touch an older person's genitals
▶ Using a child in pornography
▶ Showing X-rated books or movies to a child

### What Is Child Neglect?

This is an example of neglect.

*John worked nights at the grocery store, but the family needed more money. Ellen looked for work, but the only job she could find required her to leave home at 3:00 a.m. The children, ages 2 and 6, were alone for a few hours until John got home.*

### Examples of Child Neglect

▶ Not meeting a child's need for food, clothing, shelter or safety
▶ Leaving a child unwatched
▶ Leaving a child in an unsafe place
▶ Not seeking necessary medical attention for a child
▶ Not having a child attend school

### Why Do Abuse and Neglect Happen?

Parents and caretakers don't always know that they are being abusive or neglectful. Few adults actually intend to hurt or neglect children.

Sometimes a caretaker just doesn't know a better way to discipline a child. Sometimes an adult is just too frustrated with life and takes it out on a child.

An adult is more likely to abuse or neglect a child

▶ if the caretaker was abused as a child.
▶ if the caretaker is being abused by a spouse or partner.
▶ if the caretaker uses alcohol or other drugs.
▶ if the adult expects too much of a child.
▶ if the child is the result of an unplanned pregnancy.

Some adults don't know how to correct a child without causing physical harm. An adult who has this problem can learn new ways to discipline without hurting a child.

▷ Look for times the child is behaving well. Praise that behavior.

▷ Agree on a code word to use when things reach the boiling point. The code word signals that everyone needs some time to cool down before talking about the problem.

▷ When a child misbehaves, give the child a time-out (a few minutes alone to think about what happened.)

▷ Talk to the child about the misbehavior and its effects.

Sometimes parents and caretakers need to learn to control their own anger. They need to identify the things that make them more likely to hurt the children in their care.

Caretakers who abuse or neglect a child might be.

▷ worried about not having enough money.

▷ having problems with spouses or partners.

▷ coping with a family member's illness or death.

▷ acting the way their parents acted.

▷ stressed from their jobs or other problems.

▷ expecting unrealistic behavior; for example, thinking a 5-year-old can handle the same tasks as a 9-year-old and do them as well.

Often people who abuse or neglect children experience more than one of these situations at the same time.

Hurting a child or not filling a child's basic needs never makes things better. No matter what the problem, help is available.

### Do You Know a Child Who Is Abused or Neglected?

Brenda's teacher saw signs of neglect.

*In the preschool class, 4-year-old Brenda always seemed tired. Brenda never brought food for snacktime, and she looked hungrily at other children's sandwiches. Her classmates teased her because her hair was always dirty.*

Paul saw signs of physical child abuse.

*Paul lived next door to the Harris family, where someone always seemed to be yelling or crying. One night Paul heard glass break, then a man's shouting and a loud thump. Ten-year-old Keisha ran out the door a few seconds later, crying. Her face was swollen with the start of a black eye.*

The effects of child abuse can last a lifetime. An abused or neglected child needs help right away. Is a child you know being abused or neglected?

### Warning Signs of Abuse and Neglect
- ▶ Cuts and bruises
- ▶ Broken bones or internal injuries
- ▶ Burns
- ▶ Constant hunger or thirst
- ▶ Lack of interest in surroundings
- ▶ Dirty hair or skin, frequent diaper rash
- ▶ Lack of supervision
- ▶ Pain, bruising, or bleeding in the genitals
- ▶ More knowledge about sex than is normal for the child's age
- ▶ Hard-to-believe stories about how accidents occurred

### What Happens to Abused and Neglected Children?
Abuse and neglect have harmful effects on children. At worst, a child could die. More often, abused or neglected children live with fear or pain.

Abused or neglected children often experience
- ▶ frequent injuries.
- ▶ learning problems.
- ▶ fear or shyness.
- ▶ bad dreams.
- ▶ behavior problems.
- ▶ depression.
- ▶ fear of certain adults or places.

The effects don't end when the abuse or neglect stops. When abused or neglected children grow up, they are more likely to
- ▶ abuse their own families.
- ▶ use violence to solve their problems.
- ▶ have trouble learning.
- ▶ have emotional difficulties.
- ▶ attempt suicide.
- ▶ use alcohol or other drugs.

Abuse and neglect are hard on the whole family. Some families need help in dealing with practical problems—for example, getting help to buy groceries or learning how to discipline a child without resorting to violence. In other cases a child protection agency might move abused or neglected children away from their parents to a safe, temporary home. If abuse or neglect is severe, or if it continues, the children can be permanently moved away from their parents into a safe situation.

### How Can We End Abuse and Neglect?

Sometimes people are afraid to report abuse or neglect because they don't want to break up a family. Sometimes people are afraid to get involved in someone else's problem.

**When you report suspected child abuse or neglect, you could be saving that child's life.**

The goal of stopping abuse and neglect is to keep children safe. Part of keeping children safe is finding help for the adults who have hurt them. Adults who have abused or neglected a child have many places to turn for help.

> ► **The child's doctor** can explain children's needs at every age. He or she can recommend places to learn more about parenting and child care.

> ► **Local health and social service departments** often have parenting classes. Social service workers also can help parents get assistance to ease their financial situations.

> ► **Hospitals and community centers** often have classes on stress reduction, parenting, discipline, and nutrition.

> ► **Psychologists, counselors, and social workers** can help parents and caregivers deal with problems like drug use, anger, and previous experiences of abuse.

> ► **Religious groups** often provide food, counseling, and other types of support for anyone in the community—not just their members.

If you see that a relative, neighbor, or friend is under a lot of stress and might hurt children in their care, suggest that the person get help from one of these services. **Stop the problem before it starts.**

### What Should I Do if I Suspect a Child Is Being Hurt?

Report your suspicion to a local, county, or state child protection agency. Call a crisis hotline or find the agency number in the blue government pages of a telephone directory.

### Who Must Report Abuse?

In every state the following people are **required by law** to report suspected abuse:

- ▶ doctors
- ▶ nurses
- ▶ dentists
- ▶ mental health professionals
- ▶ social workers
- ▶ teachers
- ▶ day-care workers
- ▶ law enforcement personnel

In some states clergy, foster parents, attorneys, and camp counselors also are required to report abuse. In about 20 states **any person** who suspects abuse is required to report it.

When you make a report, the agency will make a judgment about how serious the situation is. If necessary, a child protection worker will visit the family to see whether abuse or neglect has occurred and to determine what needs to be done. The goals of child protection are to

- ▶ stop the abuse.
- ▶ give needed services to the family.
- ▶ help the family become safe and loving.

**No child should have to live in fear of abuse or neglect.**

**Protect the children you love; help stop child abuse and neglect.**

### Where to Go for Help

Several organizations can provide information and advice about child abuse and neglect:

American Humane Association

63 Inverness Drive East

Englewood, CO 80112-5117

(303) 792-9900

www.americanhumane.org


Child Help U.S.A.

15757 North 78th Street

Scottsdale, AZ 85260

(800) 4-A-CHILD
www.childhelpusa.org

American Bar Association Center on Children and the Law
740 15th Street NW., 9th floor
Washington, D.C. 20005-1009
(202) 662-1720
www.abanet.org/child

American Professional Society on the Abuse of Children
407 South Dearborn, Suite 1300
Chicago, IL 60605
(312) 554-0166
www.apsac.org

Family Violence and Sexual Assault Institute
1121 East SE. Loop 323, Suite 130
Tyler, TX 75701
(903) 534-5100
Email: fvsai@e-tex.com

National Clearinghouse on Child Abuse and Neglect Information
U.S. Department of Health and Human Services
PO Box 1182
Washington, D.C. 20013
(800) FYI-3366
www.calib.com/nccanch

National Committee to Prevent Child Abuse
332 S. Michigan Avenue, Suite 1600
Chicago, IL 60604-4357
(312) 663-3520
(800) CHILDREN C info. on getting involved/preventing abuse
(800) 55-NCPCA C info. on parenting/abuse
www.childabuse.org

National Organization for Victim Assistance
1730 Park Road NW.
Washington, D.C. 20010
Protecting Our Children From Abuse and Neglect